MEXICO'S
PRIVATE SECTOR

Recent History, Future Challenges

edited by
Riordan Roett

LYNNE
RIENNER
PUBLISHERS

BOULDER
LONDON

211

Published in the United States of America in 1998 by
Lynne Rienner Publishers, Inc.
1800 30th Street, Boulder, Colorado 80301

and in the United Kingdom by
Lynne Rienner Publishers, Inc.
3 Henrietta Street, Covent Garden, London WC2E 8LU

Library of Congress Cataloging-in-Publication Data
Mexico's private sector :   recent history, future challenges   /   edited
   by Riordan Roett.
        p.   cm.
     Includes bibliographical references and index.
     ISBN 1-55587-713-3 (hardcover   :   alk. paper)
     1. Mexico—Economic conditions—1994–   2. Mexico—Economic
policy—1994–   3. Free enterprise—Mexico.   I. Roett, Riordan,
1938–   .
HC135.M569   1998
330.972'0836—dc21   98-25921
                                                                                  CIP

British Cataloguing in Publication Data
A Cataloguing in Publication record for this book
is available from the British Library.

Printed and bound in the United States of America

∞ The paper used in this publication meets the requirements
     of the American National Standard for Permanence of
     Paper for Printed Library Materials Z39.48-1984.

5 4 3 2 1

Contents

Tables and Figures

FIGURES

Foreword

The current process of economic, political, and social restructuring in Mexico has had a significant impact on the challenges and opportunities faced today by Mexico's private sector. The transition from a protective, state-directed economic model to an open one, particularly since the passage of the North American Free Trade Agreement (NAFTA), has compelled the Mexican private sector to adjust to increased competition while simultaneously undergoing a process of redefinition of business-government relations. The structural changes brought about by these reforms have also greatly affected the international business and investment communities that have benefited from new opportunities in Mexico—these opportunities, in turn, come hand in hand with increased demands for transparency and efficient business and regulatory frameworks.

This volume provides a clear picture of the recent history and future challenges of Mexico's private sector. The authors examine the goals of economic reform and evaluate the results and the effects of economic modernization on important sectors of the Mexican economy. They also evaluate the prospects and future challenges for Mexico's private sector as we approach the twenty-first century.

This is the fifth volume in the SAIS Program on U.S.-Mexican Relations series, after *The Challenge of Institutional Reform in Mexico* (1995), *Political and Economic Liberalization in Mexico* (1993), *Mexico's External Relations in the 1990s* (1991), and *Mexico and the United States: Managing the Relationship* (1988). A separate volume was released in 1996, *The Mexican Peso Crisis: International Perspectives,* which analyzes key international policy issues affected by the 1994 peso devaluation, from the perspectives of the United States, Mexico, Brazil, Argentina, and the European Union. All of these volumes have been concurrently published in Mexico in Spanish.

The SAIS Program on U.S.-Mexican Relations is sponsored by the William and Flora Hewlett Foundation. Since its creation in 1986, the program has focused its efforts toward increasing knowledge and understanding about the critical issues that shape the Mexican-U.S. bilateral agenda among an audience of policymakers and leaders in business, media, and education. This series of edited volumes is an important component of the program.

Guadalupe Paz
Assistant Director,
SAIS Latin American Studies Program

Acknowledgments

I would like to express my gratitude to the individuals who contributed to this volume and to those who made the completion of the project possible. First, I thank my fellow authors for their thoughtful essays and for the time and patience that were required of them, as is inevitable in a project of this nature. I am especially thankful to Guadalupe Paz, the SAIS Latin American Studies Program's assistant director, for her role in planning the volume and managing all the details involved from beginning to end. Others whose efforts made this publication possible are Charles Roberts, who translated the Spanish-language chapters into English, and Donna Verdier, who bravely took on the assignment of reviewing, restructuring, and editing the manuscript.

Finally, I wish to acknowledge the generous support of the William and Flora Hewlett Foundation, which has been essential in enabling the program to continue its efforts in the field of U.S.-Mexican relations.

Riordan Roett

1

Introduction

Clint E. Smith

During the course of the past three presidential administrations in Mexico—Miguel de la Madrid Hurtado (1982–1988), Carlos Salinas de Gortari (1988–1994), and Ernesto Zedillo Ponce de León (1994–2000)—the country has undertaken a profound economic transition, a process that will continue into the twenty-first century. In the post–World War II period, the Mexican government, anxious to catch up with leading economies, accepted the conventional assumption of those times—notably espoused by the United Nations Economic Commission for Latin America and the Caribbean (ECLAC)—that by adopting a policy of import-substitution industrialization (ISI), Mexico could work to overcome the perceived disadvantages of countries exporting primary products vis-à-vis countries that exported manufactured goods.

This policy was the key to the centralized industrial policies of the Mexican state during the three decades following World War II. The implications for the state's relations with Mexico's private sector are obvious. Mexican manufacturers were at once protected from foreign competition by the ISI approach, including high tariffs and nontariff barriers to trade like restrictive import licensing, but also beholden to the state and subject to be co-opted by its all-powerful governing party.

It was not until the early 1980s that the high costs of ISI policies became generally apparent. By this time the central government subsidies and related costs for supporting ISI amounted to more than 13 percent of Mexico's gross domestic product (GDP). Recurring economic crises, beginning in 1981–1982, sharpened the examination of the efficacy of the ISI approach, and the austerity measures of the De la Madrid administration included a sharp reduction in public sector expenditures, in part at the cost of central government subsidies for "infant industries." These changes in government policy, involving a more international and market-oriented

1

approach, have had, as this book admirably demonstrates, a dramatic and probably permanent effect on the relations between Mexico's public and private sectors, and have created a whole new set of challenges and opportunities for Mexico in the new century.

The purpose of this book is to offer a diverse range of views on the history and prospects for Mexico's private sector in the year 2000 and beyond. The authors succinctly explain and analyze developments and outcomes of economic transformation in modern Mexico from their respective views as economic historians, private sector economic analysts, and academics. The authors were asked not only to describe the dramatic evolution from ISI to the current free-market government economic policies but also to assess the outlook for the field in future years.

The story begins with a commentary on the evolution of Mexico's economic modernization by Everardo Elizondo Almaguer, now deputy governor of the Banco de México, Mexico's central bank, but who comments on themes from his earlier perspective as a private sector leader. In his chapter, Elizondo makes the point that there has never been a clear-cut dichotomy between Mexico's state institutions and the private sector. The role of the state has waxed and waned in the Mexican economy but certainly must retain such vital functions to ensure that economic and social mechanisms, including the free market, operate under the rule of law. Elizondo describes the foreign trade policies, including protectionist measures, that were at the core of the state's development policy for Mexico over a period of several decades. He correctly credits the regime of President Miguel de la Madrid with initiating the foreign trade policy reforms, which were an important and necessary response to the 1982 economic crisis that was brought on during the José López Portillo period (1976–1982) by a combination of the fall in international oil prices and severe economic policy errors, including the assumption of historically high foreign indebtedness meant to be paid off by oil revenue riches. Mexico owes much, Elizondo feels, to the clear vision of President De la Madrid and his key economic advisers, who initiated the recovery of the Mexican economy in the mid-1980s. Elizondo sees for the near future a continuation of the economic and political reform process without substantial alteration, but warns that a sharp eye must be kept on the pace and extent of political reform on the road to Mexico's democratization.

The next chapter is by one of Mexico's leading economic historians, Enrique Cárdenas Sánchez, rector of the Universidad de las Américas (UDLA) in Cholula, Puebla, who provides a decades-long perspective on the evolution of Mexico's private sector during many different government regimes. Cárdenas highlights the special importance of the industrial sector as an engine of Mexican economic growth since the 1930s. During the period of transition from the traditional dependence on mining and agriculture, from the 1940s to 1980, Mexico achieved a real annual economic growth rate in the neighborhood of 6 percent. Cárdenas adds that since 1982 the Mexican economy has not been able to recover such a sustained level of real growth, although prospects currently seem brighter.

A key element in the history of the Mexican economy since the early 1980s has been the major transformation in the economy. As Cárdenas notes, "trade liberalization, privatization of public enterprises, deregulation, and openness of the financial markets are all shaping a new economic system." He links the emergence of this new economic system to the recent growth of the democratic process throughout the nation, and the weakening of the seventy-year rule of the Institutional Revolutionary Party (PRI).

Cárdenas analyzes the important role the private sector has played in financing economic growth in Mexico, but stresses the historical, sometimes shadowy, role of the state in economic affairs. Government contracts, nontariff barriers to imports for favored firms, and other means were traditionally used to support the state's influence. Thus the dramatic liberalization of the Mexican economy from 1982 to 1998 has had a powerful effect on the nature and balance of state–private sector relations in an era of regional integration and globalization.

Of particular interest to Cárdenas is industrial performance in relation to GDP with a focus on the increasing role of the maquiladoras and their impact on changing labor relations and gender issues (most maquiladora employees are women). Related productive issues, which he identifies and analyzes, are the major changes in banking and transportation sectors and the trend toward greater foreign participation. The basic course toward GDP growth is set by the soundness of the state's macroeconomic management and its attention to such structural issues as demographic growth.

Cárdenas takes a special look at the actors in this drama—the characteristics of major economic groups that participate in the process and how they interact with state institutions. He notes that "the new challenges posed by the liberalization of the economy and globalization, as well as the privatization of numerous state firms and the commercial banks . . . did have an important impact on the recomposition of the economic groups." The challenge that Mexico faces today, he concludes, is to incorporate larger segments of society into the dynamic economic process, which will lead to more broadly shared productivity gains as Mexico competes successfully in the new global environment.

Continuing on the theme of economic reforms in Mexico and their outcomes is a chapter by Jonathan Heath, a respected, independent economic analyst in Mexico City. Heath's chapter describes the rocky path that Mexico has taken as it developed toward economic modernization, including the major "stumble" of the Mexican peso crisis in 1994–1995. He describes how "reform fatigue" has set in and the withering away of popular support for reforms that have been particularly marked during the current Zedillo administration. After describing the reform measures of the De la Madrid–Salinas–Zedillo period, Heath analyzes future policy options and examines the implications of these options for the next century in terms of Mexico's original intentions and long-term goals.

Along the way, Heath describes why economic reforms were necessary; the impact of the oil boom and bust during the 1970s; De la Madrid's groundbreaking reform measures during the 1982–1988 period; and key structural changes during the Salinas period when privatization efforts intensified dramatically (more than 1,000 of the 1,200 state-owned enterprises found their ownership transferred to the private sector). He stresses that Mexico still faces many challenges, including inequitable income distribution and immense belts of poverty surrounding affluent ghettos, which he correctly describes as Mexico's most complex and important social problem.

Heath concludes that Mexico must adopt policies that will generate higher-paying jobs; restore lost purchasing power for the middle and lower classes; diversify the domestic economy; and promote sustainable and more equitable economic growth and development. These economic policies, he insists, must be joined with Mexico's evolution toward a more democratic society marked by the rule of law.

The current state of Mexico's capital markets, including private and public sector investment issues, exchange rate policies, and prospects for export growth are described in Chapter 5 in this volume by Roberto Salinas León, economic analyst and director of economic strategy at Televisión Azteca. Salinas León describes exchange-rate policy as a prominent issue since the 1994–1995 peso crisis, which will now be at the forefront of public attention as former finance minister Guillermo Ortiz takes over the reins as governor of the Banco de México and the government continues its efforts to pursue an ever more credible international monetary policy. Such a policy, Salinas León notes, is an important underpinning to the confidence of the financial sectors of the Mexican economy, particularly the stock markets, which seem "to waver between episodes of panic and euphoria," he writes. Equally important is to increase domestic savings and investment, thus dampening out foreign investment volatility.

Therefore, the central economic challenges for Mexico into the new century are investment, stability, and growth. Instead of vaguely blaming neoliberalism or market capitalism for Mexico's ills, Mexico's political leadership—from all the major parties—should focus over the coming years on how to open up private sector competition, how better to define and enforce property rights under an improved rule of law, and how to free the operation of market mechanisms while maintaining appropriate controls for the public good. Salinas León concludes that it is up to Mexico's policymakers to create a reliable regime for long-term productive investment from home and abroad.

A remarkable insight into how Mexico recovered from the 1994–1995 Mexican financial crisis and its lessons for Mexico's banking and private sector communities is offered by three officials of the Mexican National Banking and Securities Commission. They are Javier Gavito Mohar, Aarón Silva Nava, and Guillermo Zamarripa Escamilla. Their chapter examines the relationship between the private sector and official financial institutions, particularly in times of crisis. It contains an inside view of events and actions that led to the recent peso crisis, and explores the consequences of the crisis and its austere aftermath for private banks and firms and for Mexico's financial system. The authors describe the vulnerability of the financial system and how this is exacerbated by structural factors. They note that vulnerability was increased dramatically when major private firms' ratio of debt to capital climbed precipitously from 49 percent in 1991 to a shocking 83 percent in 1994, giving evidence of possible excessive risk taking by bank managers, although some banks adopted more prudent credit policies.

In any case, the National Banking and Securities Commission, in concert with other institutions, has implemented since early 1995 a series of regulatory programs aimed at supporting the health of the banking system and its borrowers. Although it is too early to evaluate the cumulative effects of these efforts, it is clear that to succeed they must encompass a fair distribution of losses among all parties and a continuing reform of the financial system, especially in the area of financial intermediation. The authors express a final caveat that private bank recovery will be gradual and heterogeneous in a time of continuing vulnerability to any future economic crises.

Raymundo Winkler, director of the Center for Economic Studies of the Private Sector (CEESP) in Mexico City, dates the beginning of the structural transformation of the Mexican economy from 1985, when Mexico sought membership in the General Agreement on Tariffs and Trade (GATT). The ongoing process involves the public and private sectors and endeavors to raise Mexico's productivity levels to make it more competitive in the global market. The beginning of the process, symbolized by entry into GATT, was marked by moving away from the protectionism of the ISI years, which in some cases quite suddenly exposed obsolescent and inefficient firms to the highly competitive global economy. The firms, now obliged to invest in improving their productivity, found that they were attempting to do so in an atmosphere of austere macroeconomic-stabilization efforts of the Mexican central government, required by a series of economic crises and setbacks. Winkler's chapter assesses the progress of efforts to achieve more productive plant operations at a time of narrow economic options.

Following a basic description of the principles, context, and rationale of Mexico's economic reform strategy, Winkler describes how the private sector undertook a generally successful reorganization and conversion of firms' equipment and machinery—necessary for the succeeding economic growth in manufacturing, export performance, and for gains in productivity and real wages. Winkler proceeds to challenge the more common criticisms made of the modernization strategy, and concludes that the liberal strategy of structural change implemented in Mexico beginning in the late 1980s has begun to produce positive results for the Mexican economy. Nevertheless, he notes, the modernization process must continue and, indeed, is crucial if the Mexican economy is to enjoy long-lasting growth, higher employment, and social progress.

In Chapter 8, Kristin Johnson Ceva, a political economist trained at Stanford and now associated with a private sector financial consulting firm, reports on the dramatic changes in the business-government relationship that have taken place since 1990 in an atmosphere of regional integration and economic crises. Her chapter contains a fascinating, detailed description of how Mexico successfully negotiated the North American Free Trade Agreement (NAFTA) in the early 1990s, with special attention to the role of the business community in the internal give-and-take as various sectoral agreements were crafted. The business-government interplay during these years was crucial to the development of a changing relationship between the private and public sectors. For example, while groups of large businesses typically played a key advisory role in the NAFTA negotiations, some smaller firms, fearing the opening of the Mexican economy to competitive forces, often joined with political and nongovernmental groups opposed to NAFTA. As Johnson Ceva notes: "Born and having prospered under the policies of protectionism and import substitution, smaller enterprises . . . had historically opposed unilateral trade liberalization and Mexico's accession to the General Agreement on Tariffs and Trade." But, finally, a strong pro-NAFTA campaign by the Mexican government, and the support of major industrial firms, prevailed. NAFTA was successfully negotiated and came into force on January 1, 1994.

Johnson Ceva also examines the political and social dynamics of groups opposed to the government's economic policies in general. One such examination is of the Barzón movement, which has grown rapidly and is now one of Mexico's best-known social actors. The Barzón, which is the Spanish word for "yoke," takes its name from a prerevolutionary song about a peasant who borrows to pay for an old *barzón* and, unable to pay for it, spends the rest of his life in debt. Originally formed by farmers in northwestern Mexico, the movement expanded rapidly to the south. The Barzón has organized innumerable protests throughout Mexico and has been effective in calling attention to the credit problems of farmers and small businesspersons. It has since expanded to include criticism of corrupt officials and bankers, and continues to be an active player on the Mexican social scene.

Partly as a result of pressures from the Barzón and other groups, the Zedillo administration has undertaken a number of new efforts to improve government–small business relations. Sectoral approaches, such as those to the shoe and textile sectors, have resulted in higher tariffs on imports from countries not covered by commercial agreements. Government programs also are making credit easier for smaller firms in such areas as textiles, leather and shoes, automotive and auto parts, electronics, steel, and chemicals.

Johnson Ceva finds that the sea change in government-business relations in Mexico has resulted in private sector demands for the correction of economic imbalances, what they call a "microrevolution" involving more attention to business sector needs, and a more efficient banking system with easier access to credit. She notes that "the previous business-government order has been shattered, but it will take time for a new order to emerge." Thus, while Zedillo appears determined to maintain the general outlines of his economic reform policies aimed at stimulating economic growth, he will have to pay ever more attention to the nation's increasingly vocal and better organized business sector.

The effects of NAFTA on the transformation of the Mexican economy over the past decade is the subject of the chapter by Deborah L. Riner, chief economist at the American Chamber of Commerce in Mexico City, and John V. Sweeney, managing director at Vector Casa de Bolsa, a financial services firm. Their analysis focuses on the private sector and foreign trade and investment since 1985, when President De la Madrid brought Mexico into GATT. This first major move reflects the fact that the most important of structural changes taking place in Mexico has been the process of opening up the country to the global economy.

Complementing the trade and investment statistics that are used in this analysis, Riner and Sweeney draw on the opinions of business leaders themselves obtained from a survey of 405 companies conducted by the American Chamber of Commerce (AmCham) in Mexico in late 1996. They argue that NAFTA has increased trade flows in almost every sector, and that larger companies, particularly in the manufacturing sector, have gained the most from the structural changes brought about by the agreement. They stress that the most wrenching changes to the economy occurred before the implementation of NAFTA, and that the agreement has only accelerated the trend of determining who the winners and losers are in a more competitive and open economy. They conclude that the implications of NAFTA go beyond trade, as the trade agreement binds governments to established obligations and limits the discretion of officials, thus providing greater certainty in the investment and business communities while making business transactions less costly and more efficient.

The direction that the world economy will take in the next century will be highly dependent on technological innovations in the workplace, including robotics and artificial intelligence, and their impact on productivity gains and increased efficiency. This is a principal argument in the chapter by Javier A. Elguea and Pilar Marmolejo from the Technological Institute of Teléfonos de México (Inttelmex). In their chapter, Elguea and Marmolejo focus on training the Mexican labor force to compete in the global economy at a time when improving intellectual capital will be the primary mark of success in a nation's gross domestic product. In the next century, they point out, economies will be "information intensive rather than labor intensive," requiring "a specialized and highly educated labor force with crucial skills and the capability to manage complex information."

Thus, the Mexican educational system is faced with a huge challenge. Elguea and Marmolejo report that a serious discrepancy exists between what Mexican schools and colleges are teaching and the material desperately required in a high-technology workplace. Far too few young Mexicans are receiving the training in mathematics, science, and technology, and prospects are not bright that the situation is likely to be remedied in the short and medium term. One obvious result of this lack of training in schools is the requirement placed on industrial firms to train newly hired employees at the site of their employment while, hopefully, the Mexican educational system gears up to meet its students' training needs to compete in the labor market of the twenty-first century. Meanwhile, both public and private sector institutions are lagging far behind other Organization for Economic Cooperation and Development (OECD) countries in educational skills training, and research and development. Although such firms as Teléfonos de México have made notable strides in investing in its human capital, these firms are relatively few and far between. The authors call for a vast reorganization of traditional educational institutions, such as schools and universities, as well as an expansion of technological institutes, and cooperating private sector training programs. Only with this huge and coordinated effort, they feel, will Mexico be able to meet the demand for economic growth in the next century.

The challenges to Mexican firms as the country took steps to open up its market, for example through accession to GATT and the successful negotiation of NAFTA, are the subject of the chapter by Arturo Fernández Pérez and Ramiro Tovar Landa. Fernández is the rector of the Instituto Tecnológico Autónomo de México (ITAM), and Tovar is a member of ITAM's economics faculty. GATT, NAFTA, and other trade-liberalization measures did, in fact, pose huge challenges to Mexican firms to cut production costs and improve their marketing efforts. Otherwise, they would face a shrinking market share and profit margin. In recent years, Mexican firms have developed a number of different strategies to meet these and other challenges, and the chapter by Fernández and Tovar explores a number of them.

One of these strategies is to improve a firm's access to capital markets—moving from self-financing, to intermediation by the banking system, and to equity markets that permit both foreign and domestic investment in the firm. The authors note that improving access to equity markets, both domestic and foreign, permit the acquisition of necessary capital and the substitution of equity for debt as the firm grows more mature. Although larger firms are usually the first to benefit from this strategy, the authors note that "the greater liquidity arising from foreign investments in the domestic capital market is key to the participation of medium-size firms."

Other strategies include mergers and acquisitions, strategic alliances, intensified export marketing, and joint ventures. Interesting and instructive case studies undertaken by the authors include Alfa, currently Mexico's largest exporter of manufactured goods; Cemex, the leading cement company in the Americas; Empresas La Moderna, an agribusiness conglomerate and leader in agrobiotechnology, with divisions in such areas as cigarette production, packaging, and vegetable seeds; Grupo Modelo, marked tenth worldwide in beer production and sales and the number-two beer exporter to the United States (after Heineken); Vitro S.A., which owns and controls more than 100 plants and seventy companies around the world that produce glass, plastic, and aluminum containers and household products; Femsa, the largest beverage producer in Latin America, led by its role as bottler for Coca-Cola; and Cifra, Mexico's biggest chain retail discount store and restaurant operator, with annual sales of about $2 billion and partnerships with such firms as Wal-Mart, which it introduced into the non-U.S. market.

The authors conclude from their long-term case studies that "globalization increases the flow of capital and technology to developing economies, thus generating higher growth rates than would be possible in a less-integrated economy." They note that, in summary, Mexico's stable and open economy has been successful in promoting efficiency gains in the businesses they studied. They insist that it must be the global marketplace itself that determines which firms succeed or fail.

Riordan Roett, director of the Program on U.S.-Mexican Relations and the Latin American Studies Program at the Johns Hopkins School of Advanced International Studies (SAIS), highlights the daunting but important tasks that remain to be done as Mexico enters the twenty-first century. Although the private sector must play a vital supporting role in the accomplishment of these goals, it is up to a modernizing Mexican state to introduce needed institutional reforms to face the challenge of globalization and growing regionalism. Meeting this challenge is made more difficult by uncertainties regarding the future of NAFTA in the context of an effort to create a Free Trade Area of the Americas (FTAA). On the domestic side, the important political changes taking place throughout the country will involve the private sector as well.

The list of needed economic reforms, Roett notes, is well known, and includes tax reform; changes in the labor laws to give employers greater flexibility to meet market challenges; the development of more efficient capital markets in an atmosphere of improving regulatory frameworks; protecting intellectual property; and in general asserting firmly the rule of law. It is also the obligation of the state, although the private sector can help out, to improve the quality of human capital coming to the workforce through better educational systems at every level.

Mexico's private sector, Roett believes, should take every advantage of the opportunities afforded by the mammoth North American market subsumed under NAFTA, but also should seek export and financing possibilities elsewhere in the hemisphere, in Europe, and in Asia. He observes that recent bilateral links with Chile, for example, have proved to be mutually beneficial. Roett concludes that the issue of globalization is critical for the Mexican private sector if it is to move to a new and successful plateau in the twenty-first century.

PART ONE

Outcomes of
Economic Reform in Mexico

2

Commentary on the Evolution of Economic Modernization

Everardo Elizondo Almaguer

The debate over the public sector's role in the economy is a long-standing one in Mexico, yet it has taken Mexico longer than other countries to take up the issue. In general, the main actors involved have never posed the polemic as an absolute dichotomy between state and market. Like the classical liberals, for example, the present-day partisans of free markets understand that a clear and respected legal framework must be in place for those markets to work.

Independent of the formalities of the dispute, in practice the most important change in the state's role in the economy in Mexico since the early 1970s took place in the mid-1980s, during the administration of Miguel de la Madrid Hurtado. It is reasonable to assume that fiscal crisis spurred change: In 1982 the public sector deficit was nearly 17 percent of the gross domestic product (GDP), and in 1985 the federal government implemented a radical liberalization of foreign trade. This reform measure was the key to the structural change.

PROTECTIONISM AND STATISM

Foreign trade policy was at the core of official development policy for several decades in Mexico, beginning during World War II. For the most part, the government simply closed its borders to selected imports to foster domestic production. The main instruments used to this end were tariffs and the so-called *permisos previos,* or preissued permits. The idea was to limit the protection to the time needed for the Mexican firms to become sufficiently competitive in the world market. The state thereby came to wield tremendous power over the nature and direction of economic activity.

The control of foreign trade was complemented by the logical exten-

sion of state activity inward. The state reserved the national market for
local firms; to this end it implemented increasingly complicated and costly
regulations on prices, investment, technological transfers, and so on,
designed to address the private sector's alleged lack of capacity, whether
financial, economic, or administrative. That rationale for the interventions,
however, failed to recognize that insufficiency of resources is a characteris-
tic of underdevelopment whose impact is not limited to the private sector.
When capital is scarce and administrative talent lacking, the assumption
that shortcomings are concentrated in one sector of the economy leads to
grave errors of judgment. Such a misguided proposition draws on the idea
that the state (its high-level bureaucracy) is capable of choosing a select set
of potential winners in the economic game. Neither economic theory nor
empirical evidence supports that notion.

The economic structure had its correlate in the structure of political
power. Of course, a symbiotic relationship evolved between the protector
state and the protected entities, and as might be expected, the connection
included organized labor. What is more, the efforts of those participating in
the scheme were geared—rationally—more to rent seeking than to efficiency.[1]

As in all cases of protectionism in Latin America, the result was a pro-
gressive distortion of relative prices, which in turn caused a deformation in
the structure of production. One of the sectors most affected was agriculture: Farmers paid prices that were too high for their main inputs (inflated
by protectionism), yet they received prices that were too low for their output (kept down by regulatory controls). Evidently, the idea was to favor
city dwellers. This result is an example of a standard phenomenon in economic policy: It is very easy to propose support measures aimed at a particular group but very difficult to recognize that the diversion of resources
implicit in the exercise necessarily takes place at the expense of another
group in society.

Except for the years between 1956 and 1972, Mexico's protectionist
period was characterized by unstable prices caused by a financial imbalance in the public sector, which was reflected in an undesired expansion in
the money supply. Regardless of the causes of inflation, its strength and
variability cut short the time that businesses could plan ahead. Thus, the
alleged myopia of the private sector regarding its investment decisions was
but a logical response to an uncertain environment.

The response of savers was equally logical and predictable. The interest rate, determined by administrative edict, was not adjusted to reflect the
change in expectations brought about by inflation. The result was often a
negative real interest rate, which discouraged saving and led to the
rationing of loanable resources (through a system of selective controls on
credit).

In the last part of the protectionist period, the instability extended to a particularly important institutional consideration—namely, the insecurity of property rights. Although official price controls clearly represented a way to change the nature of private property, the magnitude of the problem was not fully appreciated until after formal expropriations (of certain agricultural lands in northwest Mexico, for example) and, more dramatically, the nationalization of the commercial banking system in 1982. These events irremediably translated into a contraction in investment and the oft-mentioned capital flight.

Economic policy errors played a decisive role in the origins and development of the crises of the early 1980s, but the fall in the international price of petroleum was a major shock that originated outside the country. The peso fell out of step with its equilibrium level, and the public sector was overbloated both in terms of its spending and in relation to its overall indebtedness.

THE REFORM AND ITS AFTERMATH

During the first years of the De la Madrid administration, a small group of technocrats began to prepare a general assessment of the situation, and above all to pull together a consistent body of economic policy measures aimed at achieving two major objectives: stabilizing the economy and changing its structure. The reorganization of the state played a crucial role in pursuing these goals.[2]

Despite some initial hesitancy, which was reflected in an untimely recovery in 1984, it is reasonable to conclude that the administration had a clear vision of the direction of the reform. That vision was manifested in the summer of 1985, when the government implemented a profound, sweeping, and unilateral opening to foreign trade. This has been the key element in the package of changes.

The liberalization of import policy helped reduce inflation, but its main function was to realign domestic prices to finally put out the "correct" signals for resource allocation. Coincidentally, it represented an enormous step toward the decentralization of decisionmaking for the simple reason that it curtailed, and in some cases eliminated, the influence of the federal bureaucracy over business activity. The measure culminated almost ten years later when the North American Free Trade Agreement (NAFTA) came into force.

The process of bringing inflation under control beginning in late 1987 had two components. The first involved adopting an orthodox set of fiscal and monetary measures, the core of any stabilization program. The second had heterodox characteristics and revolved around a "social pact" intended to standardize and curtail public expectations of inflation, thus reducing the significance of so-called inertia-driven inflation.

Fiscal discipline relied on the contraction of total public spending, which fell by an amount equal to 17 percent of GDP over the period 1987–1991. Part of the reduction stemmed from the closing or sale of hundreds of inefficient parastatal and state-owned companies. Another part came from the final restructuring of Mexico's foreign debt, which occurred in 1989. Revenues were bolstered by a more forceful and sophisticated oversight effort. In addition, they benefited temporarily from the resources obtained in the privatization process, especially the swift and profitable reprivatization of the commercial banking system.

THE FUTURE OF MODERNIZATION

The crisis of December 1994 has had many consequences. One of special importance for the topic at hand is that it helped discredit the economic model in place. Critics across the political spectrum have caricatured the new orientation as "neoliberalism," which has come to have a highly negative connotation given its frequent association with the crisis. Their views have wide support: As political scientist Luis Rubio noted in a recent article, "an enormous proportion of Mexicans blame all evils" on the government's economic policy.[3]

Rubio's observation is a faithful reflection of the national perception. Despite the popularity of that perception, however, a careful review of the situation might yield a more balanced judgment about economic modernization. First, even the best-qualified analysts cannot agree on a definitive version of the causes of the debacle, even though serious errors in macroeconomic management obviously were made. Second, there is no doubt that the Mexican economy is presently riding the upward part of the cycle. Indeed, although it is true that production and employment plummeted in early 1995, it is also true that the recovery since then has been surprisingly swift.

It should be added that per capita income is still below the level achieved in 1994 before the peso crisis, and that in all likelihood its distribution is more skewed than before. This may suffice to explain the widespread discontent and irritation of the population. Whatever the reasons, the pace of economic reform has slowed, whereas political reform has proceeded with greater impetus.

Opinion polls conducted before the July 1997 general elections indicated that the most likely outcome for the Institutional Revolutionary Party (PRI) would be to lose the Federal District governorship and the majority in the Chamber of Deputies. This became a reality. Of the two historical developments, the second is the more consequential for framing and implementing economic policy.

A superficial review of the economic programs of the three leading parties—the PRI, the National Action Party (PAN), and the Party of the Democratic Revolution (PRD)—at the time of the congressional electoral campaigns revealed considerable differences on most of the major issues, and only a few points of agreement. There was no agreement, for example, on the rate and coverage of the value-added tax (the most important indirect tax). Nor was there consensus on the already-enacted reform of the pension system. In the area of trade policy, one of the parties, the PRD, proposed that NAFTA be revised. As for privatization, two of the parties suggested very significant changes in the process itself. These are just a few examples of the issues that must be—and are being—negotiated within the new political context.

In sum, these developments point to three trends for the near future. First, the economic reform process will be slower and more complex than in the past, because the president will have to negotiate each new measure with a divided and extremely active lower chamber (the Senate will continue to be dominated by the PRI through the remainder of the presidential term). Second, although the government of the Federal District has little influence in general economic policy, Mexico City is the largest city in the country and the political climate there will determine in part what is deemed possible; moreover, the district's prominent governor will undoubtedly be a natural candidate for the presidency in the year 2000. Finally, because the financial opening makes the economy highly vulnerable to inflows and outflows of capital, the likelihood of abrupt populist or statist turnabouts is low.

Nevertheless, the *Wall Street Journal* reported in an article entitled "Populist Backlash" that the combination of economic turmoil and political scandal in an increasingly democratic Mexico had boosted support for the leftist PRD, a party characterized as advocating a return to statist economic policies.[4] Another observer notes that "under democratic conditions, where discontent can find expression at the polls, even the most promising reform strategies may be abandoned. Either politicians . . . reverse policies that will cause them to lose elections, or they lose to competitors more attuned to the political consequences of structural transformation. . . . In some cases, egalitarian ideologies with strong populist and nationalistic overtones can be mobilized against both democracy and reforms."[5]

The danger that a "populist backlash" might lead to reversals of economic policy is mitigated by the combined strength of the executive branch and the Senate, and by the limited degree of freedom the government has to backpedal, now that Mexico has been financially integrated into the world market. It is reasonable to conclude also that the process of modernization of the state that began almost fifteen years ago, which is consistent with the core of the structural economic reform, will not be substantially altered in the immediate future. This assessment will have to be revised at the outset of the twenty-first century, however, in light of the unprecedented political developments under way in Mexico at this time.

NOTES

1. Anne O. Krueger, "The Political Economy of the Rent-Seeking Society," *American Economic Review* 64 (1974): 291–303.
2. José Córdoba, "México," in *The Political Economy of Policy Reform,* ed. John Williamson (Washington, D.C.: Institute for International Economics, 1994), pp. 232–284.
3. Luis Rubio, "¿Existe un modelo económico alternativo?" *El Norte,* May 1, 1997, p. 6A.
4. Michael Allen, Craig Torres, and Dianne Solis, "Populist Backlash: Mexican Leftists Gain Wide Support, Posing Threat to Ruling Party," *Wall Street Journal,* June 27, 1997, p. A1.
5. Adam Przeworksi, *Democracy and the Market: Political and Economic Reforms in Eastern Europe and Latin America* (New York: Cambridge University Press, 1991), p. 138.

3

Mexico's Private Sector, Then and Now

Enrique Cárdenas Sánchez

Mexico's private sector has played an important role through the years in the development of the Mexican economy, a role that is relevant to production, employment creation, and institution building. Since the 1930s the industrial sector has constituted the engine of growth, replacing the centuries-old lead of export mining and agriculture. With the rise of industry came urbanization, which changed the country's scenery and stimulated other sectors such as commerce, transportation, education, and health and other services, as well as public utilities. Economic real growth averaged over 6 percent a year until the 1982 debt crisis, with industry somewhat more dynamic. Following that crisis, however, the pace of economic growth slowed, until recently.

Since 1982, amidst a period of economic stagnation, industry and the rest of the economy have undergone a major transformation that has touched every aspect of economic life in Mexico. Trade liberalization, privatization of public enterprises, deregulation, and openness of the financial markets are all shaping a new economic system. Needless to say, such a change is accompanied by a corresponding, albeit different, transformation in the political sphere. Democratization and the end of the preponderant rule of the official party in power for more than sixty years are refashioning the political scene and its actors, though not without difficulty in some instances. The change in the political system has caused political and sometimes economic turmoil, a price that Mexican society has had to pay for its transit into a different system.

Through the years the private sector has played an important role in financing the economy. Until the late 1950s the Mexican economy was essentially able to finance itself without relying heavily on foreign lending. After that, however, the economy either had to borrow capital from abroad or attract foreign investments to finance growing levels of gross investment. From the mid-1960s until the late 1980s the private sector financed not only its own investment but also made substantial contributions to finance public investment and even public current spending in some years. Yet by the 1990s, the private sector had overspent and thus helped create the major financial crisis of 1995.

Keep in mind that contemporary industrial development of the private sector has taken place in the shadow of the state. The most important economic groups were formed years ago under state auspices; many of them grew out of government contracts or under trade protection. Only recently have such firms evolved to adjust to the new, more competitive, globalized economy. Those that were unable to evolve and adjust have disappeared.

The transformation of the private sector, particularly industry, has a counterpart in the external sector of the economy. That is, private industry has changed to a large extent along with the changes in the external sector, both in imports and exports. The driving force behind these changes was substantial trade liberalization in the 1980s, which was reinforced by the signing of the North American Free Trade Agreement (NAFTA). Since then, economic processes have changed, the location of industry and employment has changed, and salaries and wages continue to change, especially in those industries that export; productivity also differs according to these factors. Of special note, vulnerability of the economy itself has also changed.

This chapter outlines the issues that the private sector has dealt with in the past and the challenges that it must confront in the future. Industrial performance over the past twenty years, in relation to the gross domestic product (GDP) and to the various branches of industry, is examined first. Second, the private sector's role in financing the economy is explored to aid understanding of the private sector itself and its relation to the state. Next, the changing conception of the role of the state in the economy is illuminated by an examination of the industrial policy as a whole and its evolution and impact on the performance of the private sector. Following that discussion is one that evaluates the transformation and growth of the external sector, structural changes, and the full entrance of Mexico into the world economy. Last, and most important, is a look at the actors themselves—the economic groups that have participated actively in the industrialization process, their characteristics, and their ways of doing business.

PERFORMANCE

The private sector participates in practically all areas of the economy. In the agricultural area, farmers comprise two distinct groups in Mexico: private farmers and those producers often referred to as the "social sector," who are peasants working in *ejidos* and other productive structures reminiscent of a tradition dating back many centuries.[1] This latter group holds more than half of the land under cultivation, but it contributes only a fraction of Mexico's agricultural output. In mining, although there have been many instances of government involvement, a good part of production is in private hands, but development has been rather slow in the past forty or fifty years.

Historically the private sector has run most other industries, but at the height of governmental intervention in the economy, many companies were run by the public sector, though more by default than by design. Energy production, both oil and electric power, has been in the hands of the public sector since the 1960s; during the oil boom of the late 1970s, oil revenues contributed heavily to the GDP. Transportation and telecommunications—railroads, airlines, and television stations, for example—have been partly public and partly private. Commercial banks and other financial intermediaries were mostly private until the sector was nationalized in 1982; in the early 1990s the sector was privatized. However, development banks have always been government owned. Most education falls to the public sector, as do health and other services, although the private sector is making large strides in these areas, especially in higher education.

The behavior of the industrial sector can be characterized as quite successful, up until the debt crisis of 1982. For the years 1950–1981, average real growth in manufacturing amounted to 7.5 percent a year while total GDP increased at an average annual rate of 6.6 percent. Manufacturing's share of GDP increased from 17.1 percent in 1950 to 24.7 percent in 1981. Beginning in 1982, however, the economy slowed down and so did industry. From 1982 to 1997 real GDP grew only 1.8 percent annually, on average; industry performed somewhat better, growing 2.4 percent a year.

Presumably, these two periods—1950–1981 and 1982–1997—could be used to analyze the performance of the industrial sector, but they do not correspond to major changes within industry that have a bearing on performance levels. In fact, many argue that the major thrust of industrialization from the end of World War II to the 1960s was toward substituting imports of consumer goods while imports of raw materials and capital goods were welcomed to advance that process.[2] Probably because that industrialization strategy was successful, and because of the vested interests of both business and labor, the government extended protection to raw materials and capital good industries, curtailing foreign investment through the so-called Mexicanization laws.[3] Thus, with almost unanimous consensus that foreign borrowing was preferable to foreign investment, Mexico entered on the path toward foreign indebtedness.

The pursuit of import-substitution industrialization implied a growing need for foreign exchange to pay for needed imports, higher rates of investment, and, consequently, more savings. After an attempt to increase public revenues through fiscal reform fell short of its goals in the early 1960s,[4] the government had to either increase foreign borrowing or tax the private sector in some way. The government, not surprisingly, chose to do both. On the one hand, it borrowed from international lending agencies. On the other, it withdrew private savings from the banking sector by boosting legal-reserve requirements, which were transferred to the central bank and subsequently to the government through the issue of internal debt.

Because private investors were unable, and to some extent unwilling, to engage in large investment projects, the government started a series of productive ventures to secure domestic production of basic raw materials and certain capital goods. Private firms borrowed heavily from Nacional Financiera and other agencies to enter these new avenues, but they were not always successful. If these firms went broke, the government picked up the pieces and retained the whole enterprise.[5] Hence the government became involved in the production of all sorts of goods.

This trend continued through the period of "economic populism" of the 1970s—during which another attempt to increase revenues through fiscal reform failed[6]—but it finally collapsed with the restriction of foreign exchange caused by the debt crisis of 1982. At that time imports were curtailed by the price and scarcity of foreign exchange, and because productive processes had become tied to imports of a wide variety of goods and services, production declined. Industrial production fell 7.3 percent in 1983 alone.

By then it was clear that the protection strategy had been taken too far and was no longer responsive to the country's needs. Some other strategy had to be implemented—no easy task in the midst of severe economic crisis—so almost without noticing, the industrial sector accepted the dismantling of trade barriers in the early 1980s. Mexico's entry into the General Agreement on Tariffs and Trade (GATT) in 1986 marked the beginning of a new era, one that eventually was reflected in the composition of the industrial sector as firms increasingly faced foreign competition (see Table 3.1).

With the entry into force of NAFTA in 1994 and the economic crisis of 1995, the industrial sector transformed itself even further, as heavily indebted firms unconnected to the export sector suffered high interest rates and a drop in consumer consumption.[7] Those industries that were related to exports, either directly or indirectly, fared much better during the recession. Thus, the industrial sector was split between those firms and sectors that had been able to adapt to world competition and those that had not, those that depended on the domestic market alone and those that could export and supply foreign demand.

The consequences were similar for other sectors of the economy. In agriculture, for example, the opportunities to export goods expanded

Table 3.1 Manufacturing Output, by Sector, 1980–1997 (percentage of total value, except where noted)

Year	Total Value (millions of 1993 dollars)	Foodstuffs, Beverages, and Tobacco	Textiles and Leather	Wood and Wooden Products	Paper and Printing Industries	Chemical and Oil Derivative Products	Nonmetallic Mining Products	Basic Metallic Industries	Metallic Products, Machinery, and Equipment	Other Manufacturing Industries
1980	670.2	25.1	11.5	4.5	4.8	14.3	7.8	4.8	24.7	2.7
1981	714.6	24.6	11.4	4.2	4.8	14.7	7.5	4.7	25.3	2.9
1982	694.4	26.5	11.2	4.2	4.9	15.5	7.5	4.3	23.0	2.8
1983	636.0	28.1	11.6	4.3	4.9	16.7	7.6	4.4	19.9	2.5
1984	668.2	27.2	11.1	4.2	4.9	16.8	7.7	4.7	20.8	2.7
1985	711.8	26.5	10.7	4.1	5.0	16.7	7.7	4.5	22.1	2.7
1986	672.3	27.9	10.8	4.2	5.1	17.0	7.7	4.5	20.3	2.6
1987	689.5	27.2	10.0	4.2	5.0	17.3	8.2	4.9	20.6	2.5
1988	713.6	26.6	9.8	4.0	5.1	17.0	7.8	5.0	22.3	2.5
1989	770.0	26.6	9.5	3.7	5.2	17.3	7.6	4.7	22.9	2.6
1990	822.1	26.0	9.4	3.4	5.2	16.9	7.6	4.7	23.9	2.8
1991	850.3	26.0	9.3	3.4	5.3	16.5	7.6	4.4	24.9	2.7
1992	885.7	26.0	8.9	3.3	5.2	16.1	7.7	4.2	25.4	3.0
1993	879.7	27.0	8.8	3.2	5.2	15.9	8.0	4.4	24.6	3.0
1994	915.6	26.8	8.5	3.2	5.1	15.8	8.0	4.5	25.2	2.9
1995	871.4	28.1	8.4	3.1	4.9	16.5	7.4	4.9	23.8	2.8
1996	965.9	26.2	8.9	2.9	4.5	15.7	7.5	5.3	26.1	2.8
1997	783.2	24.9	8.9	2.8	4.6	15.4	7.4	5.5	27.6	2.9

Source: National Institute of Statistics, Geography, and Information (INEGI).

through NAFTA, as they did in mining and various service sectors. At the least, the threat of opening the borders forced banks and other financial services, for instance, to adapt and adjust to face competition with more weapons. Downsizing and reengineering were common in many firms. Again, those firms that did not take corrective measures and adapt confronted major challenges as foreign competitors entered the market.

The transformation of industry engendered by trade liberalization in the 1980s is revealed in at least two different ways. First, throughout most of the century imports of industrial goods—all goods, for that matter—depended heavily on domestic income and, naturally, on the level of the exchange rate. When there was a recession, imports declined correspondingly, and when there was an economic boom, imports increased. However, this strong relationship began to change in the latter half of the 1980s as income became less important and exports entered the picture as a major influence on imports.[8] That is, as exports grew after 1986, inputs had to be imported to maintain production levels and high quality, with the result that the industrial sector became more integrated with foreign inputs.[9]

Second, Sergio Fadl has shown that there was a parametric change in exports caused by the process of trade liberalization, beginning with Mexico's entry into GATT and intensifying after the enactment of NAFTA.[10] By 1997 total exports represented nearly 30 percent of GDP, more than double the figure of the early 1990s and almost three times the percentage in the early 1980s. And most of those exports were manufactured goods produced by the private sector. In fact, by 1997 manufacturing exports constituted around 75 percent of all exports.

As domestic manufacturing processes become more integrated with imports, the peso cost of domestic inputs that cannot be traded—labor, energy, and construction materials, for example—becomes less and less relevant, and the impact of fluctuations in the exchange rate on domestic firms diminishes. In short, more firms now operate on a dollar basis, including financing. Those that have not taken that step, either because they cannot or because they do not want to, are more vulnerable to such market fluctuations, which have proved so detrimental to their performance in the past. Large depreciations of the peso, along with its real overvaluation or undervaluation at times, have generated uncertainty and an incentive to speculate rather than to produce.

Financing the Economy

Over the years the Mexican economy has had to resort to foreign lending to finance its domestic needs, especially since the end of the 1950s. By the end of the 1970s, such borrowing had become untenable: Accumulated deficits mounted to an enormous external debt that exploded in 1982. Foreign resources, complemented by internal private and public savings, had long been used to finance investment. And indeed, so long as foreign lending resources were available, the economy grew rapidly; when those resources dried up, however, the economy could not sustain high rates of investment or, consequently, growth. After 1982 no more foreign lending was forthcoming, until Mexico's foreign debt was renegotiated in mid-1989. Then, as foreign lending and huge amounts of foreign investment—both in productive capacity and to a greater extent in financial instruments—poured into the country, the economy was able to resume growth, albeit at a slower pace.[11]

The relationship between domestic savings and investment illuminates the role of the private sector in generating the funds required to sustain growth. As Figure 3.1 shows, private savings were essentially enough to pay for private investment until the late 1960s. Any shortfalls in the preceding decade were made up by the public sector, although those shortfalls typically were not large. Beginning in 1968, however, private savings began to climb far higher than did private investment, which suggests that the private sector was financing an increasing portion of public investment. Throughout the 1970s and 1980s the private sector financed the government's investment to the extent that private investment was crowded out—that is, public investment was paid for at the expense of private capital accumulation. Indeed, during the 1980s only about half of private savings went toward private investment. The rest of the funds were channeled to public investment as the public sector expanded through the creation and enlargement of public enterprises and high public spending, and later as the need to repay the country's foreign debt became pressing.

This trend reversed in the early 1990s when the government eliminated its deficit and the exchange rate stimulated consumption rather than investment. In those years—until the 1995 fiscal crisis—private investment was much larger than private savings, with private consumption soaring to an all-time high just before the exchange rate devaluation in December 1994. Naturally, the economic recession acted as a brake on consumption. Private savings and investment have been kept at similar levels in recent years.

Several mechanisms were used to channel funds to the government during those years of private lending to the public sector. The most straightforward method was to increases taxes, an expedient but sometimes difficult measure. In fact, because it could not push through fiscal reform in the 1960s and 1970s, the government went through the back door and increased the legal-reserve requirement in the banking system, as discussed earlier. The result of that policy was to divert lending resources from private investment toward government programs.

However, in the early 1990s an overvalued exchange rate and

Figure 3.1 Savings Investment Gap of the Private Sector, 1950–1996

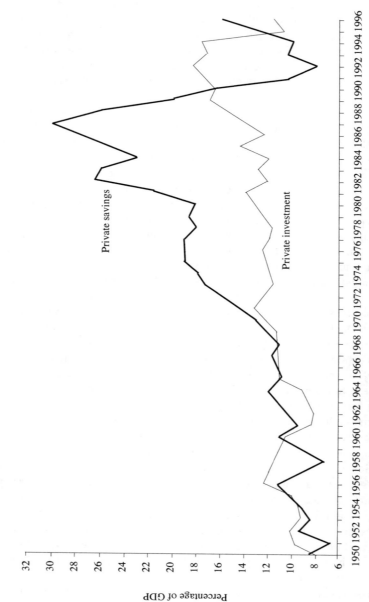

Source: Enrique Cárdenas, "Lecciones recientes sobre el desarrollo de la economía mexicana y retos para el futuro," in *México: Transición económica y comercio exterior* (Mexico City: Bancomext, 1997), p. 81.

abundance of lending resources to the general public contributed to the increase in private consumption and to the fall in private savings, leading to a serious disequilibrium in the country's relationship with the external economy. That disequilibrium, in turn, led to the exchange rate and lending crisis of 1994–1995, the resolution of which relied on borrowing more funds from abroad and on the corresponding reduction in consumption.

PUBLIC POLICY AND THE ECONOMIC ROLE OF THE STATE

The government's protectionist policies of earlier decades undoubtedly had a profound effect on the private sector. This issue has been well covered in the literature and is dealt with at length in several chapters of this book; therefore, let it suffice here to point out that the protectionism that began as a means to control imports in order to protect the balance of payments in the late 1940s became a wider, more profound, and complex policy as years passed.

In short, domestic producers were first protected from foreign competition; then, as foreign firms entered the scene to supply the domestic market and take advantage themselves of the protective measures, national investors began to be protected against foreign investors doing business in Mexico. Thereafter foreign investment was dampened through special restrictions, some of them at the constitutional level—thus, areas of the economy that previously had been open to all came under protection. Nonetheless, private investment did not react as expected, and the state stepped in.[12] More and more government agencies and companies were created to fill the vacuum left by the private sector. By December 1992, 1,155 public entities had been established, most of which were public enterprises with a majority participation of government. The state's contribution to GDP grew from 14 percent in 1978 to around 25 percent in the 1980s, largely as a result of the oil boom (see Figure 3.2).

The debt crisis brought the realization that such policies had to change—namely, that the economy should be opened to foreign competition to assure better levels of competitiveness and at the same time should be able to attract foreign investment to help cope with the scarcity of foreign exchange and productive capacity. The enormous fiscal deficits of 1981 and 1982 also prompted the government to implement strong austerity measures and to review the role of the state in the economy. The adjustment program, which implied honoring the debt, was quite costly in social terms, as real wages and levels of nourishment and health declined.[13] Public investment and government spending in social programs were drastically reduced as interest payments soared. For the first time in several decades, Mexico ran a balance of payments surplus, which meant that capital was

Figure 3.2   Public Sector Contributions to GDP, 1978–1989

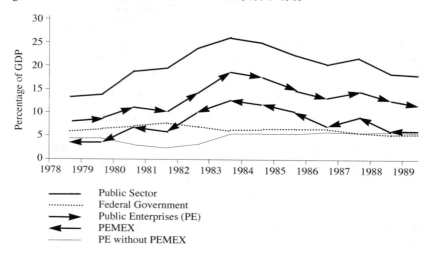

Source: Elia Marún Espinosa, *Empresa Pública e Intervencionismo Estatal en
México* (Guadalajara: Instituto de Administración Pública de Jalisco, Universidad de
Guadalajara, 1992), p. 107.

being repaid or exported, and it had to deal with a large measure of under-
utilized capacity.[14]

The administration of Miguel de la Madrid Hurtado (1982–1988)
began the process of downsizing the role of the state in the economy, and
the number of public entities decreased sharply: By 1988, those entities
totaled 412, and the public sector's contribution to GDP had dropped to less
than 20 percent. The major reduction, however, was yet to come. That was
accomplished under the administration of Carlos Salinas de Gortari (1988–
1994), as privatization gained momentum. The range of privatized companies was very wide: from sugar mills to television stations, from commercial banks and insurance companies to the telephone monopoly, and so on.
The privatization process significantly reduced the state's contribution to
GDP, although some important areas—oil, for example, under PEMEX—
remained in the hands of the state.[15] By the end of 1996 there were still 185
public sector entities.

Although it is too early to write the final analysis of privatization, it is
clear that results have been mixed. Some outcomes—for TELMEX, sugar
mills, television, steel, airlines, and food, for example—have been positive
indeed. Yet the result for the banking sector was less auspicious, partly
because the banks were hit particularly hard by the financial crisis and partly because they inherited a formidable number of bad loans upon privatiza-

tion; to stay afloat, they have had to resort to mergers and recapitalization from foreign banks. The legacy of recent strategies to rescue the banks, debtors, and other producers remains to be seen, as does the cost of those strategies to the taxpayers of this and the next generation.

TRANSFORMATION OF THE EXTERNAL SECTOR

The private sector has contributed significantly to the transformation of the external sector and consequently to the transformation of the entire economy. Indeed, the external sector has mushroomed to unanticipated levels in the past decade. Imports and exports constituted about 10 percent of GDP in 1970; in 1996 that figure had climbed to nearly 60 percent (see Figure 3.3). Obviously, Mexico's accession to GATT and NAFTA and other free trade agreements has modified the country's scenery in various ways. First, a greater array of goods and services are more widely available to domestic consumers, and Mexico's products now have nearly unlimited markets. Second, the rules of origin established under NAFTA stimulated foreign investment. Third, domestic firms have found new partners abroad in order to compete in the global economy, especially in the North American market. Fourth, the number and scope of maquiladoras have expanded rapidly; moreover, the agreement under which they operate permits them to establish themselves anywhere in national territory, which has helped create new industrial centers often far from the northern border.

The structure of international trade has also evolved in recent years (see Figure 3.4). Manufacturing now accounts for the bulk of exports (about 75 percent), and Mexico's earlier dependence on oil exports has almost vanished (oil now comprises less than 15 percent of exports, although it continues to be relevant for public finances). Within the manufacturing sector, most of the increase in exports is attributable to textiles, oil derivatives, and especially metallic products, machinery, and equipment. Clearly, the dynamism of the export sector was critical to the recovery from the 1995 crisis. For example, while the production of textiles increased 28 percent in the years 1995–1997, exports of those products increased much faster, at 65 percent, over the same period and thus strongly contributed to the economy's recovery. And a similar story can be told with respect to other manufacturing sectors.

As for foreign investment, the high expectations preceding NAFTA stimulated investments in the few years before 1994, but flows ebbed in 1995 before recovering somewhat in 1996 and 1997. Nonetheless, the flow of direct foreign investment since 1988 has amounted to $64.5 billion,[16] which has been an important complement to domestic savings and investment. Foreign investors are interested in a wide variety of economic activi-

Figure 3.3   External Sector Contributions to GDP, 1950–1996

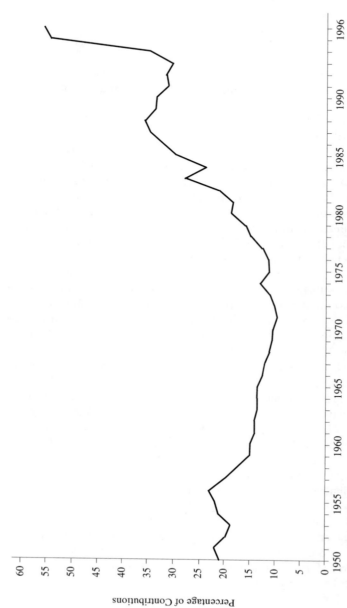

Source: Enrique Cárdenas, "Lecciones recientes sobre el desarrollo de la economía mexicana y retos para el futuro," in *México: Transición económica y comercio exterior* (Mexico City: Bancomext, 1997), p. 90.

Figure 3.4   Composition of Exports by Sector, 1972–1996

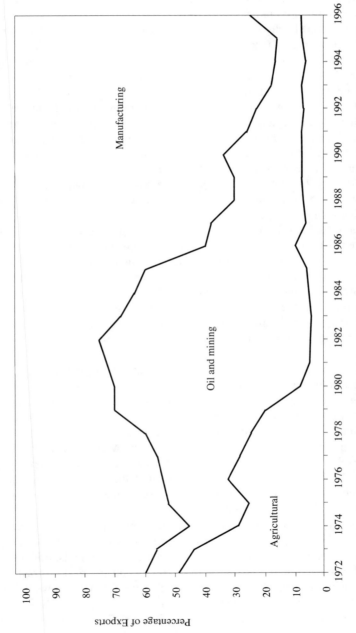

Source: Enrique Cárdenas, "Lecciones recientes sobre el desarrollo de la economía mexicana y retos para el futuro," in *México: Transición económica y comercio exterior* (Mexico City: Bancomext, 1997), p. 91.

ties, such as public utilities, telecommunications, manufacturing, and financial agencies and banks, yet a significant share of foreign investments goes to the maquiladoras; domestic investors are increasingly participating in various maquiladora industries as well.

From 1980 to the present, the number of maquiladora establishments has climbed from 620 to 2,839, many of which originally were Mexican firms producing for the domestic market. Employment in the maquiladoras has also increased enormously: Employees in such establishments totaled approximately 124,000 in 1980 and close to 1,000,000 in 1997. As mentioned previously, maquiladoras have become more geographically diverse, with their locations determined by the advantages of proximity to the firms that need maquiladora products, by the availability of good transportation, or by the incentives extended by various state governments. Specifically, although 93 percent of the maquiladoras were located on the border states in 1980, only 76 percent were situated there in 1997. Maquiladoras exported more than $45.1 billion in 1997, which represents a little over 40 percent of all merchandise exports.

Imports have kept pace with exports, and their composition has changed little over the long run. Intermediate goods make up the vast majority of imports (approximately 75 percent in the past fifteen years), whereas consumer goods account for only about 7 percent; capital goods constitute the remaining 18 percent. This phenomenon is partly attributable to the impact of the maquiladoras on imports, but because the composition of imports has not changed over time, it seems reasonable to conclude that productive processes on both sides of the border are becoming more integrated.

Regional integration between Mexico and its northern neighbor is a fact that is evidenced in many ways, including the growing integration of the Mexican financial market with its northern counterpart. Several measures — among them the closing gap in the variation of interest rates of comparable instruments, and the stock exchange in Mexico and the United States — point to the growing integration of the Mexican financial market with the U.S. market. More and more, Mexican businesses are operating on a dollar basis, borrowing even working capital abroad, with confidence that they can weather fluctuations in the exchange rate because they export a good share of their production output.

Finally, trade liberalization has effected a relocation of economic activity, which now leans more toward the border states. Such a location lowers transportation costs to the North American market and tends to increase the availability of human and financial resources and the basic infrastructure. For example, after trade liberalization took hold, financial flows to Mexico City diminished vis-à-vis the central and northern states; likewise, the southern states witnessed a reduction in financial flows.[17] For example, the Federal District received 66.8 percent of the credit flow in 1985, but in

1994 that percentage had declined to 49.5. By the same token, the industrial participation of the Federal District and adjacent states has also declined. Of course, this pattern differs among sectors: The north has seen wooden products move toward the center, whereas machinery and equipment production has clearly moved to the north, reflecting the growth in exports in that sector.[18]

Employment figures follow the same trend: The Federal District and adjacent states (Hidalgo, Morelos, and Mexico) registered a substantial decrease in employment. Although it is true that since the beginning of the 1980s employment in that area had been decreasing, the trend accelerated once the economy became liberalized. The northern region expanded its employment enormously, at the expense of the center, and by 1994 employment in the north exceeded that in the center, although in 1985 the Federal District absorbed twice as many workers as in the north.

Obviously, trade liberalization has stimulated a relocation of industry and employment toward those regions with a greater comparative advantage within the globalized context.

ECONOMIC GROUPS

Several important economic groups in the Mexican private sector have existed since the late nineteenth century, their birth and development caused in a sense by an unstable institutional framework. Or, as Gonzalo Castañeda Ramos would argue, the family governmental structure of these groups exists because there was insufficient social capital to allow the establishment of another, more corporate, governing structure.[19] In any event, those groups, as well as many of Mexico's prominent private firms, evolved under state patronage, from trade protection to "Mexicanization laws," from government contracts to concessions and actual monopolies.[20] Most of these groups were aligned with the government politically, and even in some cases through intermarriages between families of business owners and politicians.

In more recent years, various events have contributed to the development or restructuring of those large economic groups. In particular, the oil boom of the late 1970s and early 1980s produced a generous supply of financial capital for the groups, which served them well in reinforcing their alliances and actual access to capital. In 1979, for example, 68 percent of all lending resources went to only 5 percent of the borrowers in the Mexican financial system.[21] The economic boom, in turn, advanced both alliances and expansion into other business areas or vertical integration. But whatever their evolution, the group's governing structure did not change significantly as a result of the oil boom.

The new challenges posed by the liberalization of the economy and globalization, as well as the privatization of numerous state firms and the commercial banks, however, did have an important impact on the recomposition of the economic groups. They were the primary and direct beneficiaries of the privatization process. According to Castañeda,[22] those groups benefited in one of four ways: First, state firms that still had some private participation were sold to their private shareholders—as in the case of Renault, which acquired Automotores Mexicanos, and that of Siemmens, which bought Interruptores de México;[23] second, state firms were sold to economic groups that owned companies in the same branch of industry, as when FRISCO acquired Compañía Real de los Angeles and consolidated its position in mining, CEMEX bought four state cement factories, and so on;[24] third, private firms bought state companies to integrate vertically and consolidate their production chains, as in the case of the soft drink producer Consorcio Industrial Escorpión, which bought four sugar mills; and fourth, economic groups bought state companies simply to enter into new areas to diversify their holdings. Examples from the fourth group abound: Grupo Vitro expanded into consumer durable goods, Grupo San Luis entered the auto parts industry, and ICA (a construction firm) entered the heavy machinery business, to name a few.[25]

The situation surrounding the privatization of the banking sector was similar, with the long-standing relationship between industrial groups and the banks reinstalled. Old bankers with industrial interests bought a bank, or major economic groups bought a bank to establish a financial arm, or newly established stock brokerage houses had the capital to acquire a bank. As a result, the economic groups were reinforced, some were restructured, and most were able to consolidate their position.

However, when the financial crisis of 1995 struck the banks hard despite the various schemes to support the financial system, several banks were forced to sell part (and sometimes most) of their participation to foreign banks, thus causing them to lose control and have to adjust their governmental structure. Indeed, the Mexican bank owners had to relinquish—reluctantly—their total control in order to keep a financial arm within their economic group. That predicament had not arisen before, and presumably the situation is one that might influence further change in the governmental structure of large Mexican groups. But that remains to be seen.

CONCLUSIONS

The private sector and, indeed, the whole economy and society are facing a major challenge, that of adjusting, adapting, and evolving within a rapidly changing environment. Mexico's entrance into the North American market implies a dramatic change in the rules by which society and the economy have developed since 1950. Most studies indicate that three years of operating under NAFTA have produced positive effects. The volume of trade within the North American region has swelled in every direction, and the dispute-settlement mechanisms in the treaty have worked reasonably well. In fact, the dispute-settlement system grounded in NAFTA provides the forum for an equitable, respectful resolution of Mexican complaints of any sort about bilateral relations with the United States.

Moreover, direct foreign investment from not only the United States and Canada but also other countries has shown apparently permanent increases despite political and economic turmoil—some estimates put the figures at three times the level of direct foreign investment before NAFTA.[26] It also seems reasonable to hypothesize that NAFTA was one reason that the U.S. government and the multilateral financial institutions put together a financial package to rescue Mexico's ailing finances in 1995. Had the economy still been protected rather than open, it is quite possible that Mexico would not have obtained the funds for recovery so rapidly.

It is true that many firms, large and medium-size, and some small ones, have been able to adapt to competition and the new global environment; they have increased productivity and have penetrated world markets. However, the challenge that Mexican society faces today is to incorporate larger segments of society into this process: An additional number of firms need to produce more effectively to become competitive, and many more people need to be brought onto the renewed social and economic path.

NOTES

1. *Ejidos* are communally held land plots under a constitutionally mandated system of land tenure among the rural population.
2. René Villarreal argued in the mid-1970s that the "easy" stage of industrialization had finished by then. Villarreal, *El desequilibrio externo en la industrialización de México (1929–1975): Un enfoque estructuralista* (Mexico City: Fondo de Cultura Económica, 1976).
3. Rafael Izquierdo, *Política hacendaria del desarrollo estabilizador* (Mexico City: El Colegio de México–Fondo de Cultura Económica, 1995).
4. Ibid.
5. The government would usually acquire the entire concern and block its closing in order to prevent unemployment.
6. Leopoldo Solís, *Economic Policy Reform in Mexico* (New York: Pergamon Press, 1981).
7. Consumption dropped 8 percent in 1995 from the previous year's level, according to INEGI (National Institute of Statistics, Geography, and Information).
8. Silvia Quintero and Erick Luna, "El impacto de la apertura comercial en la función importaciones: México," undergraduate thesis (Tesis de licenciatura), Universidad de las Américas–Cholula, Puebla, Mexico, 1997.
9. For the macroeconomic consequences of this change, see Enrique

Cárdenas, "Lecciones recientes sobre el desarrollo de la economía mexicana y retos para el futuro," in *México: Transición económica y comercio exterior* (Mexico City: Bancomext, 1997), pp. 89–97.

10. Sergio Fadl, "El papel del Banco Nacional de Comercio Exterior como factor de apoyo del sector exportador," in *México: Transición económica y comercio exterior* (Mexico City: Bancomext, 1997), pp. 42–43.

11. For a macroeconomic history of the period, see Enrique Cárdenas, *La política económica de México, 1950–1994* (Mexico City: El Colegio de México–Fondo de Cultura Económica, 1996).

12. Ibid., pp. 61–63.

13. Nora Lustig, *Mexico: The Remaking of an Economy* (Washington, D.C.: Brookings Institution, 1992).

14. Vladimir Brailovsky, "Las implicaciones macroeconómicas de pagar: Las respuestas de política económica ante la 'crisis' de la deuda en México, 1982–1988," in *La economía mexicana: Un enfoque analítico,* ed. Gonzalo Castañeda Ramos (Mexico City: Limusa-Noriega Editores, 1994), pp. 275–331.

15. Certain areas of PEMEX operations, and the railroads, are now in the process of privatization.

16. All dollar amounts are U.S. dollars.

17. Isaac Katz, "Efecto regional de la apertura comercial," in *México: Transición económica y comercio exterior* (Mexico City: Bancomext, 1997), pp. 341–343.

18. Ibid., graphs 2–10.

19. Gonzalo Castañeda Ramos, "La empresa mexicana y su gobierno corporativo: Antecedentes y desafíos para el siglo XXI" (photocopy, 1997). Castañeda is the head of the economics department at the Universidad de las Américas in Puebla, Mexico.

20. Luis Rubio, "El sector privado en el pasado y futuro de México," in *Industria y trabajo en México,* eds. James Wilkie and Jesús Reyes Heroles G. (Mexico City: Universidad Autónoma Metropolitana, 1990), pp. 243–262.

21. Sylvia Maxfield, *Governing Capital: International Finance and Mexican Politics* (Ithaca, N.Y.: Cornell University Press, 1990), as quoted in Castañeda Ramos, *La empresa mexicana,* p. 263.

22. Castañeda Ramos, "La empresa mexicana," pp. 269–274.

23. According to Vidal, twenty-seven of the privatized firms fall into this category. Francisco Javier Vidal, "Lo que el tiempo se llevó: La industria paraestatal," in *La restructuración industrial en México, cinco aspectos fundamentales,* ed. Josefina Morales (Mexico City: Instituto de Investigaciones Económicas, Universidad Autónoma de México, 1992), pp. 118–119.

24. Ninety-eight companies belong in the group, according to Vidal, "Lo que el tiempo se llevó."

25. Ibid., p. 121.

26. Gustavo Vega Cánovas, "La promoción de las exportaciones, el TLCAN y el futuro del libre comercio en América del Norte," in *México: Transición económica y comercio exterior* (Mexico City: Bancomext, 1997), pp. 368–369.

4

Original Goals and Current Outcomes of Economic Reform in Mexico

Jonathan Heath

Mexico has undergone a noteworthy economic transformation since the late 1980s, shifting from an inward-looking, import-substitution development model to an outward-looking, market-oriented paragon. Seeking its place in the new global economy, Mexico followed the path toward economic modernization. That path has been much more rocky than originally envisioned, however, and at times the country has openly stumbled. After the peso crisis of December 1994 and the recession of 1995, "reform fatigue syndrome" set in; as a result, calls for measures to counteract the reform process gathered strength. Popular support for reform—present throughout the administration of Carlos Salinas de Gortari (1988–1994)—withered away and has been replaced by public resentment. Nevertheless, the current administration of Ernesto Zedillo Ponce de León recognizes the importance of maintaining the current economic model and is pushing ahead in the reform process.

This chapter describes the reform measures undertaken in Mexico since 1982, analyzes the pros and cons of continuing along the same path of economic liberalization, and reviews the implications of both current and proposed economic reforms. An overview of the economic policies that led to the need for reform precedes the discussion of the reform process itself. The initial attempts at reform are then examined, as are the measures undertaken by the Salinas administration. Next, the transition costs are presented, with a close look at the current status of the reform process. Finally, the outlook for further reform is analyzed against the backdrop of Mexico's original intentions and goals.

WHY WERE ECONOMIC REFORMS NECESSARY?

In the early 1940s, the aim of Mexico's development strategy was to expand the nascent industrial sector in a predominantly rural and agricultural country. The classic "infant industry" argument was invoked to justify a highly protectionist scheme with sizable subsidies for domestic producers. The industrial growth that followed brought rapid urbanization and displacement of agricultural workers to the industrial and services sectors. Despite its strong growth, the industrial sector could not provide enough jobs to accommodate the huge influx of workers caused by the combination of very high population growth and rapid urbanization. Thus, the services sector began to absorb the excess labor, although with low-paying, low-productivity jobs.

During this period of industrial expansion, Mexico's economic growth was high and inflation low, with a fixed exchange rate as of 1954.[1] Coming off an external debt negotiation in 1942 that virtually eliminated all obligations abroad, the protectionist policies allowed for very high rates of return on domestic investment. Backed by relatively conservative fiscal and monetary policies, the economy experienced an unparalleled period of growth and stability dubbed "the Mexican miracle."

By 1971, however, concerns over income maldistribution and poverty led the Mexican government to pursue a much more active role in the economy. Consequently, the fiscal deficit rose from 2.3 percent of gross domestic product (GDP) in 1971 to 9.3 percent in 1975. The resulting increase in public sector borrowing requirements and inflation caused a peso devaluation in 1976, marking the end of an era and the beginning of decades of instability.

At this point, concern over Mexico's development policy mounted higher. The import-substitution policy that Mexico had followed for nearly four decades certainly produced strong growth rates, but the policy could not succeed indefinitely: In the closed economy, the domestic savings rate was low, capital practically nonexistent, and foreign exchange modest.

Because the rate of return on investments in Mexico was high, national firms relied almost entirely on the domestic market while largely ignoring a potential export market. Exports therefore declined from almost 15 percent of GDP in the early 1940s to less than 4 percent by the mid-1970s. According to the import-substitution policy, growth in imports was supposed to decline as well, to avoid a problem in the balance of payments; however, incentives under the protectionist policy were never adequate to achieve this outcome. The resulting lack of foreign exchange led to a steady increase in external borrowing.

Economic policy changed dramatically around 1973. Before then, conservative fiscal and monetary policies had dominated the scene, providing the economy with stability and consistent growth. Because most of the population did not share in the increased prosperity, however, political pressures started surfacing. The poor were getting poorer and abandoning their rural communities. As cities swelled, so too did the problems associated with rapid urbanization, problems that previously had been almost completely ignored.

In an effort to renew economic policy and deal with these problems, President Luis Echeverría Alvarez placed his longtime friend, José López Portillo, as finance minister. An idealistic lawyer with little understanding of economics, López Portillo promoted a completely different fiscal policy, one that relied heavily on public sector involvement in the economy. Not only did the budget deficit grow, but the government started to purchase enterprises and compete with the private sector in many areas of the economy. In addition, a law was introduced that eliminated most of the incentives for investment from abroad, thereby curtailing an important source of foreign exchange;[2] subsidies and regulations were implemented on a much broader basis than before; and monetary policy was subjugated to fiscal policy, with the head of the central bank reporting directly to the finance ministry. In general terms, the government viewed the private sector as not being trustworthy to produce a sufficient number of jobs and welfare for the population as a whole.

External debt and the burden of debt service gradually increased, causing concerns that the capacity to service external debt would erode. Plagued by excessive external debt throughout its history as an independent republic, Mexico had been able to virtually wipe the slate clean of those debt obligations in 1942.[3] This had given the country precious breathing room that served as the impetus for the growth over the next four decades, but the failure of the import-substitution model to generate adequate foreign exchange ended up hindering this remarkable opportunity.

The economic strategy implemented throughout the 1960s had followed the "stabilized development" model; its three main goals were sustained economic growth, low inflation, and a fixed exchange rate. President Echeverría had decided to pursue these objectives but to distribute the benefits of economic growth more efficiently in a strategy called "shared development." However, the high budget deficit—which caused inflation and an eventual devaluation of the peso—was not compatible with stability. Moreover, the structural problem of insufficient generation of foreign exchange was never addressed—rather, it was aggravated—by the policy changes. In short, the government's more active role in the economy was not producing the intended results and was undermining the possibilities for future growth. It was becoming apparent that other reforms had to be implemented.

OIL BOOM AND BUST, 1973–1982: POSTPONEMENT OF REFORM

Concerns over the lack of foreign exchange were short-lived. After the global oil shock of 1973, Mexico stepped up its search for oil deposits and discovered large new reserves. By 1977 oil export revenues surpassed $1 billion, up from $24 million in 1973; they peaked in 1982 at $16.5 billion.[4] With the promise of a high and steady stream of dollar revenues from oil, the Mexican government initiated an ambitious investment program, borrowing heavily from abroad. By 1982 the fiscal deficit was 16.9 percent of GDP and external debt had jumped to 33.1 percent of GDP. In the meantime, however, nonoil exports had been further neglected: Their value dropped to an all-time low of 2.4 percent of GDP in 1981 (see Table 4.1).

All country risk indicators used by the international financial community showed that Mexico's level of debt was too high in 1976, thus representing a high lending risk. Even after a restrictive economic policy was put in place in 1977 to neutralize the effects of the previous year's peso devaluation, all indicators continued to register at the danger level. Nevertheless, Western banks—repositories for the global supply of excess dollars generated by the oil boom—knocked consistently on Mexico's doors.

Initial results were very good. Spurred by high investment rates, GDP grew more than 8 percent a year between 1978 and 1981. Although inflation remained high, the average annual rate for the period was less than 24 percent. The promise of a forever-high oil price and the discovery of huge oil reserves led the government to think that Mexico was well positioned to maintain its active role in the economy to help assure more equitable

Table 4.1 Nonoil Exports as a Percentage of GDP, 1940–1982

Year	Percentage of GDP
1940	14.00
1950	10.12
1960	5.78
1970	3.63
1973	3.75
1974	3.91
1975	2.98
1976	3.49
1977	4.46
1978	4.17
1979	3.75
1980	2.92
1981	2.44
1982	3.11

Source: LatinSource Mexico, based on data from the Banco de México.

income distribution and poverty reduction. The problem was that Mexico's purported privileged situation was quite vulnerable to outside shocks, which soon materialized.

In 1979 inflation in the United States reached double digits, causing a jump in the prime rate to 20 percent by 1981. Because the bulk of Mexico's debt was linked to the prime rate, the cost of debt service rose dramatically. Most banks, sensing that Mexico was already overleveraged, granted the country only short-term loans with high premiums. Despite these signals that the economic situation was deteriorating, the Mexican government refused to reconsider its development strategy; instead, it maintained an overvalued exchange rate and continued to borrow heavily abroad. In 1981 alone, the government increased its net debt by more than $20 billion in short-term borrowing, apparently assuming that it could effectively roll over the maturities on a continuous basis.

The international situation, coupled with serious domestic policy mistakes, finally caused an incontrovertible, severe deterioration of most economic indicators in 1982, when world oil prices started to weaken. By that time, the current-account deficit had grown tremendously, the fiscal budget was showing an immense deficit, the inflation rate was more than 30 percent, and economic growth was slowing down. The peso was overvalued by nearly 40 percent, and speculation rose over an imminent adjustment in the exchange rate, leading to massive capital flight. The economy as a whole was in a state of extreme disequilibrium in need of major restructuring. With its foreign exchange reserves depleted and the peso devalued three times during 1982, Mexico had to balk on its debt service payments, initiating the international financial crisis of 1982.

What reforms were necessary? First, foreign exchange had to be generated. The import-substitution model reduced the incentives for export growth, while existing legislation curtailed potential foreign investment. The result was an overleveraged economy with unsustainable country-risk ratios. A new approach was needed, one that would produce enough foreign exchange to be consistent with economic growth targets.

Second, the role of the government in the economy had to be examined. The government had been competing with the private sector, creating unfair competitive advantages and compromising its own ability to deal with more pressing social problems. A growing fiscal deficit crowded out financial resources and introduced inflationary pressures. Excessive regulations hindered new foreign investments and induced an inefficient allocation of resources. As public debt grew, so too did the cost of its service, crowding out other avenues of public spending. The government lost its ability to carry out investments in key enterprises like PEMEX (the oil monopoly), TELMEX (the telephone monopoly), and CFE (the electricity monopoly), causing a slow but steady deterioration in the country's infrastructure. The government needed to restructure its finances and its holdings in order to become more efficient.

Third, economic stability had to be achieved. High inflation induced currency devaluations, climbing interest rates, higher risk ratios, and distortions in the allocation of resources. The effects of inflation were causing firms to prefer speculative investments over productive investments.

Finally, debt ratios had to be addressed. Their high levels were inhibiting further loans, demanding large amounts of foreign exchange, and resulting in a net transfer of funds out of the country. In short, Mexico was exporting capital at the expense of economic growth.

DE LA MADRID'S ATTEMPTS AT ECONOMIC REFORM

After the first devaluation in February 1982, the Mexican government tried to stabilize the economy and set things back on track, but its policy attempts were misdirected and failed to recognize major imbalances. For example, no serious adjustments in government expenditures were made for the loss of oil revenues, and an emergency salary increase that was put into effect neutralized the impact of the devaluation and caused inflation to soar to a near triple-digit rate. Soon after the banking sector was nationalized, exchange controls were introduced, import permits on all items were established, and dollar deposits in commercial banks were converted by decree into pesos. Within a few months Mexico showed a trade surplus for the first time since 1949, albeit without instituting any measures aimed at generating foreign exchange; instead, the adjustment was carried out almost entirely through import restrictions.

After President Miguel de la Madrid Hurtado took office in December 1982, he almost immediately instituted a new stabilization program, the Program for Immediate Economic Recovery (PIRE). PIRE called for a sharp reduction in Mexico's fiscal deficit and stringent austerity measures, in accordance with the Extended Facility Agreement signed with the International Monetary Fund (IMF). In May of the following year, the government unveiled its six-year National Development Plan, which consisted of two main thrusts. The first was an all-out effort to achieve economic stability, based on the provisions of PIRE. The second called for structural changes aimed at eliminating the imbalances that had caused the financial crisis in the first place, such as the government's role in economic activity.

Between 1983 and 1987 Mexico struggled to achieve stabilization, with only limited results. Because of the very high debt overhang, foreign debt had to be restructured three times during that period. In 1983 all short-term debt was restructured, with a longer amortization schedule; further restructuring—covering interest payments, commissions, and amortization periods—took place beginning in 1984. The depth of the recession of 1983, however, brought political pressures to jump-start the economy before the stabilization efforts could be consolidated. The financial crisis, coupled with the government's initial policy response, deprived Mexico of all voluntary international lending for several years. Although the austerity program had produced a current-account surplus—which was necessary to meet amortization payments—it caused negative external savings. This, coupled with a net transfer of payments abroad from the external debt service, reduced the amount of domestic savings available for investment and economic growth.

The Mexican economy started growing again in 1984, but inflation stood at 65 percent. Therefore the peso was devalued again in mid-1985 and a renewed attempt was made to stabilize the economy. By 1985, inflation stood at 58 percent, GDP growth registered 2.6 percent, and the exchange rate depreciated 68 percent, figures that are far from reflecting a stabilized economy. Although Mexico maintained a current-account surplus, and debt negotiations allowed for new (involuntary) capital disbursements from Mexico's creditors during this period, the country was unable to continue paying its debt service. Thus, following a massive earthquake in September 1985, Mexico again called for a deferral in amortization payments and a new restructuring of its debt. This time Mexico negotiated a more viable relationship between debt-servicing requirements and its payment capacity, one aimed at lowering financial resource transfers abroad and allowing for economic growth. The terms of the debt renegotiation called for linking payments to oil prices and economic activity, in line with the "Baker Plan" (named after James Baker, U.S. secretary of the treasury at the time).

In 1986 the price of oil dropped below $10 a barrel from an average price of $25.50 the previous year. The adjustment undertaken by the Mexican government caused a 3.7 percent drop in GDP that year, with inflation reaching triple digits by the year's end. The outcome of stabilization efforts had been hindered economic growth and failure to lower inflation, despite the fact that the government had closely followed IMF recommendations. And because of the lack of foreign exchange, the Mexican monetary authorities had to implement an ongoing policy of aggressively undervaluing the exchange rate. Both the budget deficit and inflation soared as a result.

Up through 1986 the attempts at structural reform had been feeble at best. A privatization effort was initiated, although it was limited to nonpriority firms of little value. Public spending was cut back in many areas, only to be replaced by increases in debt-service payments. Public prices and tariffs were increased, but the fiscal deficit remained high. Federal government employees were laid off, but they were too few to affect the level of public spending. Thus, it was becoming increasingly obvious that stabilization efforts and structural reform had to be much more aggressive to achieve results.

NEW STABILIZATION PROGRAM

By this time Mexico was closely observing the so-called heterodox stabilization endeavors under way in Brazil, Argentina, Bolivia, and Israel. Orthodox stabilization efforts had failed in all countries, including Mexico, because the driving force behind inflation was no longer just a high fiscal deficit. Inflation had reached a stage in which it fueled itself, creating what is known as inertial inflation. For example, high inflation called for high salary increases, which in turn caused further inflation. Expectations, per se, were the driving force behind inflation.

Heterodox stabilization programs sought to cut inflation quickly and eliminate the inertial component of inflation by using strict wage and price controls, usually backed by a "social pact" whereby everyone agreed not to raise prices at the same time. Both Brazil and Argentina brought high triple-digit inflation rates down to nearly zero within a year. After a while, however, demand pressures in those countries broke down price controls and inflation returned with a vengeance. In contrast, Israel combined orthodox and heterodox elements to eliminate inflation in a very successful stabilization effort. The heterodox component brought inflation down quickly, whereas the orthodox component helped reduce the fiscal deficit, which was what caused inflation in the first place.

In October 1987 stock markets crashed all over the world, creating an extremely vulnerable situation for capital flight. Despite historically high foreign exchange reserves and a highly undervalued exchange rate, Mexican authorities devalued the peso in November. This set the stage for the introduction of a new stabilization program in December of that year. Borrowing from Israeli experience, the government used components of both heterodox and orthodox approaches, together with a social consensus agreement, in the Pact of Economic Solidarity, initiating a tradition of so-called *pactos* (agreements).

The results were immediate: Inflation dropped from a twelve-month high of 180 percent in February 1988 to a year-end rate of 52 percent. By fixing the exchange rate at 2,257 pesos to the dollar and freezing wages and certain key prices, the monthly inflation rate soon dropped. After registering an average of 8 percent per month in 1987, inflation dropped to less than 1 percent by August of the next year. The government followed up with restrictive fiscal and monetary policies, which brought down the fiscal deficit from 16.1 percent of GDP in 1987 to 12.5 percent in 1988; eventually, the deficit was eliminated altogether.

STRUCTURAL CHANGES

Between 1983 and 1988, the government pursued the structural changes called for in the National Development Plan. Privatization efforts intensified and either closed down, sold, merged, or transferred the ownership of many public enterprises. Across-the-board subsidies were drastically reduced, and the number of people employed by the federal government was decreased. The government was gradually but definitely eliminating its participation in many different economic activities through privatization, deregulation, or direct reduction of expenditures, yet many argued that the pace of reform was too slow. Most of the privatized firms had been small, insignificant enterprises with little economic impact. Economic growth rates had not yet recovered, averaging nearly 0 percent throughout most of the 1980s. Business confidence in the government had not recuperated significantly and foreign investment remained low. Country-risk indicators remained high despite several attempts to improve overall performance. Nevertheless, weary of the political costs of reforms, which often represented a radical departure from the past, the government decided to continue its gradual pursuit of reform.

In 1985 the Mexican government applied for membership in the General Agreement on Tariffs and Trade (GATT), which signaled an end to the protectionist policies of the past and marked the beginning of a new era for Mexico in trade policies. In 1987 the government decided to accelerate trade liberalization and pursue a unilateral tariff reduction, truly exposing Mexican industry to international competition for the first time. The tariff reduction, from an average of 27 percent in 1982 to 13.1 percent in 1987, proved to be larger than that negotiated six years later in the North American Free Trade Agreement (NAFTA). Nevertheless, after five years of reform attempts it had become apparent that the initial strategy was not producing the desired results, though a large amount of political capital had been spent in its implementation.

SALINAS REFORMS

In December 1988 a new administration took office, headed by President Carlos Salinas, who believed that economic reforms had to take place at a much quicker pace and that they had to be permanent in nature. After many years of attempts to stabilize the economy through a gradualist orthodox approach, the heterodox shock treatment had begun to achieve some results. Salinas decided that the same approach should be applied to the structural changes needed in the economy. A new national development plan was introduced, called the Pact for Growth and Economic Stability; the pact called for the continuation of the stability program, together with an all-out effort for "economic modernization."

The economic modernization efforts of the Salinas administration comprised four basic goals and strategies for reaching them. First, to eliminate inflationary pressures and provide a basis for stability, the government would strive for healthy fiscal accounts through a sharp retrenchment in public sector borrowing requirements. Second, to greatly reduce the participation of the government in the economy and increase total investment through private sector participation, the government would accelerate and broaden the privatization efforts of the previous administration. Third, to simplify business operations, reduce costs, and eliminate barriers to further investments, the government would deregulate a wide range of economic activities. Fourth, to increase efficiency and generate foreign exchange, the government would expand trade liberalization. To improve resource allocation, all of these reforms were to be carried out within the framework of a market-oriented economy.

Suffusing the overall plan was the need to strengthen confidence in the Mexican economy. Before the Salinas reforms, expectations had seemed stuck in a vicious circle, with inflation high, sustained growth absent, and confidence in the government eroded. By taking an aggressive stance in economic policy reform, the government managed to turn a vicious circle into a virtuous one. Within a few years, foreign banks and firms were no longer trying to evade prior commitments in Mexico; they wanted to be there to participate in Mexico's success.

The figures spoke for themselves. Inflation finished under 20 percent in 1989 and reached the single-digit level by June 1993. Economic activity grew above 4 percent (4.4 percent) in 1990 for the first time in eight years. Interest rates dropped from 159 percent in January 1988 to 11.6 percent in March 1992. The fiscal deficit went from 12.5 percent of GDP in 1988 to a surplus of 2 percent in 1991. Apparently, President Salinas's modernization efforts intimated the permanence of stability and facilitated a gradual return to much-needed sustained economic growth. Moreover, he had followed almost all of the policy recommendations of the "Washington consensus"[5]—that is, the U.S. government, the IMF and World Bank, influential think tanks, and academia.

From this point on, it seemed that Mexico could be subjected to the normal business cycle of any market-oriented economy without engendering an economic crisis, as in the 1980s. As long as the government promoted a consistent framework for macroeconomic policy, the outlook could only improve. Throughout his administration, Salinas's policies served as examples for other developing countries and as the prime example of a market-oriented transformation. Mexico became a hot market for portfolio investment and one of the most promising emerging markets.

Debt Restructuring

Upon taking office in 1988, Salinas called for a fourth and final restructuring of Mexico's foreign debt. Previous debt negotiations had extended amortization periods and reduced interest payments, but they had not effectively reduced the debt service burden, nor had they allowed Mexico to return to the voluntary international credit market. Instead, they had caused a net transfer of financial resources abroad, which was equivalent to the export of capital. In a country with relatively scarce capital, this meant that domestic investment and growth were impeded.

The negotiations this time achieved a significant reduction in payments abroad; outstanding external debt was reduced and interest payments lowered, and new capital from securities swap agreements and new loans flowed into the country. Shortly after the restructuring, Mexico returned to the voluntary credit market for the first time in seven years. Between 1989 and 1992, stepped-up privatization efforts and the sale of several large public enterprises brought over $22 billion into the federal treasury, which further reduced both domestic and external public debt. Domestic debt fell from 18.4 percent of GDP in 1986 to 7.9 percent in 1993; external debt went from 60.2 percent to 14.1 percent during the same period. As a result, Mexico's total net debt dropped from 78.6 percent of GDP to 22 percent between 1986 and 1993. Country-risk indicators started to improve dramatically and creditors substantially lowered interest premiums on new debt. In 1992 Mexico achieved a BB+ sovereign risk rating by Standard & Poor's, one notch below the coveted investment-grade minimum. This reduction in the debt burden opened up the possibility of applying further reforms and transforming the economy in the right direction.

Fiscal Retrenchment

Several factors contributed to the virtuous circle that led to a public-sector surplus (excluding proceeds from privatization) in 1992. The reduction in debt achieved in the foreign negotiations, along with the proceeds from privatization, reduced also the amount of interest paid by the federal government, which had been its largest expenditure item. And without the high demand for financial resources to finance the deficit, interest rates started dropping.

Under Salinas, the government also initiated an aggressive program aimed at reducing tax evasion. By increasing the tax base coverage and reducing tax evasion, authorities were able to cut the value-added tax rate from 15 percent to 10 percent and the top income tax bracket from 50 percent to 35 percent, while increasing the total tax intake. At the same time, taxes on certain products were either reduced or eliminated and a new tax on assets was introduced, which effectively served as a minimum income tax.[6]

On the expenditure side, spending on many low-priority items was reduced to a minimum. In fact, one representative of the Mexican government boasted that the expenditure cuts carried out in Mexico were equivalent to three times those carried out in the United States under the Gramm-Rudman-Hollings Act of 1985.[7] In moving toward a healthier financial situation, the government was able to attend to pressing social concerns, such as education and infrastructure, and to increase its attention to the poor areas of the country. In 1989 the administration introduced its principal antipoverty initiative, the National Solidarity Program (PRONASOL). Targeted to low-income urban neighborhoods and rural areas, PRONASOL deployed public funds and local volunteers to carry out such important community projects as electrification; construction of roads, hospitals, and sewage and drinking water systems; and school refurbishment. According to authorities, expenditures for such projects increased, as a proportion of total government spending, to the highest level of any previous administration.

On the downside, the government manipulated the PRONASOL program to increase its popularity in areas in which it had lost the most votes in previous elections. Studies have shown that local governments often mismanaged funds, and some even used the funds to buy votes prior to the presidential elections in 1994. In the elections in Tabasco in 1994, for example, according to newspaper reports and opposition parties' investigations, the government's candidate spent well over fifty times the allotted campaign maximum through a mixture of misappropriated funds and obscure financing techniques.

Nevertheless, the Salinas government managed to maintain a fiscal surplus in each of its last four years (including privatization proceeds). Even if the nonrecurring revenues from privatization are not included, a fiscal surplus existed in each of the administration's last three years. Those surpluses, together with a much-improved international outlook that resulted in lower interest rates abroad, contributed to the reduction of debt and debt service, helping the government increase social spending by expenditure substitution. At that time, government officials enjoyed pointing out that Mexico, if compared on the basis of its fiscal deficit and debt as proportions of GDP to members of the European Community, met the so-called Maastricht criteria, which no European country had been able to reach.

Privatization

In December 1982 the public sector officially registered 1,155 public enterprises. Toward the end of the Salinas administration, 1,018 of these had been sold, merged, or closed or were in the final stages of the privatization process. Of the enterprises that remained in state hands, many were either trust funds set up for some specific purpose or an integral part of the government's role (such as the Mexican Social Security Institute). Although the largest number of privatizations occurred during the De la Madrid administration, the more important privatizations—those comprising the larger and more complex firms—have to be credited to the Salinas administration.

Nevertheless, the giant oil monopoly (PEMEX) and the Federal Electricity Commission (CFE) remained in the hands of the state, along with railroads, airports, most seaports, and a few other key enterprises. Although PEMEX and CFE were considered to be the most difficult firms to privatize, given political and historical considerations, the government did take the first steps toward eventual privatization. PEMEX was broken up into four separate companies, run under a common holding: PEMEX-Exploration and Production, PEMEX-Refining, PEMEX-Gas and Basic Petrochemicals, and PEMEX-Petrochemicals (which comprises seven subsidiaries that handle secondary petrochemical products). This may facilitate the eventual sale of the petrochemical complexes, which should be a less sensitive matter than the sale of the other three companies. As for CFE, certain legal changes were introduced that permit the private production of electricity, as long as it is either for internal consumption or sold to the government. These changes are modest, but Salinas decided to postpone the more politically complex aspects of privatization until after concrete results had been achieved in other areas.

The sale of the telephone company (TELMEX) in 1990 was the single largest privatization effort. The government sold the monopoly under an arrangement whereby the buyers would make long-term, strong investments to modernize the country's telephone system. The government also negotiated at the same time to open up the industry to competition, especially in long-distance service, as of 1997.

The sale of commercial banks represented the largest single sector affected, with eighteen banks sold to the private sector. The sales later became the center of controversy when it was revealed that the government had overpriced virtually all of the banks (at a weighted average price of 3.1

times their book value and 14.8 times profit levels) while exercising only a poor attempt at due diligence. The government had managed most banks with social considerations, as opposed to profit motives, in mind; as a result, the banks were short on both capital and efficiency. But most important, credit-risk analysis had been either neglected or overlooked, resulting in a much larger portion of nonperforming assets than the government had admitted. The newly privatized banking sector therefore entered into a crisis that culminated with the currency devaluation at the end of 1994.

Important privatization efforts took place in other sectors as well, including airlines, sugar mills, mining, tobacco, steel mills, the dairy industry, fertilizers, newspapers, radio, television, movie theaters, trucking, and insurance. These efforts were coupled with commitments from the public sector for joint ventures and concession strategies. For example, highway construction was carried out through joint participation of the private and public sectors, a practice that was broadened to include ports and harbors and was expected to be extended to railroads and other key sectors.

As noted earlier, the most important result of the privatization effort was that the government used most of the collected revenue to reduce both domestic and external debt levels, instead of financing current public expenditures. This helped reduce interest payments and contributed to the sharp reduction in public-sector borrowing requirements between 1989 and 1992. Nevertheless, strong doubts about the propriety of these privatization efforts surfaced after Salinas left office. Many of the privatized firms had been sold to Salinas's close friends and relatives, most notably to his brother Raúl. Some firms were sold at minimal prices to close collaborators; yet others were purchased through questionable financing schemes. In the case of the banks, deals were made in which the same bank being sold gave out loans to the buyers to be paid back through future profits. In other cases, firms were sold to the highest bidders without regard to their previous experience or moral character. Taken together, these dealings hindered the process of additional privatization in the next administration.

Deregulation

Because the import-substitution development model used so long by Mexico had called for concentrated governmental intervention in the economy, an aggressive deregulation strategy was needed to transform the nation into a true market-oriented economy. As of the late 1980s the government systematically revised its regulatory environment through changes in laws and regulations, some even at the constitutional level. This process helped improve transparency and the competitive environment in many sectors of the economy. Excessive regulation was replaced by a more efficient industrial structure, which together with trade liberalization promoted competitiveness as a central driving force in the economy. Regulatory reform brought about changes in electricity, mining, health care, ports, petrochemicals, tourism, financial services, agriculture, intellectual property rights, norms and standards, transportation, telecommunications, consumer and environmental protection, the sugar and coffee industries, water supply facilities, fishing, immigration, and customs agencies, among others. By the end of 1993, more than seventeen laws had been reformed and more than forty different regulatory frameworks altered.

The deregulation process also focused on the government's discretionary powers to issue new regulations. A federal law passed in 1992 mandated that any new regulation affecting economic activity must be discussed with the private sector, consumers, producers, and any other affected body so that they might have the opportunity to comment, critique, and suggest revisions. Also required was a study on the economic aspects of any new regulation, to ensure a positive cost-benefit relationship. The government adopted the position that deregulation must be an ongoing process that continuously responded to changing technological and competitive pressures.

New antitrust legislation was introduced in 1992 to prevent monopolistic behavior and promote competitive markets. And in December 1993 the government finally introduced a new law that promotes foreign direct investment in a much more open, straightforward way than did the foreign investment law of 1989. The earlier law, which dated back to 1973, was designed to contain investment within a nationalistic framework; the new law was designed to promote investment through more flexibility and transparency.

Despite these steps toward deregulation, the latest antitrust legislation remains the number-one objection of business leaders in Mexico, with the topics of security and property rights prevailing in the absence of changes in the Mexican judicial system. The new antitrust agency seems to be subject to favoritism, not to transparent considerations. The excessive, complex fiscal structure and the undue amount of registration and licensing it imposes remain as challenges for the next administration.

Trade Liberalization

The Salinas administration decided that one of the best ways to promote competition and increase the efficiency of Mexico's industrial base was through trade liberalization. An open market strategy would not only help Mexico create a diversified export market—and thus enable it to rely less on commodity exports and build a solid source of foreign exchange—but it would also help reduce inflation by promoting competitive pricing.

Under the import-substitution policies, Mexico had a virtually closed economy. Almost all imports were subject to a stringent permit process and tariffs were as high as 100 percent. After the debt crisis of 1982, that strategy remained in force because it was thought to be the only way Mexico could force a trade surplus to meet its debt service obligations. Once the initial stabilization efforts were put into effect and the debt was restructured, however, the government started gradually to liberalize trade.

In mid-1987, one year after Mexico's entry into the General Agreement on Tariffs and Trade, the government mounted a much more aggressive trade liberalization effort. It eliminated most trade permits; dropped the maximum tariff from 100 percent to 20 percent; reduced the number of different tariffs from sixteen to five; and cut the average tariff by 14 percentage points. The government also introduced several export promotion schemes, which significantly reduced the country's dependence on oil. Within a growing export market, oil exports dropped from 74.6 percent of total exports in 1982 to 12.1 percent by 1994.

Following these bold, unilateral efforts at trade liberalization, the Salinas administration entered into discussions over a free trade agreement with the United States in 1990. Soon after, Canada joined in the negotiations that eventually led to the signing and ratification by all three countries of the North American Free Trade Agreement in 1993. The treaty went into effect on January 1, 1994.

The main objective of NAFTA was to establish a comprehensive set of rules to improve and promote market access within North America. The agreement called for the phaseout of almost all barriers to trade, a fair mechanism to settle trade disputes, an adequate protection scheme for intellectual property rights, and an opening up of financial services. The implementation of NAFTA brought Mexico into the world's largest free trade area, with an aggregate economy larger than that of the European Economic Community.

To make sure that Mexico's commitment to free trade was permanent and not just a passing fashion, the Salinas administration wanted the incentives for firms to modernize their plants and equipment to be compelling. Mexico therefore not only entered into GATT and NAFTA but also subscribed to many other treaties and organizations. In 1991 the Mexican government signed a free trade agreement with Chile and a framework agreement with Costa Rica, El Salvador, Guatemala, Honduras, and Nicaragua, which should ultimately lead to a free trade agreement with those Central American countries. In that same year Mexico signed a cooperation framework agreement with the European Economic Community and joined the Economic Cooperation Conference of the Pacific Basin. Also in the works were negotiations with Colombia, Venezuela, and Bolivia, aimed at eventual free trade agreements. In 1993 the Pacific Basin countries invited Mexico to become the first Latin American country to join the Asia Pacific

Economic Cooperation. Finally, in 1994 Mexico formally gained membership in the Organization for Economic Cooperation and Development (OECD), becoming the first country to do so since New Zealand joined in 1973.

TRANSITION COSTS

Mexico has undergone dramatic changes since the late 1980s. Profound economic and political revisions are transforming the country. The economy is shifting from an inward-looking, highly protected, import-substitution development model to an outward-looking, market-oriented structure. The political system is trying to leave behind an authoritarian regime with little regard for the rule of law and reach toward a much more democratic society. These changes are taking place within the context of a social structure with immensely skewed income distribution and huge belts of poverty. This has made the transition very painful, as different sectors of the economy and segments of society transform at disparate paces.

Mexico has paid a high, albeit necessary, price in trying to transform a large but inefficient industrial base into an efficient, globally competitive economy. The process is not simply a matter of eliminating trade barriers and reducing government intervention in the domestic economy. It is an extremely complex transformation of not only technologies and administrative processes but also values and ways of thinking. The whole entrepreneurial spirit has to undergo a major change, as do labor relations and the government's relationship to society. Given the uniquely close relationship between the political and economic systems in the past, the political system has become obsolete as the economy goes through change, dragging the pace of further reforms. This process will take time, and today Mexico has reached but the middle stage.

Michael Bruno warned us of this situation in 1988 when he wrote, "The transition strategy from a prereform regime to a postreform open economy is more important than the choice of the end product."[8] The Salinas administration launched the country on an incredible transformation with the end product firmly in mind but with scant attention to the transition process itself. Because the costs of the transition were forgotten, overlooked, ignored, or underestimated by the government, the economy ran into extremely difficult problems. The current state of the economy and the country's long-term possibilities cannot be evaluated unless the government's role in this phase is fully understood. High unemployment, low growth, banking crises, business mortality, and many other issues cannot be adequately examined outside this context, nor can the future of further economic reform. Whatever Mexico's "approval rating" with international circles, the government has to face the population's growing frustration with the lack of tangible results for the majority of Mexicans.

Because the gradualist approach of 1983–1987 had achieved only limited results but the shock treatment administered later (1988–1992) successfully reduced inflation and the fiscal deficit, authorities became convinced that the complete dismantling of all restrictions was the road to follow. A key selling point of trade liberalization was its promise of stepping up the pace of job creation. Before that could happen, however, the economy would have to go through a period of net job destruction while firms adjusted to the new competitive environment. Many firms were obsolete and would have to either shut down or downsize. Job creation could begin only after firms had expanded their installed capacity by becoming more efficient and adopting newer technologies. The Salinas administration calculated that the period between net job destruction and net job creation would be relatively short, but instead it turned out to be quite long.

The number of jobs in the manufacturing sector, according to monthly surveys by the National Institute of Statistics, Geography, and Information (INEGI), dropped for seventy consecutive months between June 1990 and April 1996. Most firms showed remarkable increases in productivity during this period as a result of their efforts to become more efficient and competitive, thus explaining how growth could coincide with job destruction. The tendency toward downsizing was not limited to manufacturing: Economic census data for 1988–1993 show that the average number of people employed per firm declined across all sectors of the economy. Although lagging considerably behind other sectors, the retail sector is also going through the same process. Starting just before the recession of 1995, the number of people employed in retail establishments has declined for thirty-one consecutive months (through March 1997).

Without a doubt, employment generation, purchasing power, and survival rates of firms suffered severely as a consequence of the brutal recession of 1995. Nevertheless, the recession in itself most likely accelerated the transition period toward a more efficient industrial base. Although many inefficient firms still exist as the economy emerges from the recession, the business sector on the whole is likely to be in much better condition to face global competition than before. For example, after reaching a peak in industrial production in October 1981, the economy took 105 months to recover and surpass that peak; after the recession of 1995, however, it took only 22 months to return to the peak of December 1994 and reach a new historical level of production.

Nevertheless, the costs of the transition should not be confused with the effects of the recession or the consequences of the peso crisis of 1994–1995. Trade liberalization and the tremendous transformation of the economy that followed are at the root of Mexico's labor problem, along with the banking crisis, the high mortality rate of firms, and other structural problems. The peso crisis and the ensuing recession aggravated those problems but cannot be considered part of their origin.

EFFECTS OF THE 1994 PESO CRISIS ON THE REFORM PROCESS

There have been many different explanations of the events leading up to the crash of the peso in December 1994 and the subsequent recession. The Bank of Mexico has emphasized political and criminal events as main catalysts in radically changing expectations.[9] Bank officials explained policy mistakes with the observation that most of those events were interpreted at the time as temporary setbacks, not strong enough to alter the positive progress of previous years.[10] The Zedillo administration has admitted to the mistake of not promoting domestic savings, while permitting the current-account deficit to grow beyond a manageable level and letting the exchange rate become overvalued. Following the same line of reasoning, some observers have suggested that once Mexico hit its international borrowing limits early in 1994, pressure on the Bank of Mexico to use its foreign exchange reserves was inevitable. Scholars in academia and prominent think tanks outside Mexico have suggested that crucial mistakes in monetary policy were made throughout the year by permitting undue expansion in net domestic credit. Others have pointed to the overselling of the Washington consensus as a magical solution to many structural problems.[11] Finally, the U.S. Council on Foreign Relations concluded that the causes of Mexico's problems were primarily domestic and that the government's decision to issue debt with short-term maturities and exchange rate guarantees was highly imprudent.[12]

Much of the early success of Mexico's reform efforts was attributable to an overall improvement in expectations. Large capital inflows arrived on the heels of the promise of reform and future improvement in economic performance. Although the peso crisis seriously damaged those expectations, the orthodox policy response and reluctance to abandon market-oriented philosophy—despite a huge political backlash—helped avoid further harm. Nevertheless, a close distinction must be made between the foreign and domestic markets.

Most foreign financial institutions reduced their holdings in Mexico during 1995, but very few actually closed the door. Instead, they closely monitored the economy, waiting for the right opportunity to jump back in. The financial institutions that did maintain operations in Mexico—with great caution and vigilant analysis—have already started to increase their investments in response to Mexico's remarkably speedy recovery from the surprisingly deep recession of 1995.

On the domestic side, investors in the more modern sectors of the Mexican economy are also quite pleased with the recovery and growing opportunities to expand their export capabilities. Years of investing in better technology, efficiency, and competitiveness has paid off: The export market has boomed and remains the cornerstone of Mexico's future. However, perceptions are quite different among owners and investors in more traditional sectors of the economy, especially the small and medium-size firms that did not transform at the same pace. Many of the owners of these firms did not have confidence in the magnitude and implications of the economic transformation, and others did not have the capability to take part in it.

The fast pace of reforms undoubtedly caused major dislocations in many sectors of the society. Many of the smaller firms that had been accustomed to government subsidies and supports felt abandoned. Rural communities and indigenous populations felt they were not sharing in the new-found growth. The traditional segments of the ruling party itself felt that younger technocrats were displacing them while their own power base was eroding. Trade liberalization did help open up the demand for a more pluralistic society, but the government determinedly downplayed these political implications.

As a result, the last year of the Salinas administration was marked by a complex series of political struggles that culminated in several assassinations and triggered the disastrous peso crisis in December. The ensuing recession underscored the unequal effects of the reforms on most of society and the need for political reforms to address growing frustrations; it also created a new environment that will make further economic reforms much more difficult.

Although the motives behind the assassinations of the presidential candidate of the Institutional Revolutionary Party (PRI), Luis Donaldo Colosio, and Francisco Ruiz Massieu, brother of Deputy Attorney General Mario Ruiz Massieu, have not been established, it is difficult not to associate them with the political conflicts that emerged from the Salinas reforms. The Chiapas rebellion exemplifies the discontent in southern Mexico, a region whose people, after the reforms, feel further from progress than ever before. The victory of Cuauhtémoc Cárdenas Solórzano, candidate of the Party of the Democratic Revolution (PRD), in the electoral race for Mexico City is another reflection of disillusionment with Salinas's promises. The difficulty the PRI had in pushing electoral reforms through Congress in 1996—reforms that all parties had previously agreed to—also demonstrates the lack of trust in the government.

The political backlash against the economic reforms, dubbed "reform fatigue syndrome," is an important consideration in pursuing additional structural changes. Even many of those who remain strongly committed to the modernization process agree that the government must begin to deliver results soon. It is hard to convince anyone—politicians or others—that further economic reforms are necessary when existing reforms have failed to produce tangible results for most of the country's people.

Opposition parties, especially the left-wing PRD, have been calling for not only a slowdown in reforms but also an outright halt in some cases and reversals in others. Although political rhetoric changes and politicians promise different things to different audiences, many statements from the PRD have caused concern, especially in light of the party's growing popularity. For example, Cuauhtémoc Cárdenas has made many statements in recent years against NAFTA and trade liberalization.

On the one hand, the PRD has emphasized the importance of maintaining a low budget deficit and a reasonable current-account deficit. On the other hand, it has pushed for new taxes, such as a capital gains tax and higher tax rates for upper income brackets—measures that would increase the government's participation in the economy. Nevertheless, the diverse statements coming from different PRD candidates indicate a wide divergence of opinion within party ranks. The greatest cause for concern within the business and investor communities has been precisely this lack of consistency, which makes it difficult to predict what changes a PRD victory might bring.

What is clear is that as long as the reforms to date continue to yield negligible results for the majority of Mexicans, expansion of the reform process will be difficult. For reforms to move forward, society in general has to be convinced that they are both necessary and feasible. What many Mexicans now believe, however, is that the peso devaluation and the devastating recession are linked to past reforms.

NEED FOR FURTHER REFORMS

After five years of what seemed to be solid economic reform and progress, the Mexican peso collapsed, throwing the economy into a deep recession and financial crisis. Instead of having the pleasant job of finishing what had seemed to be Salinas's economic miracle, Zedillo inherited the nightmarish task of tackling the crisis and restoring confidence. Given the recent history of five major devaluations between 1976 and 1998, with each followed by a crisis of confidence and a breakdown in economic activity, the task seemed almost impossible. Nonetheless, after implementation of a consistent orthodox response, the economy rebounded in 1996 with 5.1 percent growth in GDP, which in 1995 had dropped by 6.2 percent. Still, Mexico has much to prove both to its increasingly dissatisfied population and to the international community, and much work remains to be done on all of the basic pillars of reform.

Status of Reforms' Original Goals

Although the public deficit was eliminated, tax reform still remains necessary. Despite the reduction in tax rates for the higher income brackets, taxpayers enter the top bracket with relatively low incomes, suggesting the need for revision of the income structure. There is no tax on capital gains or income from interest. Moreover, the overall complexity of the tax system comes in for ample criticism from the business community. The federal budget still relies heavily on oil revenue, and a high proportion of expenditures is directed to administration rather than to much-needed investments in infrastructure.

Although most public firms have been privatized, the government has shied away from the sacred cows, CFE and PEMEX. Many argue that privatization will never be complete without including these two monopolies, but the political complexities involved in selling them will more than likely exempt them from contention for the foreseeable future.

NAFTA has definitely consolidated trade liberalization by cementing in place an agreement that will remain the backbone of Mexico's export industry for decades to come, and advancements in treaty negotiations with other countries and regions should help diversify markets. The remaining issues involve specific markets and will require either bilateral or multilateral negotiations, which are likely to be worked out over time.

Deregulation is one hurdle that reform efforts have failed to clear. Although some bureaucratic red tape has been eliminated, businesses still face a huge array of licensing, regulatory, and other measures that raise the cost of doing business. In many cases the government has cut the number of steps required to open up a new business without correspondingly reducing the number of public employees responsible for implementation. Given that the political system feeds itself on controls and regulations, the political structure of government will have to change profoundly before much progress can be made on this front.

Status of Follow-Up Measures for Reform

New measures grew out of the original fiscal goals of the reforms as Mexico's economic situation changed and priorities shifted. For example, the Salinas administration introduced the pension plan to encourage domestic savings; the plan was not accompanied by the privatization of its administration, however, and its scope was far more modest than originally envisioned. The Zedillo administration, after the devaluation of 1994, diagnosed a drop in domestic savings as the taproot of the peso crisis; trade liberalization had produced increased consumer spending but not incentives to save. Zedillo therefore set out to reform the pension plan program, as well as the social security system, to eventually build up a critical mass of longer-term savings. Nonetheless, Congress watered down many of the president's original proposals, which still face strong opposition, especially from the PRD. Compared with the Chilean pension reform, one of the biggest success stories in the recent history of reform, the Mexican revisions look quite pale.

Further measures were also required for debt management. The Salinas administration believed Mexico's debt service burden had been resolved favorably with the external debt negotiations of 1989, but the peso crisis of 1994, together with the revival of overwhelming dependency on *tesobonos* (short-term debt instruments), showed that the Mexican government still has a lot to learn. Even when capital inflows are large enough to finance a growing current-account deficit, reasonable limits have to be set on dependence on foreign capital. Allowing the currency to become overvalued, letting foreign portfolio investments become too attractive, paying insufficient attention to the term structure of debt, failing to build up domestic savings—all of these mistakes contributed to the problem, but behind them all is the shortsightedness of policymakers who did not recognize the necessity for a more flexible policy approach.

The single arena in which previous attempts at reform had failed was in rebuilding after the banking crisis. In this instance, the transition from a closed to an open economy, together with other reforms, weakened rather than strengthened the banking system. The concept of universal banking allowed brokerage houses and commercial banks to merge under one roof. The result was long-term loans financed by short-term operations. Mexico therefore must cope with a financial system that lacks the capital and technology to lead the economy into the next century. The original goals for reform in this area—privatization of banks, opening up of the financial sector, and creation of a new regulatory environment—have been transformed to finding ways to inject capital, technology, and especially managerial skills into the banks.

Still, the thorniest issue concerning all of the reform efforts since the late 1980s is the lack of tangible results. Regardless of whether the goals for reform have been met or revised, if genuine improvements do not materialize soon for most of society, the political backlash will set the country back. As the opposition parties gain ground, their driving force is a reflection of the government's failure to visibly improve the lot of the Mexican people. The costs of the reforms have been much higher than anticipated; those tangible benefits are necessary to make it all worthwhile.

The economic reform process must deliver more than rhetoric to consolidate past efforts and help insulate the economy from future financial crises. Further economic reform, however, now hinges on the political environment.

POLITICAL REFORM

Since 1970, every presidential term in Mexico has ended in crisis. Each of the past four presidents has had at least one major currency devaluation while in office,[13] almost always toward the end of the term and after elections, yet the economic strategies implemented by those presidents have differed markedly. Given this unvarying coincidence of devaluations with the political calendar, it would seem important to concentrate not on what has changed but rather on what has not, and to look beyond economic policies to understand the political nature of economic decisionmaking. Mexico has trod the path of economic reform, yet the country remains strapped with an obsolete political system that contrasts sharply with the market paradigm. Without modernization of its political system, Mexico is bound to suffer repeated economic crises.

The authoritarian nature of the political system gives near-absolute powers to the president for six years, during which unwritten but longstanding rules of partisan influence apply. Up through 1990, the ruling party took over virtually all of Congress, all governorships, and all local political positions. However, the slow erosion of that rigid system beginning in the 1970s has made it increasingly necessary to prop up voter confidence just before elections. The increased need to build confidence has strengthened the link between economic policy and the political calendar. The most notable aspect of this fortified relationship is support for an overvalued exchange rate or a fixed-rule exchange rate policy for an overextended time, which, combined with lax fiscal and monetary policy, results in an explosive outcome.

In the aftermath of the financial crisis of 1982 and the recession of 1983, Mexico suffered from high inflation rates, no growth, bad economic policy, and all-around erosion of the population's welfare. As a result, the PRI fared badly in the 1988 presidential elections, in which only outright fraud prevented it from losing power. However, the initial popularity of Salinas's policies resulted in a recovery that took place in time for the midterm elections in 1991. The turnaround lent Salinas immense popularity, which the PRI capitalized on in the 1994 elections (characterized as the cleanest elections ever held in Mexico). Nevertheless, the devaluation of 1994 and its aftermath managed to wipe out Salinas's popularity to the extent that today he is considered one of Mexico's all-time villains.

As might be expected, the crisis has also tarnished the image of the PRI. Since 1995 it has lost most local elections and, as was expected, lost its grip on Congress in midterm elections in 1997. The Mexican political system will most likely face radical changes when the dominant figure of the PRI no longer dominates; consensus politics will arrive on the scene for the first time. It is difficult to envision exactly what this will mean for Mexico's future, given that there is no precedent from Mexico's past. Political analysts have pointed out that Mexico has never managed a peaceful transition of power from one party to another in all of its history. Although a worst-case scenario definitely involves some sort of violence, the more probable scenarios present different shades of muddling through. Although many observers differ on the short-term implications of this political transition, almost all concur that it will be positive for Mexico in the long run.

All three of the major political parties (PRI, PRD, and the National Action Party, or PAN) have edged closer to the center of the political spectrum since the late 1980s in their competition for votes. This suggests that we should not expect a radical departure from current economic policy. On the positive side, this should mean that corruption will diminish and governmental efficiency will grow, because political competition forces improvements. On the downside, further reforms, especially the more politically sensitive ones such as the privatization of PEMEX or CFE, will be much more difficult to achieve because consensus building will call for a whole new set of skills that politicians have yet to learn. Nevertheless, the future of further economic reforms and the consolidation of past efforts lie today in the hands of the political spectrum.

CONCLUSIONS

Although a new period of economic expansion seems to be under way, Mexico still faces many challenges. Inequitable income distribution and immense poverty belts are the deepest and most complex social problems of all. Meanwhile, the most pressing economic problems include generating higher-paying jobs, restoring purchasing power, diversifying the domestic economy, and promoting sustained economic growth. In the political sphere the task is to evolve toward a more democratic society while ensuring the rule of law in the judicial system.

In the aftermath of the 1997 midterm elections, the biggest concern should be not so much which party wins, but whether the winners and losers alike can work toward a functional political system on behalf of the Mexican people. The test of their success in this endeavor, and the future of economic reforms, will be decided in the presidential elections in the year 2000.

Notes

1. Economic activity grew at an average annual rate of more than 6 percent between 1940 and 1982; inflation was similar to that of the United States during the 1950s and 1960s; and the exchange rate was fixed to the dollar at 12.50 pesos between 1954 and 1976.

2. The new law was designed to limit direct foreign investment so that it would not compete with domestic investment.

3. Around 90 percent of all foreign obligations were condoned, and Mexico was given a thirty-year period to pay back the rest with the first twenty years as a grace period.

4. All dollar amounts are U.S. dollars.

5. John Williamson of the Institute for International Economics in Washington, D.C., coined the phrase.

6. The asset tax helped reduce tax evasion by many firms that had claimed losses year after year, though it eventually became an extremely unpopular measure.

7. Pedro Aspe, *El camino mexicano de la transformación económica* (Mexico City: Fondo de Cultura Económica, 1993).

8. Michael Bruno, "Opening Up: Liberalization with Stabilization," in *The Open Economy: Tools for Policymakers in Developing Countries,* eds. Rudiger Dornbusch and F. Leslie C. H. Helmers (New York: Oxford University Press, 1988), p. 224.

9. *Informe Anual: 1994* (Mexico City: Banco de México, April 1995).

10. Francisco Gil Díaz and Agustín Carstens, "Some Hypotheses Related to the Mexican 1994–1995 Crisis," working paper 9601, Bank of Mexico, Mexico City, 1996.

11. See, for example, Jeffrey Sachs and Andrés Velasco, "Lessons from Mexico," New York University working paper, 1995; and Paul Krugman, "Dutch Tupis and Emerging Markets," *Foreign Affairs* 74, no. 4 (July–August 1995), pp. 28–44.

12. Marie Josée Kravis, *Lessons of the Mexican Peso Crisis: Report of an Independent Task Force* (New York: Council on Foreign Relations, 1996).

13. Technically there was no currency devaluation during the Salinas administration, though the December 1994 devaluation is ascribed to him.

5

Capital Markets and Economic Growth in Mexico: Toward a Sound Investment Regime

Roberto Salinas León

One fundamental question that emerging market economies undergoing regional trade liberalization and structural reform must confront is: What set of public policies (monetary, financial, fiscal, and institutional) should governments follow to cope adequately with the brave new world of global capital mobility? The devastating crisis generated by the peso devaluation in December 1994, and the recent wave of financial shocks in Asia, have placed this issue in the forefront of policy debates throughout the emerging market world. On the one hand, a consensus has emerged for using certain elements of macroeconomic policy as structural complements of trade and market liberalization. On the other hand, opinions about which policy initiatives might work best vary widely—for example, observers disagree on whether an exchange-rate stabilization measure is the best mechanism for price stability and capital formation.

Mexico's excessive reliance on short-run debt and volatile capital flows to finance large external accounts in the period 1990–1994 played a fundamental role in the advent of the ensuing currency and financial crisis. This experience harbors crucial policy lessons for efforts to consolidate a reliable investment regime in post-1994 emerging markets such as Mexico—namely, that capital flows are hypersensitive to volatile shifts in expectations or unforeseen external shocks. Notwithstanding the success of economic reform during the term of Carlos Salinas de Gortari (1988–1994), the policymaking process failed to address the inherent vulnerability of the large requirements of the capital account to unanticipated financial and political events. As David Hale explains, the peso crisis constitutes a demonstration of "the fragility of the post–cold war boom in securitized capital flows to developing financial markets."[1] Indeed, the Panglossian willingness to place external accounts on such vulnerable footing owed to Mexico's persistent and illogically harsh foreign investment restrictions in capital markets. Although institutional investment grew, capital markets lacked versatility in offering attractive medium- and long-term investment opportunities in the most productive sectors of the economy. The challenge was, precisely, to ensure safe and consistent flows of productive investment by abandoning entrenched political taboos and opening up restricted sectors of the society, in the framework of well-defined property ownership rights.[2]

This challenge is still relevant. Mexico's economy has witnessed a rapid and vigorous recovery after a brutal recession and a contraction of domestic consumption. Nevertheless, the authorities are treading with caution, and often warn against overstating recent improvements as more than a reflection that "the period of economic emergency" is over.[3] To analogize, the patient has moved from intensive care to intermediate therapy. This means that the patient requires diligent nourishment with new private capital flows, consistent with long-term capital formation and sustained rates of economic growth, as well as constant monitoring to avoid volatility shocks.

So construed, the development of a sound investment regime in Mexico must take a high place on the agenda of economic reform. In this chapter, I assess the problems and prospects facing Mexico's long-term effort to lessen its dependence on international capital to finance economic development. This effort embodies both positive and negative factors. On the one hand, the current administration under Ernesto Zedillo Ponce de León has the opportunity to increase domestic savings and to continue on the path of structural reform. On the other hand, it confronts important obstacles: exchange-rate uncertainty, political indecision regarding privatization and deregulation, a systematic unwillingness to further institutional reform by promoting a safe property rights regime, and fragility in the banking sector. More generally, the administration has to deal with the "paradox of recovery"—namely, the prevailing idea that the process of economic recovery is not genuine, but merely statistical rhetoric fashioned to save face among a distrustful community.

Instead of acknowledging the need for an aggressive policy to promote foreign investment, the administration has opted for a heroic attempt to sell "austerity" in terms of a painful process of recovery from "past errors." In this way, the preelectoral rhetoric of "well-being for the family" has given way to "austerity for the family." It is almost as if the Zedillo administration, in a vain effort to minimize the role of global capital flows, is admitting that the domestic investment regime cannot be trusted and therefore that Mexico must learn to grow exclusively on the basis of its own resources. This is the foundation of the medium-term plan called Programa Nacional de Financiamiento del Desarrollo 1997–2000, or Pronafide, which projects an annual growth rate of 5 percent, based on systematic increases in the domestic savings rate. The irony is that the macroeconomic numbers, so far, have exceeded the government's own projections of economic recovery.

Yet the premium on austerity is not consistent with the requirements of a sound investment regime that can neutralize the financial and structural risks of the proverbial "easy come, easy go" capital. An emerging market cannot develop without financial and commercial integration with world markets. The crucial institutional point is that the stages following the recovery need to embrace an aggressive therapy of high growth based on an unqualified commitment to create an investment climate that will yield large amounts of productive foreign capital.

THE PESO CRISIS AND GLOBAL CAPITAL FLOWS

It has become commonplace to characterize the Mexican crisis as the first financial crisis of the twenty-first century. In an article published in *The Economist,* Lawrence Summers offers important reflections on the policy lessons for emerging markets in this era of increasing competition for global capital flows and the set of measures that should be taken internally to neutralize sudden shifts in perception by the investment community.[4]

Summers says that sound policies are absolutely essential. Although suggesting an obvious truism, Summers's point is that technological advances in the world of finance have made the movement of international capital flows highly sensitive to policies pursued in different countries. A sound policy is rewarded with instantaneous capital inflows; a bad policy can be severely punished with capital outflow shocks, as happened in Mexico in 1994 when the government sought to compensate a fall in reserves (required to sustain the exchange-rate regime) with an untenable monetary policy—namely, an increase in domestic credit. In retrospect, this gamble kept interest rates artificially low; when the exchange-rate band was modified, panic ensued and capital flows fled en masse toward dollar assets. In addition, Summers claims, emerging markets should treat capital inflows as transitory, not permanent; and they should treat capital outflows as permanent, not transitory. Authorities failed to follow this conservative risk-management strategy in the months preceding the peso crash, because they were betting on a return of foreign investment, which never materialized. If the conservative strategy is followed, capital outflows that turn out to stay for good would be regarded as a windfall gain but not as a basis for pursuing policy.

A final lesson is that high rates of internal savings constitute a key ingredient for durable growth—notwithstanding the recent turbulence in the Asian economies. But such savings rates must be based on long-term policy initiatives, such as reducing the rate of inflation so that savers get positive real returns, fiscal discipline, reform of the pension system, and a more efficient and accessible financial system.[5] Summers bases his claims on an issue that has become conventional wisdom: the need to keep the growth of current-account deficits below 5 percent of gross domestic product (GDP). This wisdom, however, is based on a controversial point: a conflation of the current account with the capital account, which is discussed in subsequent sections. The complaint against high deficits in the current account is that they can lead to crisis if the terms on which they are financed are too sweet or fail to generate extra capacity to repay.

Indeed, economist Rogelio Ramírez de la O predicted that annual investment flows of $10 billion were required to finance the current account, and that this level of investment would be unlikely to continue for sustained periods of time "without a major opening of energy and financial sectors to private investors."[6] The political unwillingness to effect these reforms placed the economy in an excessively fragile position and set the stage for the type of financial disaster witnessed after the peso collapse.

The link between exchange-rate policy and Mexico's external accounts has been a source of controversy ever since the current-account deficit began to register systematic and high rates of growth amid a prima facie accumulation of currency overvaluation. In the aftermath of the peso crisis, Rudiger Dornbusch has been mentioned repeatedly as one of many who warned that a devaluation was imminent. Dornbusch and others, however, proposed devaluation as a means to stimulate exports and generate more growth. In other words, the claim was that Mexico required "competitive devaluation" to reap the advantages of the trade regime under the North American Free Trade Agreement (NAFTA), and hence that depreciation of the parity was not inevitable, but a desirable tool to enhance competitiveness.

This is the familiar argument that the former policy of maintaining a stable parity paid off at the expense of growth-inhibiting high interest rates. The Dornbusch logic was that economic growth would fail to materialize unless the peso was devalued and interest rates fell to levels that encouraged greater credit facilities and a more active economy.[7] The antidevaluation claim was that this scholastic prescription ignored the danger of a resurgence of inflation following the acute loss of confidence that a sharp devaluation creates in such a dollar-dependent economy. So far, the results overwhelmingly support the claims of the antidevaluation argument.

In the period of recovery, the principal concern surrounding the peso-dollar parity centers on the syndrome of overvaluation. The level of stability observed during 1996–1998, which is attributable to large capital inflows, has led to a real appreciation of the currency, thus fueling worries about excessive revaluation of the peso and the failure to maintain a competitive parity. As Robert Bartley observes, this concern is traceable to the obsession with the concept of a "real exchange rate."[8] The claim is that to remain competitive, Mexico must devalue the currency to offset inflation differences.

This claim suggests that without a shift to a real exchange-rate policy that adjusts the value of the peso in accordance with inflation differentials, the administration risks a meltdown of the sort experienced in 1995. This is a dubious argument. Competitive devaluation is a sophisticated form of mercantilism—an exchange-rate version of protectionism and the idea that social engineers know the correct value of the peso beyond what the market dictates. As Bartley observes, however, "what matters to the wealth of Mexico and its citizens is their collective command over world resources, and this needs to be measured by a world currency, in our era, dollars."[9] Despite signs of recovery, it will take much time to restore the dollar value of per capita income to the levels enjoyed before the peso collapse. As economist Alan Reynolds explains,

> Strange as it seems, the explicit goal of devaluation is to *worsen* the terms of trade—for example, to make Mexico trade more barrels of oil for fewer bushels of U.S. corn. Even if Mexico wanted to impoverish itself in this way, it does not work. When the peso was devalued at the end of 1994 that did not result in Mexican oil or beer being one cent cheaper in terms of U.S. dollars. After a devaluation, interest rates soar, real tax receipts collapse, and the foreign debt burden increases. This causes a squeeze on the government's budget, and on the budgets of families, farms and firms. This is no way to make a country "competitive." Economic growth depends on more and better labor and capital, neither of which are encouraged by a currency of unpredictable value. A weak currency has never produced a strong economy.
>
> Current account deficits have nothing to do with "competitiveness." They are caused by a gap between investment and domestic savings that is filled by foreign investment (which is good) or loans (which are not so good). To the extent that a devaluation might "fix" such a gap, it does so by slashing investment, not raising savings. The trade deficit shrank in 1995 because devaluation eroded the real value of incomes and savings, making Mexican households and firms too poor to afford imported (or domestic) goods. Imports of capital goods fell by nearly 35 percent in 1995. The inflationary depression also freed up capacity for exports. When construction stopped, more cement was exported rather than used to build houses or factories in Mexico. When local industries shut down, more oil and metals could be exported, rather than used for domestic production. To the extent that devaluation appears to work, in the narrow sense of shrinking a trade deficit, it does so by slashing capital investment and thereby reducing capacity to expand production, employment and exports in the future.[10]

A country with a weak currency and a credibility gap—Mexico, in this instance—has only two feasible alternatives: either a total rule-bound regime that fixes the value on a permanent basis (the so-called currency board) or a free-floating exchange-rate regime.[11] The version that seeks to combine elements in between, such as crawling pegs or real exchange-rate policies, are unviable alternatives precisely because they incorporate the notion that the government can tinker with the exchange rate without causing massive distortions in the economy. Keep in mind that, despite the popularity of his arguments, Dornbusch never predicted the peso collapse of 1994; he recommended the devaluation as a desirable tool of policy. According to this formula, Mexico needed then and needs now a scheme of annual depreciation between 15 percent and 20 percent. This, however, is exactly what the government decided to do almost two years ago: a 15 percent devaluation in the upper limit of the crawling band. The end product was not low interest rates and higher growth—interest rates hit 109 percent in February 1995 and growth ended up deep in the red for the same year, at –6.7 percent.

The peso collapse in December 1994 and the ensuing turbulence in emerging financial markets (the so-called tequila effect) have sparked a wave of speculation on the feasibility of government controls on the inflow and outflow of short-term capital. Yet the debate on controls is self-defeating: It is inconsistent to advocate capital restrictions in a country that is starving for capital and needs to undergo a long process of adjustment to regain credibility. Mexico is such a country. Conversely, discussions on the proper exchange-rate policy or the role of capital inflows in economic expansion are as relevant as ever. A crucial issue is the set of problems that must be avoided in countries that use exchange-rate policy as an instrument to fight inflation. According to Sebastian Edwards, there are four such problems, all closely interrelated: (1) the "appreciation" syndrome, which leads to currency overvaluation; (2) the relation between consumption booms and higher private debts; (3) the massive inflow of short-term capital; and (4) the sustainability of such inflows in the face of accumulating red ink in the current account.[12]

These are the very issues that dominated discussions of macroeconomic policy in the period 1992–1994, when the current-account deficit was regarded as a sign of bad times to come. Between 1991 and 1994, 75 percent of all incoming dollars were deposited in short-term portfolio assets. The danger then was that the predictable increases in current-account deficits, which had been brought about by trade liberalization, would be underwritten by "quicksilver" capital flows, which can flee elsewhere as a result of unexpected outcomes.[13] This eventually suggested the need to work harder to remove obstacles to foreign investment in financial markets, in the banking system, in sectors such as oil and electricity, and in the property rights regime. The challenge was to ensure a safe and systematic flow of productive investment.

Another popular claim suggests the need for implementing controls on short-term capital. However, the consistent practice of sound macroeconomic policy constitutes a better anchor for foreign capital flows than manufactured schemes that attempt to control short-term investments. As Alan Greenspan states, a policy that employs capital controls, taxes on private inflows, or other inhibitors of capital movements represents self-defeating options that fail to acknowledge the speed of the spread of knowledge through high-technology information systems. The challenge is not to avoid the new paradigm of global finance but to enhance transparent policies in order to minimize systemic risk, namely, the contagion effects of isolated financial disturbances.[14]

In other words, a noninflationary environment based on a commitment to credible monetary policy and price stability is the best guarantee against capital outflow shock and financial instability. A financial policy mistake (exchange-rate mismanagement, artificial expansion of credit, or asset bubbles) invites a speculative onslaught, as knowledge of potential risk is transmitted with unprecedented speed to the money managers of world capital flows. More generally, foreign capital flows seek regions with good economic policy: balanced budgets, anti-inflationary policy, deregulation, low taxes, and as little control as possible. Argentina is a good example: The freedom (that is, the absence of controls) there to switch from peso deposits to dollar deposits acts as a powerful institutional constraint on deviation from sound macroeconomic policy. If the markets sense that the central bank or the government is departing from fiscal and monetary discipline, investors have the freedom to punish the domestic financial system by switching from one denomination to another.

THE CURRENT STATE OF MEXICO'S CAPITAL MARKETS

Mexico's economy has registered a substantial improvement: Inflation in 1998 is expected to reach 12 percent, and growth has resumed pace after the 1995 contraction in output (see Figures 5.1 and 5.2). In addition, interest rates have fallen to their lowest levels since the peso crash, the stock market is active, and the peso is stable despite new fears of bouts with currency overvaluation. The numbers reflect more than a statistical improvement. A variable like the interest rate or the exchange rate is a barometer of expectations. The issue is, what are the factors that could undermine recovery in this new stage? This question is at the center of recent debates concerning economic strategy and investment expectations.

Mexico experienced fundamental changes in structural reform during the administration of Carlos Salinas. This wave of change redefined the prospects for the future. It was generally perceived that Mexico was no

Figure 5.1   Inflation Rates in Mexico, 1987–1998

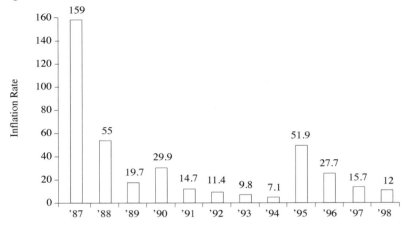

Source: Banco de México, *1997 Annual Report* (Mexico City: Banco de México, April 1998).

Figure 5.2   Economic Growth in Mexico, 1994–2000

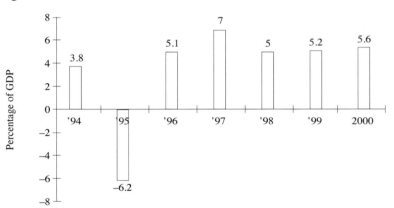

Source: Projections by the Secretaría de Hacienda y Crédito Público, *Programa Nacional de Financiamiento para el Desarrollo, 1997–2000* (Pronafide) (Mexico City: Secretaría de Hacienda y Crédito Público, 1997).

longer a nation of populism and protectionism, of debt and devaluation, of stagnation and inflation. Instead, the repudiation of "state giantism" and the commitment to open markets and commerce transformed the economy into an attractive investment regime. Nonetheless, this image collapsed with the marked political instability that eventually culminated in the massive exchange-rate collapse. The current period therefore constitutes one of the most strategically important times in the nation's recent history. Indeed, it furnishes a litmus test of Mexico's reform program and institutional scheme.

A realistic assessment of Mexico's current conditions for private investment must address two fundamental items: the short-term stability of the investment regime and the long-term prospects for sustained and stable economic growth. The first issue centers on the initiatives to maintain stability and social order now that the investment euphoria generated by the prospect of open trade within North America and the program of structural reform has been short-circuited. The second issue centers on the long-term opportunities that accrue from the shift to a pro-trade, market-oriented economy with vast resources for high growth.

The process of stabilization after the peso devaluation is characterized by three phases: (1) massive adjustments of fiscal and current accounts in 1995, with a consequent drop in domestic output of –6.2 percent of GDP (crisis); (2) steady recuperation, with income and production catching up to the levels that preceded the peso collapse (recovery); and (3) accumulation of purchasing power, whereby the benefits of stabilization will gradually trickle down to the population at large (reactivation). Thus, if all else remains equal, the post-1997 period will represent a fundamental moment for the current economic strategy, for it is a moment when the numerical benefits of macroeconomic stabilization are supposed to translate into greater income, more jobs, and improved well-being.

To be sure, recovery is indisputable. Nonetheless, the administration has failed to meet the challenge of forging ahead with structural reform— particularly in the rubrics of privatization and deregulation. This is a consequence of strong political pressures working against transformation, though, and not a lack of willingness to effect the changes. Unfortunately, mixed signals abound—the abortion of petrochemical privatization, no signals of future labor reform, and a very slow process of badly needed deregulation, to name a few. In the absence of a determined push for wholesale structural reform, it is unlikely that growth will have the institutional base it needs to sustain the high levels of economic activity that the economy needs to generate greater well-being.

THE NEW CONSENSUS ON DEVALUATION, DEFICITS, AND DOLLARS

Mexico's image as a successful emerging market collapsed after the massive peso devaluation of 1994 sent domestic and foreign investors running for cover. To date, despite improvements in growth and in the macroeconomic scenario, the investment regime still suffers the consequences of a brutal collapse of confidence. Such losses of confidence will, arguably, take much time and effort to repair. All the same, what John Williamson called the "Washington consensus" on transformation-bound economies like Mexico has faded in the wake of an unfortunate wave of emerging market blues.[15]

A new consensus, however, appears to have emerged as part and parcel of the set of lessons embodied in the recent Mexican experience. This new consensus still embraces the need for structural reform, but is based on different premises than the ones assumed by the Washington consensus, which emphasized free markets, sound money, and free trade as requisites for development. To be sure, capital is beginning to flow back into the economy at an encouraging pace, and annual growth rates are likewise positive (growth in GDP, which amounted to $40 billion in 1990, will yield, possibly, a dramatic $100 billion in 1997). In addition, exports continue to pave the way for economic recovery—they are expected to reach an astounding $120 billion by the end of 1998. The vigorous growth rate observed in the U.S. economy is an important contributor to the strong demand for export products.

This emphasis on export-led growth is a fundamental part of the new consensus. Tenets of the consensus are captured succinctly in a report issued by Bancomer:

- Developing economies should promote domestic savings to avoid high current-account deficits such as Mexico's in 1994 (some 7 percent of GDP);
- The breakdown in the capital account of the balance of payments is fundamental. The amount of direct investment inflows should account for an important fraction of net foreign saving, in order to reduce volatility. In the period 1990–1994, Mexico financed more than 70 percent of its foreign deficit with nondirect capital investment flows;
- In periods of deflation, the use of exchange rates as anchors of stabilization should be avoided, given the high risk of persistent appreciation;
- Developing countries should enhance supervision of their banking systems.[16]

Notwithstanding its popularity, this line of reasoning is somewhat paradoxical, if only because—whether one likes it or not—large new inflows of private capital must eventually translate into current-account deficits, an accounting fact that is ignored in most contemporary reports. The key issue is the nature of a current-account deficit: The focus must be on the cause of the deficit, which may be good (productive investment) or bad (fiscal expansion), not the deficit per se. Indeed, a capital-account surplus must, in

Indeed, despite commitments to a floating exchange-rate policy, there is a tacit contradiction in the official claim that it is not possible to predict a target of the parity under a floating exchange-rate regime, and the explicit commitment to avoid an "undesirable appreciation" of the currency. This tension fuels public skepticism concerning the role of the exchange rate in the efforts on behalf of stabilization and a sound investment regime.

The macroeconomic scenario has improved, and the recovery has manifested itself in a surge of imports and in currency stability. So: Why is society responding with alarm? There are two reasons: (1) a credibility gap in the management of peso policy and (2) mixed signals from the financial authorities concerning the future of the currency. The hope is that these two problems will be resolved once legislation to give the Bank of Mexico full control of exchange-rate policy is implemented.[23] This is a very positive step, addressing concerns surrounding the exercise of real autonomy, but it fails to remove the source of the tensions described above. In every case, from the formulation of the 1995 National Development Plan to the projections in the Pronafide plan, exchange-rate rhetoric is fraught with commitments to a competitive exchange rate, suggesting a policy of depreciation and exchange-rate intervention.

If Ortiz pursues an anti-inflation monetary policy consistent with the institutional mandate for stability, then he will run into an impasse. A depreciation generates an inflationary impact in the price system, which requires that liquidity be drained from the financial system to neutralize the inflationary forces, thereby driving up interest rates and stabilizing the ratio of domestic credit to foreign exchange. This, however, automatically generates peso appreciation. In effect, every episode of currency depreciation since 1994 has been accompanied by an increase of short-term interest rates.

Thus, in order to avoid exchange-rate misalignments, consistent with the criterion of export competitiveness, the new central bank regime would need to temper the force of anti-inflation policy and adopt a gradualist position. On the one hand, this outcome is flatly incompatible with an explicit constitutional instruction, thereby rendering independence useless as a tool to procure price stability. On the other hand, a serious commitment to low inflation would strengthen peso stability. This would show that the monetary authority is living up to the constitutional standard set by monetary independence, but it would call for the elimination of a policy of exchange-rate adjustments, consistent with the criterion of exchange-rate competitiveness.

The fundamental point is that the peso-dollar parity is not merely another price (the price of foreign exchange): It is a basic barometer of societal expectations and the level of confidence in the economy. The key to monetary and exchange-rate policy is credibility and communications, yet the central bank needs to build a positive track record to enhance these two ingredients of successful policy. Many challenges lie ahead.

Toward Credible Monetary Policy

Despite recent accomplishments in anti-inflation efforts, monetary policy still suffers a credibility gap. The popular consensus is that, price stabilization notwithstanding, the monetary institution in charge of procuring the purchasing power of the currency is not genuinely independent. The polemic surrounding monetary expansion on the eve of the July 1997 elections is a good example of the gap between credibility and responsibility. The central bank claimed—correctly—that unanticipated increases in money demand led it to underestimate the original targets for monetary growth. Nevertheless, suspicions of expansionism ensued in the face of the electoral contest. The increases are natural adjustments attributable to monetary demand, however: As inflation falls and growth continues, more citizens are disposed to hold domestic assets. Indeed, many of the same critics who charge the central bank with expansionism also hold that the institution follows an overly contractionary monetary policy. Both claims are mistaken.

Unfortunately, all formal explanations, whether valid or not, are construed as attempts to save face or conceal an ulterior motive. This is not a considered assessment of the particulars of the situation but a sociological statement about the status of Mexico's monetary institutions. As David Hale says, in the shadow of the peso collapse investors will unavoidably focus attention on the "quality of the monetary institutions" and the intricate details of monetary conduct.[24]

Monetary credibility is also continually tested in the area of governmental intervention in exchange-rate setting. As mentioned before, the price of foreign exchange is determined by the forces of supply and demand in a free-floating system, and thus it is impossible to predetermine the parity level. Observers systematically miss this point, perhaps because the investment community is a victim of mixed signals. But a subtle corollary, one that seems also to have escaped notice, is that accumulation of international reserves is unnecessary under a flee-floating regime—or, rather, the policy of such accumulation has no rationale from the perspective of a free-floating exchange-rate system. If the parity level does float, why sit on hard-currency reserves and prevent the money markets from absorbing new inflows of foreign exchange?[25]

So why did the government formalize a system of currency-reserve accumulation under a scheme of monthly exchange purchases? The level of reserves has reached a historic high, surpassing the $30 billion mark, which has been greeted as a highly welcome development. Nevertheless, no observer has questioned whether the policy of reserve accumulation is consistent with a floating system. Of course, in systems of fixed or quasi-fixed exchange rates, such as Argentina's currency board, Brazil's *real* plan, or the crawling peso-dollar peg put in practice in Mexico's last administration, it is essential to accumulate hard currency assets. The strong capital inflow of portfolio and direct investments during the period 1996–1997 has enabled the money markets to sustain a remarkably stable peso-dollar parity. If the inflows maintain their pace, the natural result in a free-floating system will be exchange-rate appreciation: If there is more of something (dollars), then its value (in pesos) will go down (or remain the same). In the strict technical sense, then, a floating system does not require accumulation of reserves. If more dollars come in, the lower the bids to purchase them, the lower the peso value of the parity. To recapitulate: The interplay of supply and demand in the foreign exchange market means that reserves are unnecessary.

The aim of the new scheme of international reserve accumulation strongly suggests a mechanism to control or smoothen the behavior of the parity. Indeed, according to Guillermo Ortiz in mid-1996, "In the event of a strong and unanticipated inflow of capital, mechanisms will be put in place to avoid an undesirable appreciation of the currency."[26] In other words, a direct way to "avoid an undesirable appreciation" of the peso is to accumulate reserves. This policy does not seek a strict predetermined parity, but it does represent a roundabout intervention to prevent the parity from slipping into the range of undesirable appreciation.

The government occasionally voices the popular fear of a strong peso. The justification given for increasing the ceiling of reserve accumulations is that it wishes to avoid "accelerated appreciation of the currency that could diminish the profitability of the tradable sector."[27] The contradiction is obvious: Avoiding a market-driven appreciation of the peso is inconsistent with official claims that there is no predetermined level for peso-dollar parity under a floating regime. In fact, the peso would be stronger than it is now if the central bank quit accumulating reserves. The fashionable pundits who suspect secret interventions to sustain the peso beyond levels dictated by inflation differentials have it backward: If the central bank were not amassing dollar reserves, the parity would now be lower than its current level (8.6 pesos per dollar in March 1998).

The dilemma is clear: Mexico can have either a free float or a managed parity. In the former case, reserves are expendable; in the second case, they are indispensable. The accumulation of reserves answers to a strategic criterion, not to an exchange-rate criterion. Reserve accumulation is essential, for example, as a contingency measure for counteracting any future shocks.

The decision to amass reserves, however, should take into consideration the opportunity cost that is lost in not channeling the resources toward debt reduction and the large savings in interest obligations generated thereby. As always, the issue comes down to a cost-benefit analysis: Do dollar reserves perform a more useful role than alternative uses for such monies, given present circumstances? So far, authorities have assumed that this question does not require an answer, but that assumption is gratuitous, especially when monetary credibility is at stake. An answer *is* needed: Why, if we say we have a free float, do we need to accumulate international reserves?

PROBLEMS AND PROSPECTS FOR A SOUNDER INVESTMENT REGIME

The financial and stock market sectors of Mexico's economy, together with the standard barometers such as interest rates and the peso-dollar exchange rate, seem to waver between episodes of panic and euphoria. Thus, volatility continues to play a crucial role in the evolution of long-term expectations. One fundamental measure designed to attack this vulnerability is to increase domestic savings.

In light of the financial crisis and the massive contraction of economic activity in 1995, stabilization policy can no longer be aimed at merely putting the fiscal books in order. It must encompass the conditions for a sustained increase in private savings. This is essential for restoring the health of the banking system, which is fraught with major structural and financial problems, including high levels of nonperforming loans. The revised estimates for the costs of subsidy programs for debtor and capitalization initiatives are projected at more than 13 percent of GDP, which is triple the amount originally paid in the bank privatization process. The emphasis on short-term fiscal gains over long-term efficiency gains is at the root of the banking system's fragility. However, despite the damages of past policy errors, it is critical to forge ahead with the plan to increase savings in order to encourage a healthy increase in private investment. This makes pension reform, mergers and acquisitions, and the entire second wave of privatization top policy priorities.

The new medium-term plan known as the Pronafide attempts to supply a framework of quantitative estimates for policymaking during the remainder of the Zedillo administration. The plan comes on the heels of a recommendation issued by the Organization for Economic Cooperation and Development concerning the necessity to offer greater medium-term certainty to investors and savers on the course of the main economic variables. The plan has five objectives: to achieve an annual growth rate of 5 percent or better; to generate a million jobs a year; to reactivate real purchasing power; to consolidate state rectorship; and to prevent a new crisis. There is

Kong," *Wall Street Journal,* December 20, 1996, p. A17. Examples of this obsession can be produced ad nauseam. For a simple statement of the claim, see Jaime Ros, "La Enfermedad Mexicana," *Nexos,* July 1997, pp. 57–61. An interesting and sophisticated proposal along the same lines can be found in Sebastian Edwards, "Exchange-Rate Policy in Mexico: Options and Recommendations" (University of California at Los Angeles, 1997, photocopy).

9. Bartley, "Mexico's Money Theorists."

10. Alan Reynolds, "Another Dornbusch Disaster?" (Hudson Institute, Indianapolis, Ind., 1996, photocopy), p. 3. An excellent exposition on the role of current-account deficits in emerging market development is given in Eduardo Medina-Mora, "Managing Market Expectations in Latin America: Lessons from Mexico's 1994 Crisis" (paper presented at the Forbes Magazine and Council of the Americas Conference on The Latin American Market, New York, November 7–9, 1996). The key point is that it "makes sense for emerging economies with profitable investment opportunities to import capital from richer ones" (p. 6). The issue then is not the presence of a current-account deficit per se, but the question of whether a certain level of the deficit is "sustainable." This depends, fundamentally, on the composition of capital flows (portfolio versus direct).

11. On this point, see Roberto Salinas-León, "Mexican Money Post-Mancera," *International Economy,* November–December 1997, pp. 38–41.

12. Sebastian Edwards, "Exchange Rates and Capital Flows in Emerging Latin American Markets" (paper presented at the Dallas Federal Reserve Symposium, Dallas, Texas, September 14, 1995).

13. See Roberto Salinas-León, "Don't Cry for Mexico's Current Account Deficit," *Wall Street Journal,* February 21, 1992, p. A13.

14. Alan Greenspan, "Globalization of Finance" (paper presented at the Fifteenth Annual Monetary Conference, Cato Institute, Washington, D.C., October 14, 1997), pp. 12–13.

15. John Williamson of the Institute for International Economics in Washington, D.C., first coined the phrase. It has become an enormously popular tool to describe the pro-market views advocated by beltway (Washington, D.C.) analysts, the international financial community, the International Monetary Fund and the World Bank, as well as international organizations and economists in academia and think tanks. For a good assessment of the views involved, see Paul Krugman, *Pop Internationalism* (Cambridge, Mass.: MIT Press, 1996), chapter 9, pp. 131–136.

16. Bancomer, *Reporte Económico,* Mexico City, July 1996.

17. *Special Report* (New York: J. P. Morgan, June 1996), p. 1.

18. Again, examples of this claim abound. An explicit (and thoroughly misguided) statement can be found in José Luis Calva's "Régimen Cambiario," *El Universal,* July 11, 1997, p. 11. The article endorses the highly controversial statement by Eugenio Clariond, current president of the Mexico Business Roundtable, to the effect that the fight against inflation should be subordinated to the goals of competitiveness, which in turn is understood in the crude terms of sustaining a permanent surplus in the trade accounts.

19. This data was provided by Francisco Gil Díaz, former deputy governor of the Bank of Mexico, in correspondence with the author.

20. On the inflationary impact of currency depreciation, see Francisco Gil Díaz and Agustín Carstens, "Some Hypotheses Related to the Mexican 1994–1995 Crisis," working paper 9601, Bank of Mexico, Mexico City, 1996, especially Appendix A, "On the Dynamics of the Real Exchange Rate," pp. 41–43.

21. See J. P. Morgan's *Market Brief,* "The Mexican Peso Will Continue to Surprise," May 16, 1997, p. 2. This document contains a clear and convincing case against the use of purchasing power parity models as accurate predictors of the exchange rate.

22. Ibid, p. 3.

23. See Roberto Salinas-León, "Peso Stability is Now Ortiz's New Job," *Wall Street Journal,* December 19, 1997, p. A13.

24. See David Hale, "Comments," in *Private Capital Flows to Emerging Markets After the Mexican Crisis* (Washington, D.C.: Institute for International Economics, 1996), pp. 142–146.

25. See Roberto Salinas-León, "Exchange Rate Mercantilism," *Barrons,* July 1997, for how the policy of accumulation of reserves undermines a full commitment to a genuine floating exchange-rate regime.

26. Ortiz uttered this statement in June 1996, in an interview with *Reuters,* amply reproduced by the local press. It was ironic that, just afterward, President Zedillo gave an address before the insurance sector in Mexico, where he presented one of the most forceful statements against all forms of exchange-rate interventions! Consider: "Every and any attempt to manipulate the parity of our currency would have immediately signified an artificial cheapening of our products, which entails a subsidy to the external sector and greater inflation, with a consequent negative impact on interest rates and economic activity."

27. Banco de México and Secretaría de Hacienda y Crédito Público, *Boletín de Prensa,* July 30, 1997, Mexico City (author's translation).

28. Martin Feldstein, "Overview" (paper presented at the symposium "Financial Stability in a Global Economy," Federal Reserve of Kansas City, Jackson Hole, Wyoming, August 28, 1997).

6

Recovery After Crisis: Lessons for Mexico's Banks and Private Sector

Javier Gavito Mohar, Aarón Silva Nava, and Guillermo Zamarripa Escamilla

Banks play a crucial role in the allocation of capital resources, and in most countries this function sustains productive investment. During times of widespread economic stress, however, severe distortions may arise in the functioning of financial markets due to the exacerbation of problems with asymmetric information, uncertainty, and enforcement of credit contracts. These problems and the economic agent's diminished payment capacity and liquidity imbalances, if not addressed swiftly and appropriately, can cause a financial meltdown and the disruption of major production chains.

In this chapter we examine the relationship between the private sector and the financial system under normal conditions and in times of crisis. Events and actions leading up to the December 1994 devaluation of the peso receive special attention, for this helped trigger the most severe economic crisis experienced in Mexico's recent history. The consequences of that crisis for the private sector and for the financial system are explored, as are the structural factors that underpinned the vulnerability of the Mexican financial system. Finally, the measures taken to overcome the crisis are described and their effectiveness evaluated.

ROLE OF THE BANKING SYSTEM IN INVESTMENT DURING "NORMAL" AND CRISIS CONDITIONS

Intersectoral capital flows, which are fundamental for gross capital accumulation, are mobilized through the financial system. These flows originate with decisions on aggregate savings and spending taken by firms, households, and the government. Banks, among other financial institutions, facilitate the intermediation of capital flows by collecting funds from surplus agents and deciding between targets to finance. Screening and monitoring projects to generate the greatest benefits constitute a central function of financial institutions.[1]

Bank lending thus implies a partial transfer of risk from the firm to the bank. To reduce credit risk, banks diversify their assets, in addition to requiring guarantees and collateral from borrowers. Without this mechanism of risk distribution many viable projects would not be undertaken. Furthermore, as explained by Douglas Diamond and Philip Dybvig, banks transform nonliquid assets (productive investment, such as loans) into liquid liabilities (demand deposits), allowing economic agents to distribute their consumption efficiently over time.[2]

Costs and risks are inherent to the banks' intermediation function. Among the costs are those associated with government regulations (for example, capital requirements); information gathering and processing; return on equity (shareholders' requirement of profitability); and management, transaction, and legal processes. The most significant risks are credit, market, liquidity, fraud, and operational.

Problems arising from contract enforcement and asymmetric information between borrowers and lenders constrain the efficiency with which banks carry out their selection and monitoring functions, as well as the efficiency with which they allocate capital. Under critical macroeconomic conditions, greater uncertainty magnifies these problems, jeopardizing the healthy operation of financial markets and causing financial instability. Such a situation may cause a meltdown in intersectoral capital flows, in which the liabilities of a significant group of financial entities exceed the market value of their liquid and nonliquid realizable assets. The resulting widespread insolvency is then reflected in a surge of unproductive bank assets (namely, past-due loans); a drop in corporate investment; and the urgent need to restructure solvent entities, promote mergers, and liquidate nonviable firms.

Financial crises lead to diminished levels of financial intermediation and hence to less capital accumulation and lowered economic growth, and therefore are costly for nations. Moreover, financial crises produce a deficient allocation of real resources and may also threaten the functioning of the payments system, thus engendering social costs that reach well beyond the banking business and even the financial market as a whole.

The uncertainty spawned by financial crises can spread dangerously under such circumstances if an efficient mechanism to distribute losses among different economic agents (shareholders, investors, and the government, for example) is not in place and the authorities decide not to intervene. Failure to act may have serious implications for economic growth, in which case banks may tighten the credit supply and seek recovery by burdening good borrowers with higher interest rates to offset the banks' loan portfolio losses.

The resulting credit crunch, coupled with higher intermediation costs, harms market performance generally and distorts the decisionmaking process for investment projects. Even firms with viable projects can be driven to insolvency by the liquidity problems that follow a credit crunch, and both firms and banks may become insolvent if incentives to adopt riskier behavior intensify. Because the performance of the economy's business sector determines the value of bank assets, problems in the real sector are readily transmitted to the financial sector.

If, however, the public authorities decide to intervene, they must distinguish among banks that should keep operating and those that would likely go out of business sooner or later. Such a decision is subject to two types of error: First, sound banks might be misclassified as likely failures, and, second, unhealthy banks might be judged promising. In either case erroneous predictions entail a double cost: the expense of wasting real resources, and the toll of sending a wrong signal to economic agents and further distorting incentives.

Banking crises around the world share several features, despite the distinct political systems and regulations of different countries. In general, crises arise from the convergence of several of the following factors: financial liberalization processes; unsound management in the financial sector; lack of adequate regulatory and supervisory practices; unfulfilled favorable expectations regarding economic performance; vulnerability of the real sector; external, monetary or production shocks; and adverse macroeconomic environments.[3]

To avoid a systemic crisis in nearly all countries that have experienced solvency problems in the banking system, the authorities have chosen to act rather than to rely on market-driven solutions, which would inevitably lead to the closing down of some banks. Authorities offer diverse arguments in support of the decision to act, mainly related to protecting small depositors and the payments system, avoiding a disruption of productive processes, maintaining or restoring the public's confidence in the financial system, or minimizing negative externalities.

According to the Asian Development Bank, the process of resolving a financial crisis in most countries involves four tasks.[4] First, the problem must be fully recognized and diagnosed, keeping in mind that both banks and governments have incentives to conceal the magnitude of losses—banks want to protect their capital and governments want to preserve investor confidence. Second, measures to avoid major losses should be implemented together with a strategy to restructure not only loans but also, if necessary, whole companies and financial institutions. Then, third, those losses must be distributed among economic agents. Finally, the profitability and viability of firms and banks should be restored.

MEXICAN BANKS AND THE PESO CRISIS OF 1994

The origins and consequences of Mexico's financial crisis of 1994 have been much debated. In the years preceding the crisis, market-oriented reforms had not delivered the anticipated level of economic success, but no consensus had arisen that the strategy be changed. Up to 1994, observed results from these reform policies seemed in general satisfactory,[5] but by the end of 1994 the Mexican economy was in fact in a vulnerable condition. Economic growth and real interest rates had not evolved as expected, and the government's liquid reserves were too low to deal with short-term liabilities. Firms and households also were seriously overindebted.[6]

These conditions had been brewing for several years. Between 1982 and 1988 the level of private sector debt decreased because of an array of adverse conditions, including contraction of domestic aggregate demand, high and volatile interest rates, foreign exchange uncertainty, and low availability of loanable funds. This trend reversed in 1988, however, when the macroeconomic setting became more favorable. The deep structural change that took place in Mexico during the following years delivered a leaner public sector with healthier finances, stable macroeconomic indicators, and financial liberalization. In addition, new policies to deregulate economic activities and to speed up the trade-opening process stimulated the business sector to restructure its operations to become more competitive in a free-trade environment.

Foreign and Domestic Capital: Explosive Growth in Supply and Demand

When abundant international capital flows migrated to Latin America, Mexico ranked notably among recipient countries: Between July 1990 and the third quarter of 1994, close to $114 billion flowed into the country.[7] Moreover, in 1993 Mexico captured 22 percent of all foreign capital flows directed to developing countries, although its share of the total gross domestic product (GDP) of emerging markets was only 8 percent.[8]

The experience of developing countries, including Mexico, suggests that sizable inflows of foreign capital can destabilize the domestic market in various ways.[9] They can engender, for example, financial fragility, if the foreign capital is highly concentrated in liquid financial assets; inflationary pressures and an expansion of the current-account deficit, if large inflows are not offset by sterilization measures; appreciation of the real exchange rate; heightened problems of asymmetric information, mainly in recently deregulated financial systems; and misallocation of real resources, restricting the contribution of external savings to economic growth.

As for the domestic supply of loanable funds in Mexico, financial penetration (measured as the ratio of the broadest monetary aggregate, or M4, to GDP) reached a record peak of 45 percent in 1994, compared with 27 percent in 1988 and 30 percent in 1971, the previous historic peak.[10] From 1988 to 1994, the evolution of M4 revealed a growing volume of savings being intermediated by the financial system, with commercial banking the most dynamic component. Although this expansion of the money supply did not necessarily mean that fresh resources were released into the economy,[11] it did show that the public had more confidence in the financial system and was more willing to mobilize a higher share of savings through it.

Meanwhile, the ratio of public sector borrowing requirements to GDP went from a 10 percent deficit in 1988 to nearly a 1 percent surplus in 1993, and healthier public finances freed up substantial resources that were directed to finance the private sector. Most of the proceeds from the privatization of state-owned firms over that period were allocated to the reduction of public sector debt.[12]

In this environment the commercial banking system's financing to the private sector, as a percentage of GDP, rose from 7 percent in 1988 to 24 percent in 1992[13] — surpassing tenfold the growth of GDP over this period and strongly enhancing the leverage of the private sector. By 1994 this ratio had risen to 32 percent.

The Role of Firms' Expectations

At the outset of the 1988 stabilization program, real interest rates had reached historically high levels. It was generally believed that as inflation fell under the new program, interest rates also would drop. Owners of many small and medium-size firms without access to international capital markets or the domestic stock market therefore turned to bank credit to initiate new investment and expansion projects, perceiving their high cost as merely a temporary condition.

Contrary to expectations, however, the fall in real interest rates was not permanent, and rising rates since 1992 accelerated both past-due loan problems in the banking system and a liquidity crisis in the business sector. Like interest rates, banking deposit rates rose, which together with wider financial margins (partly attributable to the higher levels of past-due loans and to the additional reserves that banks had to create) led to a substantial increase in real lending rates.

In terms of credit supply, favorable midterm expectations encouraged banks to enlarge their loan portfolios; the most vigorous components within this credit expansion were mortgage and consumer lending, which showed the highest growth rates. Regional and multiregional banks took advantage of this situation to gain an increased market share.[14]

Disequilibria in the Economy

As a consequence of the liquidity crisis and the narrowing of maneuvering margins,[15] a self-fulfilled panic set in at the end of 1994 as the government assessed the need to devaluate the peso.[16] The problem did not lie in the fundamentals of the Mexican economy, however, but in the public's perception of an imminent risk of a financial meltdown.

Guillermo Calvo and Enrique Mendoza offer an interesting thesis to explain the severity of the Mexican financial crisis.[17] Their rationale is based on the so-called herd behavior of investors,[18] in a setting of a semi-fixed exchange-rate regime and a major imbalance among short-term debt, international reserves, and monetary aggregates. Economic disequilibria followed the expansion of domestic credit (which was supposed to counter the effect of falling international reserves) and the switch of public debt from peso denominated to dollar denominated. These economic policy measures were especially risky in light of the financial system's fragility, which had been induced in the first place by the significant foreign capital inflows, rapid financial liberalization, and overwhelming credit expansion of the late 1980s and the early 1990s.

VULNERABILITY OF THE FINANCIAL SYSTEM: STRUCTURAL FACTORS

The intensity with which the Mexican crisis struck did not result only from unfulfilled macroeconomic expectations and a series of shocks affecting the economy during 1994. Two structural factors that further hampered the vulnerable position of the real and financial sectors were overindebtedness of the private sector and implementation of risky and inefficient bank policies.

Private Sector Overindebtedness

In 1990 the Mexican private sector returned to international capital markets after a nine-year absence. Resources obtained from foreign sources subsequently skyrocketed through loans and portfolio investment from a negative balance of $1.2 billion in 1989 to a peak surplus of $19.9 billion in 1993.[19] During these years the private sector (firms and households) shifted from net supplier to net demander of financial resources within the and 1996 the government sought to mitigate the impact of the financial crisis on society.

Measures Implemented

The objectives of the measures the government implemented were to curtail the transmission of the banking crisis to the business sector, to restore depositors' confidence, to protect the payments system, to foster the restructuring and capitalization of troubled banks, to support institutions rather than shareholders, and to minimize the fiscal cost.[33] Some of the measures were aimed at strengthening the solvency and liquidity of banks, whereas others offered mechanisms to relieve pressures on debtors' capacity to pay—most notably, the programs for restructuring loans in *unidades de inversión* (units of investment, or UDIs). All of the implemented measures were characterized by significant flexibility, that is, the programs were adjusted in accordance with the evolution of the problems caused by the crisis.

For example, the drastic contraction of debtors' disposable income made it clear that the initial mechanisms for loan restructuring had to be strengthened. The first agreement for immediate support of bank debtors (Agreement of Immediate Support to Bank Debtors, or ADE) was implemented in September 1995; its two main components were the reduction of interest rates and a package of benefits for small and medium-size borrowers, through the restructuring of loans in UDIs. The program also sought to reward payment discipline.

In addition, banks were finding it extremely difficult to attract new capital, even though the legal reforms of early 1995 had been designed specifically to foster such capitalization. Capitalization of the institutions could not be deferred. Their financial situation, as well as society's confidence, had to be reinforced. Moreover, because deposit insurance covered virtually all banking liabilities, the potential cost to the government had to be minimized. The government therefore set up a program through the bank deposit insurance trust (Savings Protection Banking Fund, or FOBAPROA), which allowed all commercial banks that were not under government intervention or in a "special situation" to sell loans to the trust, provided bank stockholders injected fresh capital into their institution. FOBAPROA has the task to orderly dispose of the assets acquired from the capitalization and loan purchase program, as well as those of intervened banks.

Other Measures

In a second round of support measures for debtors, a program to alleviate the problems of the mortgage portfolio was announced in May 1996. Like other programs, this one is aimed at encouraging a payment culture by setting up a ten-year scheme of discounts on monthly installments; the government is absorbing the costs of the discounts.

In September 1996, the Financial Support Program for the Agricultural Sector (FINAPE) was put into effect to assist debtors in the agriculture and fishing sectors.[34] The program reduces up to 40 percent of debtors' total payments or monthly installments and makes available up to twelve billion pesos for financing profitable projects.[35] The latest government program to support debtors was implemented in October 1996; this one benefits 98 percent of the micro, small, and medium-size firms with outstanding bank loans under six million pesos. Under the Support Program for Small and Medium Enterprises (FOPYME), partial prepayments allow reduction of the principal, as well as of interest for a specified time, and banks are committed to providing up to thirteen billion pesos in new financing.

The cost of both FINAPE and FOPYME is shared by the government and the banks. The distribution of the cost will depend on the net flow of resources from the banking system to the supported sectors—the more resources the banks make available to these sectors, the less the banks' share of the cost. Banks thus have an incentive to provide new financing.

Concomitant to the support measures, the government initiated a profound regulatory reform to enhance the safety, self-regulation, and efficiency of the financial system. Among other important measures implemented since 1995 are those that improve supervisory practices, enhance risk management, and assure adequate internal controls (all these following a consolidated approach); require that financial institutions value their securities portfolio at market prices; establish accounting criteria consistent with international standards; and set up new capitalization rules for banks and brokerage firms that cover market risks as well as credit, in accordance with international standards.

RESULTS OF THE SUPPORT PACKAGE

The emergency measures implemented by the authorities helped the financial standing of households, firms, and banks, and the measures for restructuring past-due loan portfolios have given many debtors the means for recovering their financial viability.

Financial Indicators

The capital and reserve requirements of banks were addressed in three ways. First, the private sector has injected (or committed to do so) sixty billion pesos of new capital into the institutions, an increase equal to 176 strengthen human and technological resources—will lead to efficiency gains and better financial margins, and thus enable profitability indicators to follow a positive though moderate path. Nevertheless, it is worth noting again that the recovery of banks' financial statements will come gradually and heterogeneously, in that banks are vulnerable to macroeconomic shocks. Also, the consolidation of financial institutions through sales, mergers, and liquidations is expected to continue for some years. The outcome will be a smaller number of financial institutions, although stronger ones operating in a more competitive environment.

In the meantime authorities will continue their efforts to improve the "rules of the game" concerning factors that shape financial operations—asymmetric information, transaction and contractual costs, and legal processes, for example. Measures will be implemented to promote strong prudential regulation and self-regulation, more effective supervision, a more competitive system, and improved foreclosure processes.

Specific measures that confirm the regulatory agenda of the authorities will

- reinforce corporate governance in financial institutions and in issuers of securities for the protection of savers and shareholders;
- reform the safety net provided by the government to discourage excessive risk taking;
- improve disclosure by financial intermediaries and strengthen the role of external auditors, rating agencies, and credit bureaus; and
- update the bankruptcy law and improve its enforcement mechanisms.

All of these measures will contribute to a more efficient, sounder system of financial intermediation, which will in turn promote savings and their efficient allocation toward productive investment.

NOTES

The authors are affiliated with the National Banking and Securities Commission (CNBV) of Mexico and are solely responsible for the opinions presented in this chapter, which are not necessarily those of the CNBV. We are grateful for the comments of Mónica Flores del Villar and Isaac Volin, as well as the collaboration of Lucila Aguilera, René Plata, and Susana Ross.

1. More specifically, banks monitor projects on behalf of depositors by performing "delegated portfolio management," thus taking advantage of their economies of scale to reduce transaction costs for small investors. See Douglas W. Diamond, "Financial Intermediation and Delegated Monitoring," *Review of Economic Studies* 198 (1984): 393–414.

2. Douglas Diamond and Philip Dybvig, "Bank Runs, Deposit Insurance, and Liquidity," *Journal of Political Economy* 91, no. 31 (1983): 401–419.

3. Although economic instability alone does not necessarily lead to a banking crisis, there is ample consensus that in the long run, a stable macroeconomic environment is imperative for sound performance in the financial system, which is always vulnerable to macroeconomic shocks.

4. Asian Development Bank, *Managing Financial Sector Distress and Industrial Adjustment: Lessons for Developing Countries* (Manila, Philippines: Asian Development Bank, 1992).

5. Even though some authors had warned about the risks arising from the high current-account deficit and the overvaluation of the peso, scholars as well as government and foreign analysts considered this situation to be a natural outcome of the ongoing structural change, productivity gains, and dynamic restructuring of the productive sector. Imports comprised mainly capital goods, whereas exports showed an unprecedented growth beyond that attained even by the "Asian tigers." See Francisco Gil Díaz and Agustín Carstens, "Some Hypotheses Related to the Mexican 1994–1995 Crisis," working paper 9601, Bank of Mexico, Mexico City, 1996.

6. Javier Gavito, Aarón Silva, and Guillermo Zamarripa, "Mexico's Banking Crisis: Origins, Consequences, and Countermeasures," in *Regulation and Supervision of Financial Institutions in the NAFTA Countries and Beyond,* ed. George M. von Furstenberg (Boston: Kluwer, 1997), pp. 228–245.

7. Between 1983 and 1989, Mexico had endured a net capital outflow of $15 billion. (All dollar amounts are U.S. dollars.)

8. David Folkerts-Landau, Ito Takatoshi, and Marcel Cassard, *International Capital Markets: Developments, Prospects, and Policy Issues* (Washington, D.C.: International Monetary Fund, 1995).

9. This issue has been explored thoroughly in Guillermo A. Calvo, Leonardo Leiderman, and Carmen M. Reinhart, "Inflows of Capital to Developing Countries in the 1990s" (International Monetary Fund, Washington, D.C., 1996, photocopy); Guillermo Calvo and Enrique Mendoza, "Petty Crime and Cruel Punishment: Lessons from the Mexican Debacle," in *American Economic Review* 86 (1996): 170–175; Folkerts-Landau, Ito, and Cassard, *International Capital Markets;* and Alejandro Díaz de León and Moisés Schwartz, "Crisis Management and Institutional Change Aimed at the Prevention of Future Crisis," in *The Banking and Financial Structure in the NAFTA Countries and Chile,* ed. George M. von Furstenberg (Boston: Kluwer, 1997), pp. 184–198.

10. All ratios related to GDP have been calculated with the new GDP series, using 1993 as the base year. For those years for which data were not available, we used an overlapped series.

11. See Gavito, Silva, and Zamarripa, "Mexico's Banking Crisis," for a full explanation.

12. Total net public debt, consolidated with the central bank (Banxico), plummeted from 69 percent of GDP in 1987 to 20 percent in 1993.

13. That ratio continued to increase in 1993 and 1994, though at slightly lower rates. At the end of 1994, a significant increase occurred because of the exchange rate adjustment of foreign currency balances.

14. Between January 1990 and September 1994 the loan portfolios of commercial banks, classified according to their geographical coverage as national, multiregional, or regional banks, grew annually in real terms by 19.8 percent, 50.2 percent, and 40.4 percent, respectively.

15. The level of international reserves was too low, the increase of domestic interest rates to avoid capital outflows was perceived as ineffective, and the market had disregarded a new issue of dollar-denominated debt—all while the government's short-term commitments were compelling.

16. On December 20, the sole announcement that the upper band of the exchange rate had been "adjusted" delivered the wrong signal to investors, suggesting that the government either had lost its capacity to support the exchange rate parity or was not willing to continue doing so. Speculating against the peso then became a reliable bet.

17. Calvo and Mendoza, "Petty Crime."

18. Ibid. Such herd behavior stems from the allocation to a single country of substantial portfolio investment resources that become highly volatile with small changes in expected returns; the cost and information asymmetries that make capital flows quite sensitive to rumors; and the adoption of extremely severe fiscal adjustment, a measure that heightens expectations of a recession.

19. Banamex, "Deuda privada en el exterior," *Examen de la Situación Económica de México* 72, no. 844 (1996): 97–101.

20. In 1989 the private sector supplied financial resources (therefore it was a net saver) equal to 1.6 percent of GDP; in 1990 that level dropped to 0.6 percent. The private sector reached net demander status in 1991, with financial resources at −8.2 percent of GDP; levels in 1992, 1993, and 1994 were −14.1 percent, −6.2 percent, and −6.6 percent, respectively.

21. Between 1994 and 1996 banks financed, on average, 83 percent of the total debt resources mobilized through the financial system as a whole.

22. The share of consumer and mortgage past-due loans in the total past-due loan portfolio of the commercial banking system increased from 14 percent in December 1991 to 31 percent in mid-1994. This is true even when only the amount of unpaid installments was considered to be the past-due balance, as specified in earlier Mexican accounting standards (now, the entire loan amount is the past-due balance when partial payments are delinquent).

23. These figures are based on data for the deciles 7–10 of the income-expenditure survey, which represents more than 90 percent of total debt service expenditures and more than three-fourths of households that have access to bank credit. Because some items are not identifiable, such as principal installments on credit cards, the figures do not include all items that should be considered under total household debt service (interest and principal installments).

24. "Las 500 empresas más importantes del año," *Expansión* 24, no. 597 (August 1992): 307; and "Las 500 empresas más importantes del año," *Expansión* 27, no. 672 (August 1995): 200.

25. Many firms and individuals were overindebted, however.

26. See Guillermo Ortiz, *La reforma financiera y la desincorporación bancaria* (Mexico City: Fondo de Cultura Económica, 1994); Sergio de la Cuadra and Salvador Valdés, "Myths and Facts About Financial Liberalization in Chile: 1974–1983," in *If Texas Were Chile: A Primer on Banking Reform* (A Sequoia Seminar), ed. Philip L. Brock (San Francisco: Institute for Contemporary Studies, 1992); Frederick Mishkin, "Asymmetric Information and Financial Crisis: A Developing Country Perspective," Federal Reserve Bank of New York, March 1996; and Victor Herrera and John Chambers, *Bank System Report* (New York: Standard & Poor's, 1996).

27. This is common among countries when the deregulation process is rapid; see *OECD, Economic Surveys: Mexico 1995* (Paris: Organization for Economic

Cooperation and Development, 1995); and Aristóbulo de Juan, "A Sum Up, or False Friends in Banking Reform" (paper prepared for the annual meeting of the European Bank for Reconstruction and Development, London, April 1995).

28. The first credit bureau in Mexico was authorized in July 1995 and began operations only in 1996. In addition to the deficiencies of information about the profile of borrowers, the credit boom for mortgages happened when prices for housing were at a peak, making it riskier for expected defaults. Theory and experience reckon that when the value of the underlying asset of a mortgage falls in relation to the value of its related loan, it is rational for the borrower to default (independent of the borrower's payment capacity). So mortgages in Mexico before 1994 were supplied in a risky environment, which assumed that it was highly improbable that the price of assets would keep climbing.

29. The credit, *préstamo quirografario,* is known as an unsecured business loan, even though the signed covenant transforms into a formal loan backed by a promissory note. This type of credit operation is usually intended for the short-term financing of working capital.

30. Under former accounting standards, between 1990 and 1994 the past-due loans ratio increased from 2.5 percent to 7.3 percent.

31. A study that includes 94 percent of the resolved banks in the United States between 1979 and 1987 found that management-driven weaknesses played a significant role in the decline of 90 percent of the resolved and problem banks in the sample. See *The Changing Business of Banking: A Study of Failed Banks from 1987 to 1992* (Washington, D.C.: Congressional Budget Office, 1994).

32. A highly concentrated banking system and its correlate risks, derived mainly from interbank loans, make the event of bad news for a single institution to be perceived as true for the whole banking and financial system. This perception results in widespread doubts about the global solvency of the system, which causes informed investors to exit the domestic market whenever full and credible deposit insurance is not in place. When these investors are, in turn, just a few agents who hold most of the banking sector's liabilities (high wealth concentration), their decision to exit causes major liquidity problems.

33. For a detailed description of the support measures adopted up to March 1996, see *La crisis bancaria en México: Orígenes, consecuencias y medidas instrumentadas para superarla* (Mexico City: Comisión Nacional Bancaria y de Valores, 1996). Measures adopted between April 1996 and the first semester of 1997 are described in *La crisis bancaria en México: Evolución reciente y medidas instrumentadas hasta el primer semestre de 1997* (Mexico City: Comisión Nacional Bancaria y de Valores, 1997).

34. Mexico's agricultural sector is mostly underdeveloped, both in economic and social terms; productivity rates are low—the sector accounts for 23 percent of the economically active population and only 7 percent of GDP.

35. This reduction rate applies to the initial 500 thousand pesos of the outstanding loan, thus benefiting in full 89 percent of the borrowers in this sector. The reduction rate diminishes progressively for larger debts.

36. These banks are Banamex, Bancomer, Serfín, Bital, Banorte, Atlántico, Promex, and Bancrecer/Banoro.

37. Secretaría de Hacienda y Crédito Público, *Criterios generales de política económica* (Mexico City: Secretaría de Hacienda y Crédito Público, 1997).

38. From 1991 to December 1994, the group of eight banks, not intervened or in a special situation, injected 6.5 billion (constant November 1997 pesos) of additional capital resources; this figure, added to amounts for reinvested profits and

7

Structural Change in the Mexican Private Sector: Strategies and Results

Raymundo Winkler

Beginning in 1985, when Mexico sought entry into the General Agreement on Tariffs and Trade, the country's government and business sector began a process of structural transformation of the economy to a more open, market-oriented system. The ultimate goal of the endeavor was to raise the economy's standards of productivity and efficiency to levels that would enable Mexico to compete successfully in the global economy. That has been no easy task. Even before the economic opening, but especially after the country's protracted protectionism was dismantled through lowered tariffs and other nontariff measures, the obsolescence and inadequate size of the Mexican productive apparatus was apparent.

Moreover, since the early 1980s the economy has faced both acute and prolonged instability, reflected in high budget deficits and rapidly rising inflation. To eradicate the threat of hyperinflation, a strict stabilization program was put into place in late 1987, which in only a few years has brought annual inflation down to less than 10 percent for the first time in two decades. In short, the strategy of structural change was carried out under a program of macroeconomic stabilization, which made it more difficult for firms to invest in the productive apparatus necessary for the new competitive environment.

This chapter assesses the progress of efforts to bring structural change to the productive plant of the Mexican private sector. It also explores this controversial, important question: Has the development strategy of structural change based on free-market or liberal economic principles failed? If the answer is yes, then what is the viable strategy for modernizing the national productive apparatus? If the answer is no, how can the strategy be reinforced or fine-tuned?

The chapter is divided into three sections. In the first is a description of the basic principles, context, and rationale of the reform strategy. The analysis in the second section challenges some of the more common criticisms made of the modernization strategy, and the third section presents general conclusions and a proposal for reinforcing structural change.

STRATEGY FOR STRUCTURAL CHANGE

Official rhetoric aside, the fundamental outlines of the strategy for structural change were very simple and direct. First, tariffs were reduced rapidly and nontariff barriers were eliminated to expose private firms to international competition. The government emphasized this measure when it began the stabilization program in 1987 as a way to expand the supply of goods with new participants and to deter rising prices in markets that include monopolies or oligopolies. Second, and with more immediate results, tax benefit and financial aid programs for companies were dismantled, as were subsidized prices for inputs produced by state enterprises. These measures were not ideologically motivated. Rather, they were an effort to put public finances in order, which could not be accomplished without cutting unjustified government expenses. Part of the task of reordering public finances was improving the financial health of the bloated and costly parastatal sector, which was the major contributor to the government's budget deficit.

The privatization of many state enterprises, such as the iron and steel industry, brought a definitive end to the practice of subsidizing certain industrial inputs. The decline in the price-to-cost ratio for public enterprises such as Petróleos Mexicanos (PEMEX) and the Comisión Federal de Electricidad (CFE), among many others, led to a dangerous decapitalization as well as to pressures from foreign governments to reduce such preferential prices, which are considered unfair trade practices. Both of these developments translated into higher operating costs for the enterprises.

To offset the negative effects of this new environment, policymakers promised what, in their view, would be sufficient for Mexico to adapt to competition and develop its own potential: a stable macroeconomic environment characterized by low inflation and interest rates, predictable parity (on occasion, almost fixed), access to supplies and foreign capital goods on favorable price and quality terms, and a new approach to economic regulation.

The strategy included a significant reduction of the tax rates on firms, from a maximum of 50 percent in 1988 to 34 percent in 1994. This measure was accompanied by the repeal of various tax exemptions and an intense oversight effort to bolster payment of taxes and reduce tax evasion and avoidance. In addition, some investment depreciation schemes were kept in place, especially for investment outside the principal metropolitan areas (Guadalajara, Mexico City and environs, and Monterrey).

To sum up, the strategy to modernize the productive apparatus involved rapidly dismantling the old industrial policy (and eliminating tax incentives, public subsidies, and soft loans) and replacing it with this principle: The industrial policy is that there is no industrial policy. That is, it was left to market forces, operating in a stable macroeconomic environment, to determine which sectors and enterprises would be competitive in the open economic environment.

The change in the development strategy was abrupt and costly. Almost unexpectedly, firms faced an avalanche of imported goods of all kinds. Foreign goods were favored by three conditions in addition to lowered tariffs and the elimination of nontariff barriers: (1) the appreciation of the peso, which drove down the relative prices of foreign goods and drove up the prices of exports; (2) the ample supply of foreign exchange in Mexico, fostered by the inflow of financial investments in unprecedented amounts; and (3) the increase in available income, which was earmarked for purchases of goods (many of them imported) that had been deferred by the crisis of the early 1980s.

Moreover, the promised stable macroeconomic environment was late in coming (if it came at all). Restrictive fiscal and monetary policies from 1988 to 1993, in combination with the initial effects of the stabilization program, yielded high effective interest rates. In other words, the cost of capital always included a high-risk premium, which made it difficult to make the investments essential for modernization and expansion of the productive plant. In addition, the great uncertainty prompted by the negotiations over the North American Free Trade Agreement (NAFTA) in 1992 and 1993, and especially in the months preceding NAFTA's ratification by the U.S. Congress, brought about the temporary suspension of investment plans on the part of Mexican and foreign firms. The history of 1994 and the subsequent crisis in 1995—which undid the advances in stabilization— complete the picture of recurrent macroeconomic instability.

The deregulation of economic activities that began in 1988 covered only a few regulations and some small industries. That deregulation was undertaken at all was a major step forward, but its scope was far from encompassing most of the productive apparatus in depth and breadth. The administration that took office in late 1994 (that of Ernesto Zedillo Ponce de León) made another stab at deregulation, this time with the goal of establishing a new regulatory framework. Unfortunately, this attempt reflects the same shortcomings of earlier ones.

If a liberal modernization or free-market strategy is to be successful, it should at least enjoy a context of basic macroeconomic stability and predictability. This has not been the case in Mexico. From 1985, when the process formally started, to 1995, only exceptionally (and debatably) did such an economic environment exist. The years 1985–1987 marked the most critical period of instability and disorder in Mexico's public finances. Between year-end 1986 and February 1988, annual inflation rose from 105.7 percent to 179.7 percent; the currency was devalued 155.7 percent; and the public deficit averaged 14.2 percent of gross domestic product (GDP).

Cumulative inflation from 1988 to 1994 was 262.7 percent, despite the presumed success of the stabilization program that began in late 1987. As noted above, effective interest rates were extremely high during almost all of the years of the administration of Carlos Salinas de Gortari (1988–1994), especially from 1988 to 1991. In mid-1993 annual inflation finally dropped to less than 10 percent and remained there until the end of 1994. Nevertheless, the political environment—and then the economic environment—began to deteriorate sharply, culminating with the peso devaluation crisis of late 1994 and the worst recession in decades in 1995.

INITIAL EFFECTS AND RESULTS

The history described above is not unimportant. To ignore it or downplay the significance of these unstable conditions, and then to conclude that the free-market strategy as such is incapable of fostering the modernization of the productive apparatus, would be a mistake and a misinterpretation. No strategy for economic modernization, liberal or otherwise, can succeed in a markedly unstable environment. This argument is crucial, at least in Mexico at this time, if one is to debate the current problems in good faith.

Even given this unfavorable environment, it is useful to evaluate in more detail the results of the new strategy for developing the productive apparatus. In principle, the lack of detailed information about sectors, industries, and firms makes it difficult to conduct a comprehensive and reliable analysis. Those studies that have attempted to do so end up referring to large aggregate figures, although the conclusions drawn from them too often pass for exhaustive intra- and interindustry analyses.[1] The following analysis uses standard information, while taking into account pertinent limitations of the data.

General and Sectoral Growth

The litmus test for evaluating the modernization program is the rate of general economic growth, as measured by GDP. The widespread opinion is that the performance of the Mexican economy from 1985 to 1994 was mediocre, in spite of the large inflows of external capital during that period.

Before reviewing the numbers, various considerations should be taken into account. The first and most obvious is whether ten years is enough time for an economy to show the sustained spectacular growth (say, 6 percent or 7 percent annually) that would be indisputable evidence of the strategy's success. Certainly, measured against the excessively optimistic expectations created by the authorities (which many people unwaveringly believed), the results were disappointing.

A second consideration concerns the need to specify the degree of industrial plant deterioration at the time the process started. Many studies demonstrate the obsolescence of Mexico's productive apparatus, its lack of competitiveness, and its failure to register technological advances—all the result of almost a half century of isolation from international competition. It was naive, at the very least, to suppose that the productive plant would adapt to the new competitive environment rapidly and without costs, successfully holding its own in the face of first-rate imported goods. In fact, one of the first stages of the market strategy was precisely to eliminate partially or completely (in the Schumpeterian sense or otherwise) sectors and firms incapable of succeeding under the new conditions. Again, only extreme naiveté would lead one to expect that the Mexican industrial apparatus would modernize rapidly.

At the same time, those sectors, industries, and firms that sought to adapt to the new environment displaced those that were unable to or did not want to modernize. How was this done? By importing the raw materials and intermediate and capital goods that would enable them to increase their competitiveness. The process of industrial reconversion was expensive, but it was also natural, rational, logical, and advisable from an economic standpoint. In no way, as critics frequently claimed, was it the result of bad faith, shortsightedness, or irresponsibility on the part of a group of authorities, or of an intrinsic defect in the liberal strategy.

In the technical slang used in Mexico, the free-market strategy "disarticulated productive linkages," which severely hurt the potential for growth and development of the productive apparatus. The assertion is true, but what matters is whether the linkages should have been, or deserved to be, kept in place. In fact, the continued existence of these linkages, which had been created and sustained by overblown protectionism, could not be justified in a competitive environment. To allow them to continue would imply that the whole productive chain would have to limit its access to goods of the quality and price essential for its modernization. To sing praises to the old industrial structure is to overestimate the true value of the obsolete and inefficient industrial apparatus. To call for its survival or its return to a privileged place is to demand that modernization of the industrial plant be set back or slowed down.[2]

With these caveats in mind, the assertion that growth has been mediocre can be examined more closely. Most evaluations simply calculate the average annual rate of GDP growth from 1985 to 1994. The result is 2.5 percent, slightly greater than the population increase (2.1 percent) over the period; much below the historical average; and insufficient to generate enough new jobs for those entering the workforce each year, let alone tackle the already high rates of unemployment. Yet the average for this period obscures the evolution of the economy over time. Most important, the years 1985–1987 were not only the first in the process of change but also those in which the Mexican economy was prisoner to considerable macroeconomic instability; an earthquake in Mexico City caused serious financial repercussions, as well as loss of life; and international oil prices collapsed, which was responsible for the equivalent of a 7 percent decline in GDP.

I therefore believe that the pertinent period for evaluation is 1988–1994. The latest data on those years show that average annual growth of GDP was 3.5 percent.[3] This average covers bad years, such as 1988 (with 1.3 percent growth) and 1993 (when the uncertainty surrounding NAFTA paralyzed investment and the economy grew only 2 percent), as well as good years, such as 1989, 1990, 1991, and 1994, with growth rates of 4.2 percent, 5.1 percent, 4.2 percent, and 4.5 percent, respectively. These figures suggest that, as anticipated, as the processes of structural change ripened, strong growth began to materialize. Average growth in the 1988–1994 period was not spectacular but does reflect the gradual advances stemming from the reforms. Indeed, it is equivalent to almost double the rate of population increase for the period (1.9 percent). Nevertheless, the devaluation crisis of late 1994 brought the trend to a dramatic halt.

The performance during 1988–1994 of the nine major categories that make up GDP reflects different degrees of adaption to the strategy or, in other words, the selection of winning and losing sectors. Those sectors registering growth rates higher than the 3.5 percent that the entire GDP averaged over the period were construction (4.7 percent); transportation and communications (4.5 percent); commerce, restaurants, and hotels (4.4 percent); financial services, insurance, and real estate (4.2 percent); and manufacturing (4.1 percent). In contrast, the sectors with less-than-average growth were agriculture, forestry, and fishing (1.0 percent); mining (1.4 percent); and community services (2.5 percent). The electricity, gas, and water sector grew at about the same rate (3.4 percent) as the GDP average.

The performance of sectors within the manufacturing industry, which is the basis for transforming the productive apparatus, is even more representative of the process of industrial reconversion. As Figure 7.1 shows, the most dynamic average annual growth (7.1 percent) from 1988 to 1994 occurred in metal products, machines, and equipment; the category "other manufacturing industries" trailed fairly closely at 6.6 percent. Some sectors

Figure 7.1   Average Annual Growth of GDP for Sectors Within the Manufacturing Industry, 1988–1994

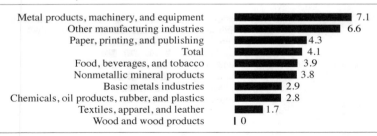

Metal products, machinery, and equipment	7.1
Other manufacturing industries	6.6
Paper, printing, and publishing	4.3
Total	4.1
Food, beverages, and tobacco	3.9
Nonmetallic mineral products	3.8
Basic metals industries	2.9
Chemicals, oil products, rubber, and plastics	2.8
Textiles, apparel, and leather	1.7
Wood and wood products	0

Sources: Prepared by the Center for Economic Studies of the Private Sector (CEESP), Mexico City, with data from the Instituto Nacional de Estadística, Geografía e Informática (hereafter INEGI).

hovered around the average growth rate of the manufacturing industry as a whole (4.1 percent), and others showed below-average or no growth. Overall, although the pace of expansion of the leading industries and sectors is not exceptional, it is far from poor and does show gradual improvement.

Advances in Productivity and Rising Real Wages

Another relevant indicator of the manufacturing industry's performance is worker productivity. Despite criticisms of this type of calculation, measurements of productivity are considered required references in both the economics literature and in the practices of most countries.[4] For Mexican industry, the advances have been significant since the mid-1980s. From 1985 to 1987 the average annual gain in productivity was 2.1 percent. During the period 1988–1994 the pace accelerated to 5.9 percent, far greater than in the industrialized economies and in most developing countries. Figure 7.2 details the rates at which productivity increased for sectors within the Mexican manufacturing industry.

The number of workers employed in industry dropped 14 percent from 1988 to 1994, which some argue is attributable more to the improvements in worker productivity than to increased production or better efficiency. Yet the reduction in the manufacturing labor force, contrary to what one might think, could just as easily be attributed to increased efficiency in the use of resources (capital and labor) and improved organizational and business management techniques. Indeed, in strictly economic terms this relationship is precisely what one would expect of a successful modernization process. It is, moreover, the first step toward increasing profits for the productive units, which in turn will eventually lead to the strengthening and

Figure 7.2   Average Annual Growth in Productivity Within Sectors of the
Manufacturing Industry, 1988–1994

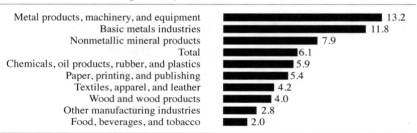

Sources: Prepared by the Center for Economic Studies of the Private Sector (CEESP), Mexico City, with data from INEGI.

expansion of the productive plant and, ultimately, the creation of more jobs.

The downsizing of the workforce in manufacturing also suggests a surplus of labor in relation to the new machinery, technology, and organizational processes typical of an environment marked by global competition. The recomposition of labor relations in Mexico changed the practices and institutional agreements between firms and unions that prevailed in the previous, closed economy. In the closed economy, excess labor or overstaffing was tolerable; in the new environment, practices are more flexible and strictly tied to the needs of the productive process, leading to gains in productivity and efficiency. It should be noted that these changes were brought about through freely negotiated agreements between companies and unions, without formal modification of the legal framework that governs labor-management relations.

One sign that the gains in labor productivity have been beneficial to the economy (which, incidentally, contradicts speculations about the technical validity of these estimates concerning calculations such as worker productivity) can be found in the evolution of real wages in manufacturing. Between 1982 and 1987 real wages in manufacturing had declined at an average annual rate of 6.8 percent.[5] Beginning in 1988, however, real wages tended to stabilize, and over the period 1989–1994 they increased significantly, if not steadily. The cumulative increase from 1988 to 1994 was 40.4 percent, for an average annual rate of 5 percent.[6]

In most Mexican manufacturing firms, wages are negotiated under bargaining agreements between the firms and labor unions. In the period 1988–1994 it was by consensus among business organizations, labor, and government authorities that prices and minimum wages were determined.[7] The consensus was also to negotiate contractual wages in a framework of freedom of action by unions and companies, and there is evidence that this is what really happened. In other words, remuneration in manufacturing has reflected market conditions. Therefore, and unless individual firms have acted irrationally, deciding in a sudden outpouring of benevolence to pay wage increases in real terms, the improvement in remuneration must have been based upon concrete gains in productivity and efficiency.

Response of Private Investors

The reorganization of the business sectors and companies, as well as the conversion of firms' equipment and machinery—both of which were necessary for adapting to the new incentives and competitive framework—were mainly responsible for economic growth overall and in manufacturing, in particular, and for the gains in productivity and in real wages. Conversion required considerable investment, as in the case of replacing the antiquated industrial base. In other cases investment was aimed at expanding already-existing capacity, and in still others, at creating new industries (for example, certain aspects of telecommunications). The response of the Mexican private sector to this new incentives system may be interpreted as either favorable or unfavorable, depending on the amounts and direction of investment in the productive apparatus.

The change in private investment trends from 1982–1987 to 1988–1994 was radical and very favorable. From 1982 to 1987, private investment plummeted, with a cumulative decrease of 23.6 percent. The economic crises of those years—unleashed by another balance-of-payments emergency when the country could not meet its external debt obligations, and the subsequent intensification of macroeconomic instability—explain this fall in investment. Sluggish investment, in turn, accounted for the scant economic growth.

In 1987 that trend began to reverse, and dramatically so beginning in 1988. From 1988 to 1994, private investment increased at an average annual rate of 9.3 percent. According to some estimates, such investments amounted to approximately \$306 billion.[8] As a proportion of GDP, private investment grew from an average annual rate of 11 percent in 1985–1987 to 13.9 percent in 1988–1994. Of the latter total, 52.7 percent was for acquiring machinery and equipment, and 47.3 percent for the construction and expansion of facilities (see Figure 7.3). In other words, the largest share was for modernizing machinery and equipment; the structural change strategy was expected to yield this result.

This boom in private investment has been called into question because of its supposedly modest impact on the general growth of the economy. As previously noted, however, investment did gain momentum, which was reflected in better economic performance. Although there are valid reasons to be skeptical about the positive impact of increased private investment on

Figure 7.3   Private Investment as a Percentage of GDP

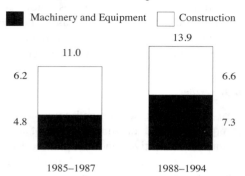

Sources: Prepared by the Center for Economic Studies of the Private Sector (CEESP), Mexico City, with data from INEGI.

the economy, most new investment went toward retrofitting the old plants, not to expanding modern installed capacity. New machinery and equipment may confer the potential for greater capacity, but such modernization is not enough, by itself, to increase production in the short run, especially considering that new projects require a natural maturation period before their full benefits materialize. In general, the full potential of modernization processes can be realized only over several years.

Another important element in understanding the modest response of economic growth to these investments is structural. Several studies have demonstrated the trend of the Mexican productive apparatus toward capital-intensive processes, which translate into a capital-to-output ratio that is lower than that for labor-intensive processes (elasticity). In other words, the capital requirements for generating a unit of output increase over time, and thus the investment effort has been insufficient to contribute significantly to general economic growth.

These indicators can be interpreted as reflecting an inefficient use of the lion's share of the productive resources of Mexico, in which capital is scarce (and therefore its cost high) and cheap labor is abundant. This line of reasoning would argue for abandoning the present scheme and inducing labor-intensive technological processes. In principle, doing so would generate a higher rate of growth and at the same time create many more jobs.

But the issue is extremely complex—taken alone, it would require exhaustive studies. For the purposes of this chapter, keep in mind these two relatively simple considerations that tend to be scorned by some who advocate productive processes with a high labor-to-capital ratio: First, those studies that compare the capital-to-output ratio in different historical periods refer to productive processes from the initial stages of industrialization, when any increase in the capital base generated production gains more than proportional to the mix of added factors. Industrialization of the Mexican economy lasted several decades, but by the late 1970s it had begun to show clear signs of exhaustion, as increased investment in fixed capital came to a halt and the learning curve reached its peak. Second, the new conditions of international competition demand levels of efficiency, scale, and quality for most goods and services that are not compatible with the technologies of the 1970s or 1980s, which were less capital-intensive and had a higher capital-to-labor ratio.

To pursue this alternative strategy would constrain the global competitiveness of the Mexican economy. By focusing on the production of low value-added goods, this path would diminish the potential both for growth and, ultimately, for generating employment.

Export Performance

Finally, successful export performance is overwhelming evidence of progress in the structural change strategy. After all, an increase in foreign sales demonstrates the ability to penetrate highly competitive international markets and thus is one of the clearest signs of increased efficiency in a given economy. Overcoming the lengthy period in which the Mexican productive apparatus was more or less unable to export was a great strategic challenge.

As shown in Figure 7.4, Mexico's export performance has notably improved over the past decade, given that the country went from a petroleum-based, almost monoexport economy to one in which manufactured goods make up 83 percent of all exports. The value of foreign sales increased from $24 billion in 1982 to almost $100 billion in 1996, for an average annual growth rate of 10.4 percent over the fourteen-year period. These figures place Mexico among the ten leading exporting countries in the world. Over the same period, exports of manufactured goods skyrocketed from $6.2 billion to $81.2 billion (20.2 percent annually). From 1988 to 1996 the average annual increase in foreign sales of manufactured goods was 17.4 percent, three times the pace of export growth globally. The unilateral economic opening bore fruit, for it helped to open new markets, which better-quality and competitively priced Mexican goods are entering.

The exports include all kinds of manufactured goods. Of course, those goods are concentrated in relatively few industries and firms, which some critics interpret as an anomaly. In fact, however, the Mexican situation is no different from that of most high-export economies. Worldwide exporting is synonymous with specialization and concentration, as no one country can be competitive in a wide array of industries. The global trend toward

Figure 7.4   Value of Mexico's Foreign Sales of Manufactured Goods and All Other
Exports, 1982–1996

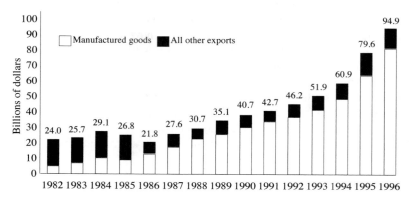

Sources: Prepared by the Center for Economic Studies of the Private Sector (CEESP),
Mexico City, with data from INEGI.

specialization in a relatively limited group of products has become further
accentuated since the late 1980s, and Mexico is no exception.

Critics have also claimed that because the domestically produced content of Mexican exports is low, the impact of the export sector on the rest of
the productive apparatus is limited. This is also true, but again the phenomenon reflects the logic of specialization and intense competition in global
markets. Under present conditions, the manufacture of exportable goods
that can successfully penetrate international markets (and, increasingly,
even those goods that are not exported) needs to incorporate intermediate
components and inputs, and machinery and technology of better quality, as
well as lower prices than are available in any one part of the world.
Consequently, not only do Mexican exports have a high imported content,
but the same can be said to a greater or lesser extent of all economies. This
observation is bolstered by the fact that economies that show a surplus in
their trade balance are the exception. Those countries with the most exports
are also the largest importers, particularly of intermediate goods, components, and capital goods. This does not mean that the priority objective of
economic policy—to increase the domestic content of exports—should be
abandoned. The process of increasing the domestically produced content is
bound to be gradual and difficult; however, and above all, as in other countries, it has very tight constraints.

It should also be noted that the quickest growth in Mexican exports
(1988–1996, as shown in Figure 7.4) occurred despite a major revaluation

of the peso during most of that period (through 1994). In other words, the increase in exports was not based on a weak currency, as was the case in many developing nations in the 1970s and 1980s. We can therefore conclude that the successful export performance was the result of efficiency gains in the productive apparatus. Specifically, the accumulated increase in the productivity of the manufacturing industry was more than sufficient to offset the strengthening or appreciation of the peso.

CONCLUSIONS AND PENDING TASKS

The devaluation crisis of late 1994 and the unprecedented recession that followed in 1995 have caused many people to conclude, too hastily, I believe, that Mexico's free-market strategy for economic modernization has failed. The results and advances described in this chapter challenge that conclusion. The devaluation crisis arose from the convergence of several circumstances still being debated, but the performance of the productive apparatus since the new system of free-market incentives was initiated was not one of them.

In particular, it is said that the modernization strategy tends to produce high and unsustainable current-account deficits. The evidence? In 1994 Mexico's current-account deficit reached 7 percent of GDP and the economy was unable to withstand it. This argument is only part of the story, however. In effect, the importation of capital goods and intermediate inputs worsens the trade balance, but a large share of those imports (approximately 42.3 percent) went to support export growth, and the rest (57.7 percent) was used to improve production (with machinery and components) of goods for the local market, which compete with foreign goods.[9]

At the same time, the rapid increase of the current-account deficit is a consequence of an age-old problem of the Mexican economy, one that is not directly related to the modernization strategy: that is, the considerable foreign exchange required to service Mexico's foreign debt. In 1994, for example, debt service alone accounted for 39.8 percent of the current-account deficit. Excluding it, the current-account deficit would have amounted to 4.3 percent of GDP, which, by international standards, is not exorbitant. The burden of servicing the external debt (in addition to its amortization) is a formidable constraint on the country's growth potential, to the extent that it establishes a very high floor for disequilibrium in the current accounts. Thus, whatever the nation's economic policy, the problem of foreign debt demands further attention if Mexico is to advance, even slowly.

The principal conclusion of this chapter is that the liberal strategy of structural change implemented in Mexico since 1988 has begun to produce positive results for the Mexican economy. When the nation recovers from the recession and financial instability of 1994–1995—which it has been doing faster than most analysts predicted, with the newfound strength of the productive apparatus contributing to the recovery—the progress and maturation of the structural change, interrupted suddenly in late 1994, will return.

Nevertheless, the modernization process is far from over. The Mexican economy is still subject to structural constraints that should be removed or reworked to unleash its growth potential. Among the most pressing needs is to make the national government a more effective advocate of efficiency and economic growth. More specific reforms would be (1) to establish a modern institutional framework, one that protects property rights and guarantees the strict and timely performance of contracts freely entered into by economic actors; (2) to implement a modern system of regulation, consistent with the requirements of a market economy, so as to reduce transaction costs and facilitate the development of all stages of productive activity; (3) to allow private firms, both national and foreign, to participate in sectors still reserved exclusively for the state (power generation, among others); (4) to loosen labor market regulations; and (5) to structure the tax system to encourage investment and domestic savings.

This set of pending reforms is crucial if the Mexican economy is to make the most efficient use of its scarce resources. These measures will help bring about vigorous and long-lasting growth, create better-paying jobs, and ultimately overcome the long-standing lag in the well-being of most of the population.

NOTES

1. One such study, for example, is *La industria mexicana en el mercado mundial: Elementos para una política industrial,* 2 vols., edited by Fernando Clavijo and José I. Casar (Mexico City: Fondo de Cultura Económica, 1994).

2. "Privileged" is meant in the sense that, as was the case when the Mexican economy was closed to open trade, those companies could sell their products or goods regardless of their quality or price.

3. BAINEGI database, National Institute of Statistics, Geography, and Information (INEGI) of Mexico.

4. The most common criticism of this type of calculation is that it is a very general approach that does not take into account specific problems or situations of firms in particular.

5. BAINEGI database, INEGI.

6. Ernesto Zedillo, Third State of the Union Address, September 1, 1997, Mexico City.

7. Minimum wages are set by government, labor, and the companies. Contractual wages are negotiated freely between unions and the companies.

8. Bank of Mexico 1994 data. All dollar amounts are U.S. dollars.

9. Economic indicators database, Bank of Mexico.

8

Business-Government Relations in Mexico Since 1990: NAFTA, Economic Crisis, and the Reorganization of Business Interests

Kristin Johnson Ceva

Efforts at regional integration in North America have wrought substantial changes in Mexico's business-government relations and in the types of economic policies being promoted by both sectors. Based in part on extensive interviews with business and government leaders, this chapter traces the nature of those changes from the beginning of negotiations over the North American Free Trade Agreement (NAFTA) in 1990 to the present.

Although most of the presidential term of Carlos Salinas de Gortari (1988–1994) found much of Mexico humming a consistent tune of business-government harmony and general business support for Salinas's neoliberal economic agenda, a growing voice of resentment, discontent, and even discord has emanated from the business community since the negotiations started. Opposition parties and new social movements began openly to criticize the administration for its handling of the negotiations and for economic imbalances caused by the government's protection of certain large business groups and banks. Many small and medium-size firms, and some large ones, have participated in those parties and movements, as well as contributed to the debate through a variety of new and traditional business associations.

One common call is for the government to focus not only on macroeconomic issues but also on the microeconomy. Another is for the government to develop an adequate industrial policy, one that could help Mexican firms become more competitive in the context of trade liberalization and regional integration. This more critical view of public policies, and the heightened advocacy of changes for the microeconomy, have been referred to as the "microrevolution."

GROWING DISCORD DURING THE NAFTA NEGOTIATIONS

To better understand how business and government began to diverge over
regional integration strategies, it is important to consider how NAFTA was
negotiated, what stance various types of businesses took regarding the
agreement, and how business and government interacted during the negotiations.

NAFTA would consolidate a process of economic opening in Mexico
that had begun in the mid-1980s, under the administration of Miguel de la
Madrid Hurtado (1982–1988). A small group of policymakers within the
Salinas administration was involved in the negotiations, closely counseled
by business leaders. On the one hand, the negotiations illustrated the close
nature of the business-government collaboration that had characterized the
Salinas years. On the other hand, they also placed front and center a system
of business representation that for the most part excluded small and medium-size firms, that is, one that did not adequately represent the growing
diversity of business interests in a liberalized economy.

Large business groups, or *grupos,* whose members were best positioned to compete within a free-trade area, generally supported the government's intent to negotiate NAFTA, as did the Business Coordinating
Council (CCE), Mexico's premier business federation.[1] But smaller firms
and microenterprises, still primarily oriented toward production for the
domestic market, remained marginalized from many avenues of business
representation, and most knew very little about how the terms of the free-
trade agreement might affect them.

Born and having prospered under the policies of protectionism and
import substitution, smaller enterprises—commonly affiliated with the
National Chamber of Manufacturing Industries, or Canacintra—had historically opposed unilateral trade liberalization and Mexico's accession to the
General Agreement on Tariffs and Trade (GATT), which occurred in 1986.
And since that time the smaller producers have suffered severely, particularly from Asian competition in clothing, shoes, leather products, metal
products, and toys.[2]

Vocal opposition to NAFTA by small and medium-size firms was fairly
marginal, however, for several reasons. First, President Salinas and his
trade ministry officials put a tremendous effort into publicity to preempt
potential opposition, conducting meetings about NAFTA with hundreds of
business groups before the formal negotiations began. Rodolfo Cruz
Miramontes (coordinator of the industrial sectors for the Coordinating
Body of Foreign Trade Business Associations, or COECE) maintains that
"at first, most people did not know what NAFTA was, and we had to define
a free trade agreement for them. After the government provided an explanation of NAFTA and outlined its advantages, we received less opposition

from industry."[3] A second explanation for low levels of opposition is the lack of accurate information at that time—apart from government publicity about the benefits of NAFTA—about free trade among small and medium-size businesses. Discussion and debate of NAFTA's potential effects was quite limited in Mexico, especially compared with the wide-ranging discussions then taking place in the United States and Canada.[4] Third, many small-business owners saw no alternative to NAFTA and simply hoped that its terms would give them some advantages vis-à-vis their Asian competitors.[5]

FORMING A TRADE ADVISORY GROUP: COECE'S ROLE IN THE NEGOTIATIONS

When the Mexican government announced its intent to negotiate NAFTA in June 1990, it invited the CCE to participate in the negotiations. The government soon learned, however, that neither its own agencies nor the CCE had the detailed sectoral information necessary to serve as the basis for decisionmaking on the terms of the agreement. The Secretariat of Commerce and Industrial Development (Secofi) therefore encouraged the formation of a new business trade advisory group that would be organized by economic sector. Formed in late 1990, the Coordinating Body of Foreign Trade Business Associations was responsible for coordinating the writing of sectoral monographs by 176 subsectors, including detailed information on each sector's potential to export, its vulnerability to imports, and what remained to be done in each sector to increase competitiveness.

Rationales for Forming the Trade Advisory Group

Governments may form a trade advisory group (TAG) for several reasons. In addition to serving particular informational needs, a TAG may also function as a meeting ground to rally support and consensus for trade negotiations and policy. More broadly, they may also serve a political role, exerting influence that may support the state's efforts at control and legitimation.[6]

The business community has its own incentives for forming TAGs. First, a TAG represents one more institutional mechanism through which businesses can influence public policies that are likely to affect them. Second, a TAG may offer opportunities to acquire and disseminate information that other societal groups do not have. Finally, business leaders can make important contacts through such an institution, not only with domestic government officials but also, in the case of negotiating trade agreements, with foreign government and business leaders.[7]

Although the business sector may strongly support the formation of a

TAG, small and medium-size firms are unlikely to receive adequate representation within these structures:

> Despite their enormous importance, and the peculiar needs they have, small and medium-sized firms in the TAGs are clustered together with large firms and treated as members of separate industry groups, i.e., textiles, apparel, furniture. In this institutional framework the needs of small and medium-sized firms as well as large firms are seen as similar and dependent on the characteristics of the particular sector of the economy to which each belongs.[8]

Thus, the TAG structure may foster greater sectoral identity and networking, particularly on issues of common interest to most firms in the sector, but in the context of trade liberalization the needs of the smaller firms will most likely differ from those of the larger ones in their sector. This is particularly true in developing countries such as Mexico, where economic activity is concentrated in a small number of very large business groups. In particular, the smaller firms are less likely to have access to credit for new investments and more likely to need additional training in marketing and management to face new competition. As a result, the lack of representation of the smaller firms may ultimately work against the express goals of the TAG. Paradoxically, TAG structures may bring about the unintended consequence of fomenting divisiveness between business sectors, between small and large firms, and between certain sectors or firms and the government.

COECE's Role in Promoting Business Interests

Between 1990 and 1993 Mexico's trade advisory group, COECE, represented the Mexican business sector in the NAFTA negotiations and advised government officials negotiating the treaty. The sectoral monographs that COECE coordinated attempted to identify the probable effects of NAFTA in each sector and drew conclusions on these topics: concessions that should be sought from the United States and Canada in the negotiations; what Mexico could concede (and not concede); and what infrastructure or prerequisites Mexico needed to be competitive. Through these monographs the government tried to identify a single negotiating position for each subsector of the Mexican economy.[9]

The process of writing sectoral monographs drove the structure of the trade advisory group: An ad hoc sectoral organization was established, first representing forty major sectors (each selecting its own leader) and eventually representing two hundred subsectors. Secofi, the commerce secretariat, developed a matching reciprocal structure to act as the interlocutor on the government side and to field the demands of each business sector during the negotiations.[10]

COECE's organizational structure was patterned after the Canadian Trade Advisory Committee and was much more horizontal than that of the hierarchical CCE. In fact, COECE represented a not insignificant break with the traditional verticality of Mexican business associations since the 1950s. The organization also included other business associations not formally represented within the CCE, such as export organizations.[11]

COECE developed a considerable amount of strength and autonomy during the negotiations, and for two years it was the most influential business organization in Mexico. Moreover, the business sector became the most significant interlocutor with government throughout the negotiation process through a communication structure known as the *cuarto de junto,* or "room next door," whereas labor participation remained largely circumscribed. From the initial negotiations through March 1992, COECE organized 1,333 meetings between the Mexican negotiating team and businesses. In addition, new business-government committees were created throughout the negotiations to deal with specific trade-related questions and issues.[12]

At first COECE, with its sectoral structure, appeared to be much more representative than the CCE in organizing the entire business community. Nevertheless, large firms still had the most influence over the sectoral studies that COECE undertook in preparation for the negotiations. Many of the sectoral reports were written by local consulting firms under contract to industry associations dominated by large firms. And most of the debates about the findings of the studies went on at the highest levels of the business-state coalition, with questionable input from smaller firms.[13]

As the negotiations got under way, "big companies slowly took over the whole negotiating process, both by paying their executives to be committed to the process full-time, and by presiding over the most important negotiating tables."[14] Carlos Alba, a Colegio de México researcher who has written extensively on the subject, maintains that "big business was overrepresented in COECE, particularly in the *mesas,*" or roundtable discussions.[15] According to COECE's director, Guillermo Güémez, the most significant points of contact between business and government occurred at those roundtables. Eighteen *mesas* had been formed, in addition to the sectoral groups, to address various technical issues such as dispute resolution procedures, tariffs, and dumping.[16] The roundtables included a coordinator and experts on each technical subject and thus were arranged by topic, not by sector. Because of the preponderance of technical experts from large firms, those firms were able to exercise a great deal of influence over the *mesas*. As the business leader in charge of the automotive sector explained, "We needed people who could talk about questions of rules of origin, market obstacles, tariffs, safeguards, and disloyal practices. Small businesses did not have the requisite language."[17]

Not all businesses accepted the less-than-fully-representative structure of COECE, and it was not only the business elites who debated the micro-economic effects of NAFTA. Although open opposition to NAFTA was minimal at the outset, it grew as the negotiations progressed. Various points of conflict and tension arose on the part of business during the NAFTA negotiations, rooted in both the increasingly polarized business sector and leaders' frustrations with the inefficiencies in the current system of business representation.

Mexican businesses are profoundly heterogeneous with respect to the size of their establishments, geographic region, and relations with international markets. Their positions on many aspects of trade liberalization have therefore varied widely, and the threat of increasing foreign competition only widened the gaps. Numerous conflicts arose between exporters and nonexporters, among regions, and especially between large and small firms about many specific terms being negotiated.[18] Moreover, some small and medium-size producers openly complained that COECE never truly represented them at the negotiating table.[19]

Several of these firms also maintained that control over the negotiating process had been seized by the firms qualifying under the Registry of High-Exports Enterprises (or ALTEX, a government program for firms with high levels of exports, mostly made up of large *grupos*). Eventually, interest grew among small and medium-size firms, regional groups, and export firms to strengthen their own means of representation.[20]

These discussions brought into high relief the competitiveness, or lack thereof, of Mexican firms. As the prospect of heightened competition grew imminent, many of the smaller firms became more keenly aware of the obstacles they faced in becoming competitive in an increasingly liberalized economy, including their lack of technology, low quality of product, and lack of access to credit and capital.[21] Representatives from the more vulnerable sectors, such as textiles, trucking, and government procurement, protested against the speed at which reforms were being phased into their sectors and the lack of adequate financing for economic adjustment.[22] Although most small and medium-size firms did not oppose NAFTA per se, their grievances continued to focus on their lack of representation in COECE, the speed and timing of the reforms, and the lack of adequate support to meet increasing competition.

The NAFTA negotiations also sparked a debate between business and government as to their respective responsibilities for promoting the competitiveness of Mexican enterprises. Firms began to identify themselves as either winners or losers in the process of economic liberalization, in terms of both the individual firm itself and its economic sector. As a result, the smaller enterprises came to formulate new ideas about what economic policies would best meet their needs and interests in the context of liberalization and regional integration, and their business organizations became more critical of the government's inattention. Many resented in particular the government's management of the NAFTA financial negotiations.

THE ROLE OF THE FINANCE MINISTRY
AND THE BANKS IN THE NEGOTIATIONS

Although Secofi controlled the NAFTA negotiations on behalf of all other sectors, the Secretariat of Finance and Public Credit (Hacienda) took direct control of matters concerning the financial sector. According to interviews with NAFTA negotiators, Secofi and Hacienda had disagreed over which agency should have jurisdiction for the financial sector and the degree to which the finance sector should be liberalized. Secofi had intended to negotiate for the finance sector in the same way it did for the industrial and agricultural sectors, making use of the COECE organization. Secofi officials also hoped to liberalize the financial sector to a much greater degree than did their counterparts in Hacienda.

After a clash between the two agencies, Hacienda was able to bypass both Secofi and COECE. Its officials (some of the same ones who had orchestrated the bank reprivatizations in 1990) formed a compact team to conduct all of the finance negotiations. And unlike the elaborate sectoral and *cuarto de junto* structures set up by Secofi and COECE, business-government interactions in the financial sector took place between this small Hacienda team and the leaders of the major *grupos financieros* (financial conglomerates).

The team fought for high levels of protection for the Mexican banks. Its initial position included no opening until 1998, with 1 percent of the total market to be opened in that year, reaching 7 percent by the year 2010. After tough negotiations with the United States, the countries agreed on a thirteen-year transition period, including the so-called 4 percent rule: No individual foreign bank could own more than 4 percent of the total market share, beginning in the year 2000, with a safeguard clause carrying through 2007. Because of the oligopolistic nature of the Mexican banking system (each of the three largest Mexican banks represents well over 4 percent of the total market share), this rule meant that no foreign bank would be able to acquire a large Mexican bank.[23]

Under the final agreement, the financial sector liberalization achieved was limited, especially compared with the extent of liberalization achieved under NAFTA in other sectors. Hacienda officials argued that the new *grupos financieros* needed time to consolidate their market position before facing international competition. Many economists argued, however, that a greater degree of competition was precisely what the Mexican financial system needed.[24]

Although the new bank owners had their own obvious interests in avoiding international competition, Hacienda officials had strong political interests—for a variety of reasons—in keeping the banks in Mexican hands. First is what Alberto Musalem, Dimitri Vittas, and Asli Demirguc-Kunt call the "efficiency vs. ownership dilemma."[25] State officials may recognize the efficiency gains possible from increased competition, but they are also concerned about the possibility of increased capital flight and questionable local commitment with the entrance of foreign-owned banks.[26]

Second, Hacienda officials believed it would be easier to deal with Mexican bank owners than foreign owners in securing support for government initiatives and programs. As one former Hacienda team member recalled, "As for myself and the other finance negotiators in NAFTA, we did not see bank protection as a question of protection of our sovereignty. We wanted the three largest banks to be always in Mexican hands, for the purpose of management and control."[27] Third, many Mexican observers insist that their government fought for high levels of protection for the financial sector to allow the new bankers to recoup their investments, acquired at steep prices (3.52 times the book value, on average).[28] There is a widespread belief that the bankers and the government had a tacit agreement when the banks were reprivatized: The purchasers would pay high prices for the banks, and in return the government would subsequently fight to protect the banks during the NAFTA negotiations, to ensure high rents in the sector for a number of years.[29] Under this scenario, not only would the bank sales supply much-needed funds to reduce internal debt, but the finance ministry itself would retain an acceptable level of political control over the banking system.[30]

Protection of the financial sector from domestic or international competition or both may cause serious economic disequilibria in developing countries attempting an overall project of economic liberalization. When a government pursues a gradual financial liberalization during which certain barriers to entry still remain, domestic banks can keep their profit margins high while slowly writing off bad loans and recapitalizing. However, because financial services can be viewed as intermediate goods used in the production of final goods, any estimation of the effects of protecting the financial sector must take into account economywide effects. Gradualist transition policies restrict domestic producers' access to cheaper credit and better financial services, thereby constraining their competitiveness because their costs of financial intermediation are higher than those faced by foreign producers.

"If the real sector is at a more advanced stage of liberalization, as in Mexico, protecting the financial sector or allowing its gradual transition taxes the real sector which faces international competition in pricing its output. . . . This tax is also disproportionally borne by small producers."[31] In short, small and medium-size firms confront the problem of exposure to international competition without recourse to internationally competitive sources of capital. Large firms are not as affected because they have much greater access to international financial markets. All told, then, the impact of Hacienda's and the banks' role in Mexico's financial opening under NAFTA must be evaluated by examining their effects on other business sectors as well.

BUSINESS REACTIONS TO NAFTA'S FINANCIAL TERMS

The political fallout from NAFTA's terms regarding Mexico's financial sector was significant. There was great resentment on the part of many industries over bank protection and how they saw the *apertura* (opening of the market) in general. Through a variety of channels, business firms have protested against the high costs of financing charged by the reprivatized banks and against the government's protection of an inefficient banking sector. Not surprisingly, the discontent has been particularly audible among small and medium-size businesses, which remain outside the *grupo* networks. Their owners have maintained that when the economy was closed, they could more readily pass on high finance costs to consumers in the form of higher prices. Within a more competitive open economy, however, their principal concern has become the cost of financing.[32]

With the cost of credit up to four times higher than that available to their U.S. counterparts, Mexican firms complained that the excessive protection given to the banking sector would only prolong their difficulties in adapting to an open economy. Many argued that the government should allow for the establishment of new banks and open the market to foreign competition, so that Mexican interest rates would drop toward international rates.[33]

A firm's access to affordable credit plays a fundamental role in its ability to develop its productive apparatus, to plan long-term productivity improvements, and to invest in the modernization of machinery and equipment. Most small and medium-size firms in Mexico, being squeezed out of the commercial bank credit market, have had to rely on financing from development banks, primarily through Nacional Financiera (Nafin). Nevertheless, estimates for 1992 show that Nafin was able to provide financing to only 4 percent of the nearly 1,309,000 small and midsize business establishments in Mexico—and to these, at interest rates up to 22 percent; the rates available from commercial banks were around 37 percent.[34] According to a 1993 survey by Canacintra's Center of Economic and Political Studies, fully one-half of its members (primarily small and midsize firms) reported that they were experiencing a liquidity crisis that threatened their existence.[35]

Another difficulty in relying on Nafin has been its status as a second-story bank, which means that its credit is actually administered by the commercial banks using Nafin resources. The commercial banks perform the risk assessments and decide which firms will receive the credit, but their risk evaluation focuses almost exclusively on collateral, not on the potential viability of the applicant's proposed project. Thus, the banks have often neglected to ascertain whether the loans will be used for productive investments or simply for credit card or auto loan payments. Moreover, the commercial banks have sometimes taken advantage of the situation by falsely claiming that Nafin resources are not available or that the paperwork will take months to complete if processed through Nafin. A bank may then offer a direct loan to the small firm, but of course at a much higher interest rate.[36]

Adolfo Valles Septien, president of the National Association of Manufacturers (ANIT), which represents microenterprises and small firms, publicly decried the Mexican government's protection of the banks within NAFTA:

> The aim of setting the opening of financial services at seven years and limiting the participation of foreign capital in NAFTA constitutes an excessive protection of the Mexican banks and condemns the productive sectors in Mexico to continue paying heavily for financing, and the savers and investors to receiving low rates of return. . . . The privatized Mexican banks have been the greatest obstacle to the industrial sector during the modernization process. Financing in Mexico is at least twice as expensive as in other countries, which represents an enormous disadvantage for the productive sectors that must face these higher costs of production, and without a doubt places Mexican firms as sure victims of their foreign competitors.[37]

He also claimed that the high costs of credit and excessive requirements for bank loans were not likely to change until Mexican banks face authentic competition, both domestic and foreign.

José Antonio Murra Giacomán, the vice president of Canacintra, also voiced his frustrations with NAFTA's finance terms: "How is it possible that a Mexican enterprise that exports to the U.S. may locate financing in dollars at 9 percent through Bancomext, while the firm that does not export can obtain financing—that is, if the firm can even obtain a loan—only in *cetes* plus fifteen points? [And] even the firms that export have to sustain a subvaluation of the dollar of between 15 and 20 percent, which markedly limits their margins of utility."[38] Murra Giacomán warned that the decapitalization of the industrial sectors puts the consolidation of Mexico's economic modernization at risk.

Proposals by various industrial sectors of the Canacintra in the state of Nuevo León, written as a response to the proceedings of the NAFTA finance negotiations, urged a fiscal reform that would both aid in the development of smaller businesses and open the Mexican banks to international competition by providing industry with better access to competitive rates of finance. Rubén Medina Villarreal, president of the industry association Metal-Mecánica, remarked, "The development of a country should rely on the small and medium businesses, which generate the majority of jobs; they represent 90 percent of the productive capacity of Mexico. . . . We cannot acquire equipment with higher technology, because the cost of financing prevents any investment projects."[39]

POLITICAL CONSEQUENCES OF THE NAFTA NEGOTIATIONS

The foregoing debate also spilled over into debate among political parties. In fact, the National Action Party (PAN) has used the banking issue to differentiate itself from the ruling Institutional Revolutionary Party (PRI). According to Felipe Calderón Hinojosa, secretary general of the PAN,

> Over the long term the party believes that NAFTA will bring growth in employment and investment. The PAN supports open markets, a competitive system, and is aware of global changes. Thus, we believe NAFTA is positive in the long term. However, we believe that within specific sectors there are problems, as well as many short-term problems in general. One error the PRI has made, and which we criticized at the time, was that the commercial opening was not accompanied by sufficient financial opening, due to favored groups of the PRI. A big part of the problem in lack of financing to firms is the oligopolistic system of the banks.[40]

Calderón continued:

> Salinas's argument for needing big industrial-financial conglomerates to confront the *apertura*, even if true, never worked in the financial sense. There is no efficiency in the financial system. And the only option for small and medium firms in this type of model is to form part of productive chains. Salinas, however, created and supported big firms and never worked to integrate the small and medium businesses into productive chains. In countries like Spain and France there are more means of getting financing for [the latter] firms, since the financial system is more diversified.[41]

The PAN candidate for the August 1994 presidential elections, Diego Fernández de Cevallos, remarked on the perils of bank protection, during the historic televised presidential debate of May 12, 1994: "Financial opening is urgently needed in this country. The government has committed a crime, in opening the border to competition for Mexican agriculture, for Mexican small, medium-sized, and microenterprises, while it has protected a banking oligopoly. This is a crime that cannot continue. We need to capture internal and external savings to capitalize agriculture and the small, medium-sized, and microenterprise."[42] Fernández de Cevallos also claimed that the new bankers, far from contributing to national development, had taken advantage of the government's protectionism for their own exclusive benefit.[43]

The economic policy platforms of the PRI and PAN parties had grown more similar since the late 1980s, after the PRI implemented many of the economic reforms to reduce state intervention that the PAN had been advocating since the early 1980s. However, the PAN began a more concerted effort toward the end of the Salinas administration to assert itself as a better promoter of small and medium-size businesses than the PRI. The PAN led efforts to "democratize" capital during the bank reprivatization process and has also opposed special privileges to large *grupos* and the protection of the banks under NAFTA.

MICROREVOLUTION AND THE INDUSTRIAL POLICY DEBATE

Business organizations, including both new radical associations and traditional associations within the CCE, gained prominence toward the end of the Salinas administration by promoting a new discourse more critical of the administration's economic policies.

New, independent organizations of small-business owners, such as ANIT and Concamin (National Confederation of Microindustries), were created in the early 1990s. These groups, among the few to oppose the agreement openly, waged a noisy public campaign warning of the dangers that NAFTA would present for small and midsize businesses. They also voiced their members' distrust of the government stemming from the lack of information flowing to them about the substance of the NAFTA negotiations. ANIT and Conamin leaders have been highly critical of the lack of representation of small firms in business organizations such as the CCE and COECE,[44] particularly outspoken against government policies in the banking sector, and demanding of greater state support and promotion of small business.

In addition to spawning the activism of new independent groups, the

NAFTA negotiations engendered a new discourse among traditional business associations and the formation of new alliances within the giant CCE itself, particularly between 1992 and 1994. Until early 1992 most of the traditional business associations that made up the CCE had promoted NAFTA as a mechanism that industry could use to increase Mexican exports and raise the standard of living of Mexican citizens. Even Canacintra, the traditional business association most active in promoting small businesses, had claimed that Salinas's economic programs would eventually benefit all sectors of society and that the structural changes in progress were simply part of a new development model that would lead to healthier public finances, inflation levels, and trade balances.[45]

But starting in late 1992 and growing in intensity through 1994, the rhetoric shifted to a focus on the microrevolution: a new concentration on the structural barriers facing smaller businesses, which NAFTA's terms seemed likely only to exacerbate. In particular, the business associations wanted to make their concerns known to the presidential candidates before the August 1994 elections, especially in light of an increasing trade deficit and stagnant economy.

Thus, some of the traditional associations, particularly Canacintra, Concamin, and Coparmex (Employers' Confederation of the Republic of Mexico), moved from being promoter-participants in the NAFTA negotiations to becoming more critical of the Salinas administration's economic policies, especially its lack of an industrial policy that targeted not only the macroeconomy but also the microeconomic issues facing businesses in their everyday operations.

The government's reply to this criticism was perhaps best summarized in later remarks by Jaime Serra Puche, minister of Secofi during the Salinas years: "NAFTA *is* our industrial policy; we don't want the government to replace business initiative with an industrial policy. We already did our work, now you do yours"[46] (emphasis added). Most businesses did not find an industrial policy within NAFTA, however, and many were not convinced that the government had done enough to promote the competitiveness of Mexican firms outside the largest *grupos*. In debates during the last two years of the Salinas administration, Serra Puche largely diverted the specific questions raised about what an industrial policy should contain by engaging in a more philosophical discussion about efficiency and competitiveness. More specifically, the Mexican government claimed that an industrial policy, particularly in a vertical form, was not appropriate under the current neoliberal economic model.

According to Fernando Clavijo, coordinator of economic advisers to President Salinas, it was a mistake not to begin a concerted industrial policy in 1992:[47]

Until 1990 or even 1991 the lack of a defined policy to increase competitiveness at least similar to that of our principal competitors in the international market seemed reasonably justified. For one thing, macroeconomic
disequilibria left little room on the political economy agenda to pursue
long-run strategies, like industrial policy. . . . Yet by 1992 the panorama
had changed radically. Inflation was under control, public finances were
at a surplus and the public and private sectors had regained the confidence
of international markets.[48]

Clavijo suggested that from 1992 to 1994 society began to reconsider the
question of industrial policy and the necessity of helping the business sector become more competitive. Nevertheless, he argued that Secofi's
Programa de Competitividad, announced in 1992, was very limited, particularly regarding sectoral policies.[49]

The business organizations that have championed the microrevolution
emphasize that they do not want to return to the protectionist industrial policy of the past, but that the government's economic development efforts
cannot stop with achieving one-digit inflation. Concamin president
Fernando Cortina Legorreta, in what was termed by several news sources
as a very unusual public statement, claimed in September 1993 that "we
accept the cost of economic opening, only if the government adopts a new
attitude in the microeconomy." He also maintained that a new industrial
policy was needed to do away with the concentration of production and the
existence of oligopolies.[50]

Business associations advocating microrevolution called for greater
competition in the banking sector, improved infrastructure to meet the
demands of an open economy, greater legal protections against unfair trade
practices such as dumping, and simplified government documents, for both
taxation and exporting.[51] Many of these proposed measures can be termed
"horizontal" industrial policy, meaning a nonsectoral approach whereby all
firms are treated equally. They are simply measures that seek to enable all
firms to better compete within an open market.

Some business leaders, however, also advocated the adoption of a
"vertical" industrial policy, one designed according to the needs of individual industrial sectors. According to Gilberto Vázquez, a director of
Concamin, a sectoral industrial policy was in order: "The U.S. and most
countries give subsidies, so why shouldn't we? We cannot compete in terms
of cost of capital or in costs of infrastructure. To Concamin industrial policy means selective credit and strategic sectors. The European Community
gives credits to countries like Portugal, but the NADBank idea is not the
same."[52] In other words, because NAFTA itself offered no support for vulnerable business sectors, many business owners believed it was up to the
Mexican government to develop support mechanisms within the parameters
of the trade agreement.[53]

New Alliances Among Business Associations

As some business organizations began to publicize their demands for a microrevolution, new alliances began to form within the CCE itself. The most outspoken member organizations within the CCE in the period 1992–1994 were Canacintra, Concamin, Concanaco (Confederation of National Chambers of Commerce, Services, and Tourism), and Coparmex. A new alliance formed by Canacintra, Concanaco, and Coparmex was formalized in a document they published in March 1994, entitled "Proposals from the Private Sector for the *Sexenio* of 1994–2000."

A similar document had been elaborated for the presidential *sexenio* (six-year term) 1988–1994, but only by Concanaco and Coparmex. The addition of Canacintra in this alliance is important for several reasons. Because of the large number of small and medium-size firms within Canacintra, it has historically been the most powerful political voice of those businesses. It was therefore notable that, in contrast to the earlier document, the new proposal was much more explicit in demanding an authentic industrial policy and in outlining the responsibilities of the state in promoting the competitiveness of individual firms. More specifically, the proposal advocates the adoption of an industrial policy that targets the particular needs of individual sectors, provides solid means of financial support, modernizes infrastructure, further deregulates business activities, and promotes representative business associations and an adequate implementation of the competition law.

The new alliance is also notable because Canacintra had in the past maintained a very different posture from that of Coparmex and Concanaco, which have historically represented what Matilde Luna terms the "liberal conservative" faction of the CCE.[54] This faction has been characterized in the past by its radical stances and political confrontation with the government—particularly concerning the 1982 bank nationalization—and greater numbers of PAN opposition party members. Its influence over the years since the CCE's creation in 1975 has alternated with that of the "technocratic" faction, represented by the CMHN (Mexican Council of Business Executives), the AMB (Mexican Association of Banks), the AMCB (Mexican Association of Brokerage Houses), and the AMIS (Mexican Association of Insurance Institutions).

However different Canacintra's platforms have been from those of the liberal conservatives in the past, these organizations had in common a greater representation of small and midsize firms than in any of the organizations in the technocratic faction, which is led by the exclusive CMHN (comprising Mexico's most powerful *grupos*). Toward the end of the Salinas administration the liberal conservative faction of Coparmex and Concanaco once again took a critical stance against the government, but this time, ironically, it was not to criticize state intervention but to demand increased state action in promoting the competitiveness of smaller firms.

The CCE's reactions to internal debates over the microrevolution have been mixed. While recognizing the importance of policies to stimulate the microeconomy, the federation also remained firm in its support of the Salinas administration and the continuity of its economic model. The latter position ignited criticisms from additional groups of small businesses, including the IMMPE (Mexican Institute of Medium and Small Enterprises).[55] Thus, it became increasingly difficult for the CCE to speak on behalf of all its member organizations. With respect to the credit situation, for example, it was hard for the CCE to advocate that the banks lower their margins, because banks had become part of the CCE after the reprivatization process.

POLICY ADJUSTMENTS BY THE SALINAS ADMINISTRATION: A SECOND STAGE OF FINANCIAL REFORM

While these controversies waged, most of the Salinas administration's actions to promote microrevolution took the form of horizontal industrial policy, such as attempts to institute more competitive practices in banking and industry. Secofi officials at first remained committed to their view that microeconomic reform was principally the responsibility of the business owners themselves.

Their position softened somewhat in 1993, however, as business demands continued into the election season (a presidential election was scheduled for 1994) and small businesses continued to fail at alarming rates. As one brokerage executive put it that year, "The big concern of the government is that the domestic financial system is not responding to the credit needs of the real economy. On the contrary, the banks are concentrating resources, making loans to the very wealthy or to high-rated corporations that can borrow in the U.S."[56]

It was not until fall 1993, after the NAFTA negotiations had ended, that more direct action emanated from the government. As the *Wall Street Journal* noted,

> The friendly treatment the Mexican government has given private bankers here during the past two years is ending. . . . It's an election year. The ruling party wants credit to flow. Mexico's central bank isn't about to loosen monetary policy, risking higher inflation and a sinking peso. So the government is going after the private banks, trying to get them to cut their high lending rates. . . . Regulators here have tolerated loan rates that would be considered usurious by international standards. But no more. Mexican finance officials are scolding the banks publicly.[57]

President Salinas announced the beginning of a second stage of financial reform, including an increase in the number of domestic bank licenses, diversification in financial intermediaries, and increased banking and securities regulation. Although the government insisted that this stage had been planned, others argued that it was an emergency strategy designed to neutralize the negative impact of bank intermediaries. In efforts to cheapen credit and begin to crack the banking cartel, the government fostered some new competition when it granted more than twenty new banking licenses in 1993. It also instructed the development banks, particularly Nafin, to distribute credit more freely to smaller firms in 1994.

The government also created several mechanisms (albeit limited) in 1993 for the support of small and midsize businesses, mainly oriented toward improving technology, and it sponsored several laws to promote competition, including the Antimonopolies Law and the Federal Law of Economic Competition.[58] These government initiatives suggest that the changing alliances of the small and medium-size businesses and their ability to alter the CCE and public discourse very likely had some effects on economic policymaking. The government also had to counter support promised by opposition parties for smaller businesses during an election year.

All told, the opposition to the Salinas administration's economic policies, by social actors both new and old, offers an important lesson about economic liberalization and regional integration. Although the government expects opposition to these policies when its intent to negotiate a free-trade area is announced, some businesses may not have sufficient avenues to voice their concerns over the integration process. Others may have false expectations about liberalization, because of incomplete information or overinflated government promises of the likely benefits. As the negotiations proceed and the specifics of the agreement are decided, the winners and losers soon become apparent. Businesses are forced to evaluate their situation more closely and may take actions to improve it through heightened participation in a variety of social organizations. Thus, even after the processes have been successfully concluded, new demands for reform arise.

ECONOMIC CRISIS AND CHALLENGES
FACING THE ZEDILLO ADMINISTRATION

The Salinas strategy for economic liberalization rested on the notion that the country would go through a period in which firms prepared to become internationally competitive before transformation into an export-led economy. Meanwhile, the government counted on billions of dollars in increasingly volatile foreign investment to finance a growing current-account deficit. This period came to an abrupt halt with a devaluation under new president Ernesto Zedillo in December 1994.

This devaluation and ensuing economic crisis intensified many of the tensions in business-government relations (and within the business community itself) that had begun during the NAFTA negotiations. Within weeks after the crisis, 1.5 million people were thrown out of work. One of the most detrimental effects of the economic crisis for many citizens was that it also produced a severe banking crisis. Interest rates immediately skyrocketed and Mexican citizens who had borrowed under the relaxed lending policies of the privatized banks suddenly faced the prospect of paying these interest rates or losing their homes, cars, and other possessions. Firms of all sizes found it impossible to pay the interest rates required on their corporate loans and were faced with a steep depreciation of asset values. The economic crisis brought a collapse of the internal market and an alarming growth of poverty.

The main thrust of the government's economic programs after the devaluation has been focused on macroeconomic stability, with tight monetary policy contributing to scarce liquidity in the private sector. In 1996 the Zedillo administration touted a recovery, particularly to foreign investors. The current-account deficit decreased from approximately $29 billion in 1994 to $600 million in 1995.[59] Although the annual rate of inflation averaged 52 percent in 1995, it fell to 27 percent in 1996. The government also decided to proceed with privatization of ports, airports, railways, electricity, and gas distribution.[60]

Despite the improvement in macroeconomic variables, real wages fell 25 percent during 1995–1996, and there was little discernible increase in consumer spending. The private sector's confidence in the government was severely eroded as a result of the crisis, as businesses at all levels grew increasingly skeptical of government plans and of the likelihood that the recovery in macroeconomic variables would reach the microeconomy. Industry representatives argued that the Zedillo administration should have developed more programs to promote the productive firms after the crisis, and they criticized the government for spending large amounts of money to bail out the banks.

Groups within civil society were also outspoken in their criticisms of the Salinas government and of the elite business-government alliance that had been constructed under the previous administration. These groups attempted to influence the economic policies of the Zedillo administration, and their strident criticisms and demands became important factors in the restructuring of business-government relations.

The Barzón Movement

One of the most notable of the groups critical of the government's economic policy management is the Barzón, one of the most rapidly expanding social movements in Mexico. The Barzón, which comprises citizens fighting for favorable restructuring of more than $3 billion in debt, has been very outspoken against government finance policies and has publicly demanded state action with regard to a variety of economic policies.[61] This movement was originally formed by a small group of farmers in northwestern Mexico in 1993 who refused to pay what they considered to be unfair bank debts, but expanded rapidly after the 1994 devaluation to include small businesspeople and consumers in urban areas as well.

The Barzón has staged many widely publicized protests and has been quite effective in calling attention to the credit problem faced by small businesses. Juan José Quirino, the organization's national coordinator, maintains that the movement became more radical as Barzón members lost their livelihoods. Barzón leaders have also remarked that they hope Mexican banks will be exposed to more international competition so that foreign banks will show Mexican banks how to loan money correctly. The credit problem is what first united the Barzón, which, its members profess, is independent of any particular political opposition party.

Quirino notes that "this is a middle-class movement. The middle class is being destroyed by the economic policies of the government."[62] About 40 percent of the Barzón's membership now comes from small businesspeople in the cities. Though different estimates have been made concerning Barzón membership, the movement expanded from about 60,000 before the crisis to 500,000 in the weeks following the crisis. Debtor groups recently estimated that between one and two million Mexicans with past-due loans have organized to protest the conditions of payment, with the average Barzonista carrying debt between $83,000 and $166,000.[63]

In February 1995 the Barzón shut down banks in three states and staged a protest outside the central bank in Mexico City. They demanded that the government create a special rescue fund for small and medium-size businesses and agribusinesses, as 95 percent of the Barzón's members were automatically excluded from the government's first plan to restructure bad loans through UDIs.[64] On Labor Day of 1995 (May 1), Barzonistas occupied banks again, as part of demonstrations by workers over wages and unemployment.

The government did not demobilize the protest; as Williams argues, "Many of the protesters were businesspeople and professionals—the same constituency that had initially supported the market reforms of the Salinas era. . . . There was also the question of the impact if hundreds of thousands of consumers were to declare moratoria on payments."[65] Such chaos would also threaten investor confidence in Mexico, particularly if it were accompanied by violent public demonstrations against the federal government.

In addition to more radical tactics, the movement has also taken advantage of debtor rights via the legal system. Although they recognize their debts and their obligation to repay loans, Barzón members argue that they are unwilling to pay what they consider to be usurious interest rates, or to remain uninformed of their legal rights with respect to banking transactions. Bankers have begun to take the movement more seriously after the Barzón's agreement with the Mexican Bar Association, which has ensured that all debtors understand their legal rights and have access to legal representation during foreclosure proceedings.[66]

In April 1995 the Barzón delivered 400,000 remittances of debt to Nafin and the Superior Court, declaring their debt obligations to be invalid. These documents charged bank managers of fraud through usury; one top Barzón leader warned that "this will be a constitutional war against bank terrorism."[67] This legal representation has helped to give the movement increased social legitimacy. The Barzón has met with high-level government officials in the Zedillo administration, including Zedillo himself.

The Barzón did not stop with protests about the financial system but went on to provide a profound critique of the neoliberal economic model in general. Many businesses have participated in social movements such as the Barzón to express their concerns about economic policies in the new context of liberalization and regional integration. The "Ballad of the Barzón" illustrates this: "Neoliberalism is to blame. It's drowning us in this great abyss. We'll unite the people under a new economic model that will bring us together in a grand project. We are Barzonistas. Our deepest hopes are to raise citizen awareness and to save our country."[68] The movement has blamed corrupt politicians and bankers, a lack of democracy, trade liberalization, and financial speculation as the primary causes of the economic crisis.[69]

Although the Barzón may hold the highest profile of the middle-class movements, it is certainly not the only one. Comprometidos por México, in Monterrey, advises hundreds of people on disputes with utility companies. Mujeres por México has battled Teléfonos de México, the national telephone company, over its rates and billing practices. Some of these civic groups have also been folded into the Barzón, such as All for Chihuahua, a broad-based civil organization. According to Emíliz González, leader of All for Chihuahua, "Here in Mexico, it is very clear to us that when a social struggle has just one front, just students, for example, the government can brush it aside as if with a feather. With just peasants, we're gone. Our government runs this society by sectors. But a pluralistic movement like this one is very difficult to control. It's not the same to crush businesspeople as it is to crush peasants. This complicates things enormously."[70]

In real bargaining terms, the Barzón has not been able to achieve its goals of lowering interest rates on consumer and commercial loans to the satisfaction of its members, and NAFTA has remained intact. The debt relief programs offered by the government have been criticized by the Barzón for insufficiency, as well as for being negotiated between bankers and government officials without significant input from debtors' groups. Barzón members have complained bitterly about a lack of seriousness on the part of the government to consider their alternative debt relief proposals. At the same time, however, the Barzón has been more successful in influencing policy at the state and local levels, in terms of gaining at least partial settlements of their demands on debt and farm subsidies and in being included in actual negotiations in some areas. Moreover, despite repeated occupations of banks, highways, and government offices, the movement's leaders and members have not received harsh treatment from police.[71]

The Barzón mobilization may have its greatest impact on the political arena. This movement has pulled together a large number of middle-class individuals, including business professionals, many of whom had no previous experience in civic organizations or in public protests. The Barzón has demanded that the voice of consumers and small businesses be heard as attentively as those of the banks and the government. The Barzón has clearly influenced the levels of citizen participation in a highly centralized political system and has heightened a debate about how to shape the future Mexican economic model. Although the movement insisted at the beginning of its mobilization that it had no ties to political parties, by the July 1997 midterm elections twenty-three leaders chosen by the movement ran as candidates of the PRD (Party of the Democratic Revolution), the left-of-center opposition party. However, some supporters of the PRD warn that the Barzón represents a dangerous populist backlash; they feel that this movement works against their goal of articulating a viable economic alternative to neoliberalism.[72]

Business Associations Under Zedillo

In addition to organizations such as the Barzón, formal business associations have continued to present proposals to the government advocating economic policy changes that they feel are necessary for elevating the competitiveness of firms. In the first months of 1995 four associations, including the CCE itself, proposed six different programs containing more than 100 specific policy suggestions to reactivate the economy.[73] Prominent in the proposals are issues concerning the federal budget, financing, interest rate reduction, promotion of internal savings, deregulation, and promotion of exports. Business organizations have also demanded lower value-added taxes and other taxes on firms and a more readily comprehensible tax system. They achieved consensus that the government should design a long-term industrial policy but also provide for temporary measures to help small and medium-size firms meet the economic crisis.

Perhaps the most surprising of the proposals is that of the CCE, entitled "Proposals for the Sustained Growth of the Mexican Economy." Because the CCE was one of the most ardent supporters of the Salinas administration's economic policies, its sudden harsh critiques of neoliberalism represented one of the most dramatic reversals in business association discourse. In addition to presenting dramatic statistics on employment and productivity, the document also discussed the growing current-account deficit under Salinas. "In spite of the elevated dynamism of non-petroleum exports, the commercial balance suffered an accelerated deterioration because of an even greater dynamism in imports. . . . An overvalued exchange rate and an accelerated and indiscriminate commercial opening ended with the displacement of national production. . . . In this process, the small and medium firms were the most severely affected due to their limitations."[74] The document also argued that only a small fraction of the productive plant has been capable of competing successfully in the new environment and that exports continue to be highly concentrated in only a few sectors and firms.

Finally, the report states that "the application of policies and measures of a general character have had unequal effects, sharpening the contrasts between sectors and firms. It is not equitable, or efficient, to give equal treatment to unequals, not only because of differences of size, but also because of differences in access to resources, markets, information and capabilities."[75] The CCE maintained that the neoliberal model initiated in the past is still a viable one, but that it is vital to initiate adjustments and further reforms, including sectoral programs, promotion of exports, better access to credit, and recognition of the heterogeneity of the Mexican private sector.[76]

In April 1996 business leaders criticized the Zedillo administration's economic policy management in a report released by the CCE's economic studies center (CEESP, Centro de Estudios Económicos del Sector Privado). While acknowledging the need to continue efforts to promote economic stability, the report criticized the administration for placing too much emphasis on macroeconomic performance. These criticisms represented an escalation in the demands of the business community for a microrevolution. The report argued that the government must stimulate growth in the private sector through direct action to promote investment and consumption; to achieve this, privatization of national railroads, petrochemical plants, seaports, and airports must be expedited.[77]

Some business leaders also criticized the Zedillo administration for placing too much emphasis on bailing out the banking system. The government estimated in November 1996 that the cost of state programs to aid banks and debtors would eventually total 8.4 percent of gross domestic product, or GDP (slightly more than $27 billion); independent analysts have calculated that the total could reach as much as 20 percent of GDP.[78]

Influential industrial leaders also expressed their strong displeasure at the lack of continuity in economic policy and the inability of government officials since 1970 to manage the economy without recurring crises.

POLICY ADJUSTMENTS BY THE ZEDILLO ADMINISTRATION

Although groups such as the Barzón and many business organizations have charged that the Zedillo administration has not paid enough attention to their demands and proposals,[79] the administration has made several important changes in economic strategy as compared with the Salinas years. After the devaluation, the Zedillo administration had the difficult job of convincing foreign investors that Mexico would offer a stable and profitable investment environment in the future and simultaneously placating a domestic constituency that demanded economic growth and lower interest rates. Zedillo has responded to this dilemma by trying to keep inflation under control while promising various industrial stimulus packages to domestic businesses. This has been a difficult task, as those economic signals that bolstered foreign investor confidence often made domestic business groups criticize the administration for not doing enough to ease their distress.

The Salinas administration focused on national ownership of large, strong industrial and financial groups able to face international competition, but the Zedillo administration has been unable to maintain this focus, largely because of the effects of the devaluation and economic crisis. The desperate need for capital after the devaluation forced even the most powerful of Mexican business groups, including the banks, to sell large stakes to foreign partners. These foreign takeovers are causing painful transitions for Mexican businesses, even for the once indomitable Mexican dynasties.

Government-Bank Relations After the Devaluation

The devaluation and ensuing banking crisis significantly changed the nature of government-bank relations. The overwhelming need for capital to meet the massive banking crisis left the government with no choice but to allow greater levels of foreign participation in the banking system. The need for foreign capital was so strong that officials in the finance ministry agreed to allow foreign investment levels above the maximum levels they fought so hard to establish in the NAFTA agreement.

In January 1995 Zedillo announced an initiative to reform seventeen articles of three laws regulating financial intermediaries, with the objective of capitalizing banks by incrementally raising the maximum level of foreign participation.[80] The government maintained that the need for capital was so great that these changes were imperative to capitalize the banking system and keep national banks from failing.

In addition to the need for capital, the government also recognized the urgent need for upgrading the risk evaluation and technological capacities of national banks, which also could be improved by foreign participation. As Eduardo Fernández, president of the National Banking Commission, announced at the annual National Stockmarket Convention in April 1995, "Without a doubt, when stabilization of fundamental financial variables is achieved, we will see strategic alliances of national and international institutions which will strengthen the health and competitiveness of the financial system."[81] In May 1995, the government authorized the entrance of twenty-one new foreign financial institutions, announcing that more foreign participation would help small and medium-size businesses and other productive firms by bringing down interest rates.

Foreign institutions have been able to make powerful inroads into both commercial and retail banking. Although analysts predicted that foreign institutions would focus exclusively on the corporate sector, this has not been the case. In 1996 Spain's Banco Bilbao Vizcaya led the charge into retail banking after its purchase of Grupo Financiero Probursa, and the Spanish Banco Santander later bought Grupo Financiero Inverméxico. Even large Mexican banks, though not losing Mexican control, have been forced to seek outside help; Bancomer sold 16 percent of its shares in March 1996 to the Bank of Montreal. Most analysts agree that the foreign presence in the financial system will continue; *The Economist* has reported that "in Mexico, foreign banks, which were barred from taking part in the botched bank privatizations five years ago, are now being welcomed with open arms. Since the peso crisis, they have paid around $2 billion between them for a clutch of troubled banks. Foreigners now control 10 percent of the banking system. Some local bankers think that the figure might rise to half the total within a few years."[82] Ramírez de la O argues that within three years, the Mexican banking system could very well have the highest concentration of foreign-owned banks of any system in the world.[83]

In addition to changes in levels of foreign participation permitted in the banking system, the government also began to provide stricter regulation of the financial system. Changes in regulation during the Zedillo administration have included the weekly reporting of macroeconomic statistics and international reserve levels, providing greater transparency about government economic policy. The government has also strengthened the power of bank supervisors, who are "trying harder to break the cosy relationship between banks and big businesses by leaning on bank managers who lend to friends in industry at special rates."[84] Mexico agreed that banks would adopt internationally accepted accounting standards in 1996, so Mexican banks must now provide more realistic information about their financial

the Consejo Asesor en Comercio Internacional (CACINTE). This new group was composed of thirty people chosen by COECE, mostly important businesspeople and former leaders of business associations. CACINTE's main task was to unify positions and to legitimate decisions.

18. Luna, "Las asociaciones empresariales," pp. 21–22. See also Cristina Puga, "Las organizaciones empresariales en la negociación del TLC," in *Los empresarios ante la globalización*, ed. Ricardo Tirado (Mexico City: UNAM and the Instituto de Investigaciones Sociales, 1994).

19. Pastor and Wise, *Political Economy*, p. 481.

20. Luna, "Las asociaciones empresariales," p. 13.

21. Cristina Puga, "Medianos y pequeños empresarios: La difícil modernización," *El Cotidiano* 50 (September–October 1992).

22. Pastor and Wise, *Political Economy*, p. 481.

23. See Luis Rubio and Alain de Remes, *¿Cómo va a afectar a México el Tratado de Libre Comercio?* (Mexico City: Fondo de Cultura Económica, 1992), pp. 208–217. Note that under the administration of Ernesto Zedillo Ponce de León, this rule changed from 4 percent to 6 percent.

24. Vicente Galbis, "Financial Sector Liberalization Under Oligopolistic Conditions and a Bank Holding Structure," *Savings and Development* 2 (1986): 117–140; and Alberto Musalem, Dimitri Vittas, and Asli Demirguc-Kunt, "North American Free Trade Agreement: Issues on Trade in Financial Services for Mexico," PRE working paper 1153, World Bank, Financial Sector Development, Washington, D.C., July 1993. See also Javier Gavito and Ignacio Trigueros, "Los efectos del TLC sobre las entidades financieras," in *Lo negociado del TLC*, ed. Georgina Kessel (Mexico City: Instituto Tecnológico Autónomo de México [ITAM] and McGraw Hill, 1994), who argue that "a balance between the necessity of consolidating national financial intermediaries, and the possibility of augmenting the degree of competition in the Mexican financial system, seems to indicate that the opening is too generous toward them (the banks). Even though it is difficult to evaluate, for example, the time that the Mexican banks would need to reach conditions of international competitiveness, the restructuring of financial institutions is typically done in periods of no more than three years" (p. 223).

25. The efficiency benefits of foreign participation include the transfer of technology and skilled management, the introduction of new services and products, training and employment benefits for the local population, and greater access to international markets (Musalem, Vittas, and Demirguc-Kunt, "North American Free Trade Agreement," p. 2).

26. As Del Castillo and Vega point out, these concerns are particularly pressing for developing countries (*Politics of Free Trade*, p. 221). Musalem, Vittas, and Demirguc-Kunt argue, however, that many of these concerns have not been empirically documented, and they point out that "one of the key questions regarding the liberalization of DFI in financial services is whether national authorities are justified to be worried about the ownership and control of financial institutions" ("North American Free Trade Agreement," p. 3).

27. Author's interview with a NAFTA finance negotiator who prefers to remain anonymous. The interviewee added, "I need to be able to sit down with the owner of Banamex, Mr. Hernández, who is my friend, who pays taxes, whose kids go to school here, who owns other businesses here, who is a Mexican. I need to be able to tell him that he needs to support me in any number of different situations— for example, to support government initiatives and pacts, and particularly in crisis situations. When the owner of the bank is Mexican, we in the government have

more elements of control. When the owner is John Reed, who is not a personal friend, whose family lives in the U.S., who doesn't have other businesses here, I cannot negotiate with him for his support the way I can with Mr. Hernández."

28. Chris Aspen, "The Auction's Over: What Lies Ahead for Mexico's Newly Private Banks," *Business Mexico,* August 1992, p. 44.

29. According to a former president of Coparmex and member of the Banamex board of directors, "The government definitely made an explicit promise to the bankers that if they bought the banks at very high prices, they would be given an opportunity to recoup their investment quickly" (interview with José María Basagoiti, May 31, 1995). The fact that many Mexicans suspect the existence of this quid pro quo was verified in several interviews, including those with César Flores Esquivel, president of the Asociación Mexicana Automotriz during the NAFTA negotiations, May 15, 1995; Celso Garrido N., Universidad Autónoma Metropolitana, March 2, 1995; and Gustavo Lomelín, editor of *El Financiero,* May 16, 1995.

30. Although the government had improved the external deficit through negotiations in 1989 with foreign creditors, internal debt payments still posed a serious problem. The reprivatization process brought the government 38.7 billion pesos, or about $12 billion, and the money earned through the sale of the banks was used toward the retirement of internal debt. See J. Antonio Zúñiga and Salvador Guerrero Chiprés, "La venta de los bancos, para reducir la deuda interna: Hacienda," *La Jornada,* May 26, 1990, p. 15.

31. Musalem, Vittas, and Demirguc-Kunt, "North American Free Trade Agreement," p. 17.

32. Carlos Acosta Córdova and Fernando Ortega Pizarro, "Prioridad de los banqueros, cuatro años después de la reprivatización: obtener utilidades," *Proceso,* May 23, 1994, p. 35.

33. Alain de Remes, "Debe el estado permitir la competencia financiera," *Excélsior,* July 3, 1993, p. 1.

34. Jorge Castañares Priego, "Desventajas ante el TLC," *El Nacional,* September 23, 1992, p. 24.

35. Vicente Gutiérrez, "Cuesta el dinero en México trece veces más que en Estados Unidos," *Excélsior,* May 3, 1993, p. 1.

36. Author's interview with Jorge Mattar, CEPAL regional adviser on Economic Development, June 2, 1995.

37. "Protegen demasiado al sistema bancario," *El Norte,* May 13, 1992.

38. Carmen Alvarez, "Molesta a empresarios negociación financiera," *El Norte,* October 8, 1992. Note that Bancomext is a Mexican development bank that obtains funding on the external market and then loans to exporters; *cetes* are peso-denominated short-term government bonds.

39. Juan Antonio Lara, "Demanda IP apertura bancaria," *El Norte,* May 12, 1992.

40. Author's interview with Felipe Calderón Hinojosa, secretary general, Partido Acción Nacional, May 17, 1995.

41. Ibid.

42. Acosta Córdova and Ortega Pizarro, "Prioridad de los banqueros," pp. 30–31.

43. Ibid.

44. Amalia Frías Santillán, "La desinformación aumenta la vulnerabilidad de México: ANIT," *Uno Más Uno,* July 28, 1992.

45. Alonso Gómez U., "La política económica de México, respuesta a la altura del cambio mundial: Canacintra," *Excélsior,* February 8, 1992.

46. Luis E. Mercado, "Política industrial," *El Economista,* March 30, 1995, p. 11.

47. Author's interview with Fernando Clavijo (coordinator of economic advisers under Salinas), May 3, 1995. He argues that those within the government who advocated an industrial policy were largely ignored. Clavijo and José I. Casar coedited a two-volume book on industrial policy, *La industria mexicana en el mercado mundial* (Mexico City: Fondo de Cultura Económica, 1994), which was one of the first books published during the Salinas administration that dealt with this subject in the context of a liberalized economy.

48. Clavijo and Casar, eds., *La industria mexicana,* pp. 16–17.

49. According to a 1992 Secofi document, "Sectoral programs do not confer monetary benefits, access to credit, or effective protection. The role of Secofi is to understand the problems, and in some instances to reduce information costs, create alternatives and to help with concrete actions in the matters of deregulation, customs and standards" (Clavijo and Casar, eds., *La industria mexicana,* p. 18).

50. "Urge nueva política industrial: Concamin," *La Jornada,* September 19, 1993, p. 35.

51. Isabel Becerril and Leticia Rodríguez, "Urge resolver discrepancias entre macro y microeconomía," *El Financiero,* December 6, 1994.

52. Author's interview with Gilberto Vázquez, director of the Unidad de Apoyo al Acuerdo de Libre Comercio, Concamin, January 27, 1995.

53. The National Convention of Industrialists in 1994 focused on the need for a well-defined sectoral industrial policy to modernize Mexican firms and promote the microeconomic revolution. See Isabel Becerril and Leticia Rodríguez, "Política industrial promotora de la inversión, exigen empresarios: Necesario un diseño que rebase la frontera sexenal," *El Financiero,* December 6, 1994, p. 31.

54. Matilde Luna, "Los retos de la globalización: La reforma microeconómica," in *Los Empresarios,* ed. Ricardo Tirado, pp. 211–217.

55. "Apoyaremos a quien asegure continuidad: CCE," *Excélsior,* September 27, 1993, p. 28.

56. José de Jesús García, "Se modifica la relación entre bancos y el gobierno federal," *Excélsior,* October 8, 1993, p. 1. The banking executive asked to remain anonymous because his firm owns one of the larger banks.

57. Craig Torres, "In Mexico, Banks Face Pressure to Unite," *Wall Street Journal,* October 5, 1993, p. C22.

58. Luna, "Los retos," p. 217.

59. All dollar amounts are U.S. dollars.

60. Mauricio González Gómez, "Memoranda on the Recent Performance of the Mexican Economy," prepared for the Group of Associated Economists, July 22, 1997.

61. The Barzón takes its name from an old song about harsh conditions in the countryside during the Porfiriato, before the Mexican revolution. The song speaks of a hacienda peasant who must borrow from his boss to pay for a yoke (*barzón*) in poor condition. The peasant then remains in debt for life, all for the sake of a yoke, as interest payments accumulate faster than he can pay them off. See Heather Williams, "Planting Trouble: The Barzón Debtors' Movement in Mexico," Current Issue Brief Series 6, Center for U.S.-Mexican Studies, University of California, San Diego, 1996, p. 6.

62. Dudley Althaus, "Mexican Middle Class in Crisis: Desperate Citizens Form Group to Halt Economic Downslide," *Houston Chronicle*, February 26, 1995, p. 18A. Economists consider a family in Mexico to be middle class if its per capita annual income is $5,000, which is more than $2,000 over the national average. A middle-class family generally owns a home and at least one car, and the head of the household is a white-collar worker. See Enrique Rangel, "Middle-Class Militancy," *Dallas Morning News*, December 16, 1996.

63. Andrew Wheat, "The Mexican Debtors' Revolt," *Multinational Monitor* 17 (June 1996).

64. UDIs (*unidades de inversión*) are financial instruments that link debt interest rates to the rate of inflation. They were not designed to inject fresh capital into the system, and they imply a different form of accounting for debts. Many of the Barzón members held credit card debt (which was not eligible under the program), did not have the requisite of viable economic projects, or did not owe enough money to be considered "irrecuperable." Lourdes Edith Rudiño, "Fuera del esquema de UDI 95% de los miembros de El Barzón," *El Financiero*, April 5, 1995, p. 8.

65. Williams, "Planting Trouble," pp. 18–19.

66. The president of the bar association publicly accused the banks of acting abusively and breaking the law. Lourdes Edith Rudiño, "Legítimas las demandas de El Barzón contra la banca," *El Financiero*, April 27, 1995, p. 9.

67. Matilde Pérez U., "Entregará El Barzón 400 mil escritos de consignación de pagos," *La Jornada*, April 24, 1995, p. 13.

68. Williams, "Planting Trouble," pp. 8–9.

69. This chapter focuses on the social organizations with which businesspeople have expressed their differences with the government's economic policies, but other forms of social discontent, such as the new guerrilla movements, should not be overlooked. The Zapatistas have been particularly outspoken against NAFTA, beginning their rebellion in Chiapas on the first day of NAFTA implementation, January 1, 1994.

70. Wheat, "Mexican Debtors' Revolt," p. 43.

71. Williams, "Planting Trouble," p. 43.

72. Lucy Conger, "Tilting at Neoliberalism," *Institutional Investor*, May 1997, p. 103.

73. For a review of these programs, see Leticia Rodríguez López, "Ignora el gobierno las demandas de la IP para reactivar la economía," *El Financiero*, May 27, 1995, p. 6.

74. Héctor Vázquez Tercero, "El CCE y sus propuestas de política económica," *El Financiero* Comercio Exterior section, May 22, 1995.

75. Ibid.

76. Norma Vargas Saldívar, "Recomienda la cúpula empresarial hacer más eficiente la sustitución de importaciones," *El Financiero*, May 15, 1995, p. 27.

77. "Business Leaders Renew Criticism of Zedillo Administration's Economic Policy and Urge Government to Increase Public Spending," *SourceMex*, April 3, 1996.

78. Standard & Poor's has calculated that the cost will eventually total 12 percent of GDP ($30 billion), and the independent economic consulting firm Ecanal estimated a higher total of 20.3 percent of GDP. Even the government's conservative estimate of $27 billion for the bailout of the banks is staggering, and more than twice the amount that the government received from the privatization of the banking system ($12 billion). See Rogelio Ramírez de la O, Ecanal Special Report 1, "The Budget for 1997: Uncertain Cost of Rescuing the Banking System," February 1997, p. 2.

79. See Leticia Rodríguez López, "Ignora el gobierno las demandas"; and Armando Flores, "Desconfían empresarios de la política industrial," *El Economista,* May 8, 1995, p. 1.

80. Mauricio Flores, "Reformarán leyes de intermediarios," *Reforma,* January 18, 1995. This new law also changed the limits set by NAFTA. NAFTA stipulated that before the year 2000 a single foreign bank could not control more than 1.5 percent of the market and total combined foreign ownership could not exceed 15 percent total market share, but the February 15 law increases these numbers to 6 percent and 25 percent, respectively.

81. Alicia Salgado, "Acelerado proceso de fusiones y alianzas bancarias, en puerta," *El Financiero,* April 10, 1995, p. 4.

82. "Survey: Banking in Emerging Markets," *The Economist,* April 12, 1997, p. 34.

83. Author's interview with Rogelio Ramírez de la O, president of Ecanal, April 21, 1997.

84. "Survey: Banking," p. 19.

85. "Zedillo's Mexico," *Institutional Investor,* March 1997, p. 13.

86. "Survey: Banking," p. 19.

87. Ibid.

88. Mireya Olivas, "Herminio Blanco Mendoza: La clave es la competitividad," *El Economista,* May 11, 1995, p. 33.

89. This was done in an effort to curb strong competition from Indonesia, North Korea, and Thailand. María Luisa Alós and Osiel Cruz, "Apoyan calzado y textil," *Reforma,* April 10, 1995, p. 15A.

90. Yadira Mena, "Modifica estrategia: Apoyará Bancomext 10 ramas productivas," *Reforma,* March 31, 1995, p. 22A.

91. G. Flores et al., "Macroplan de rescate financiero para empresas medianas y pequeñas," *El Financiero,* March 19, 1995.

92. Elena Gallegos and Emilio Lomas, "Se simplificará la ley para crear empresas, anuncia Herminio Blanco," *La Jornada,* May 10, 1995, p. 43. Although many small and medium-size firms have applauded the formation of the council, some also criticized the makeup of the council for having more representatives from government than from business. María Luisa Alós, "Disgusta a la IP perfil de consejo," *Reforma,* May 11, 1995, p. 15A.

93. Conger, "Tilting at Neoliberalism," p. 103.

PART TWO

The Outlook After NAFTA

9

The Effects of NAFTA on Mexico's Private Sector and Foreign Trade and Investment

Deborah L. Riner and John V. Sweeney

The period from the late 1980s to the present has seen a profound transformation of the Mexican economy. Even before the word NAFTA appeared in the political vocabulary, the environment in which companies do business had changed dramatically. The implementation of the North American Free Trade Agreement (NAFTA) formalized and accelerated a process of economic opening that had begun in 1985, when then-President Miguel de la Madrid Hurtado made the unexpected announcement that Mexico would join the General Agreement on Tariffs and Trade (GATT). That rupture of the barriers protecting Mexican firms from foreign competition changed the rules of the game for companies: Political connections and price increases, though helpful, would no longer be enough to guarantee businesses' success.

The NAFTA treaty went beyond GATT to establish procedures for resolving trade disputes among its parties; more than 70 percent of Mexico's trade is covered by these procedural mechanisms. NAFTA also converted implementing regulations into the less easily altered form of international treaty obligations, thereby conferring greater certainty and restricting the discretion of government bureaucrats. Greater certainty and limited discretion both are inestimable advantages in the pursuit of investment and the jobs that investment creates.

Since the mid-1980s the opening of the economy has been perhaps the most important of all the profound structural changes that have taken place in Mexico. Exports of goods and services rose from 7 percent of gross domestic product (GDP) in 1980 to 14 percent of GDP in 1990 and an estimated 28 percent of GDP in 1996. The value of merchandise exports rose 123 percent between 1991 and 1996, from $43 billion to $96 billion.[1] As measured by the value of its exports, Mexico is now the sixteenth largest exporter in the world, up from twenty-eighth in 1980; and it could well rise to the top twelve by the turn of the century. At the same time, the composition of exports has changed radically since the mid-1980s, reducing Mexico's vulnerability to external shocks produced by sharp movements in the country's terms of trade. In 1985 petroleum accounted for 67 percent of merchandise exports, whereas the share of manufactured products was only 24 percent. By 1996 manufactured exports constituted 84 percent of the total, yet petroleum had declined to 12 percent, despite the high international price of oil.

Not all the effects of NAFTA can be measured in economic terms. Despite ongoing, contentious bilateral issues such as migration and drugs, relations between Mexico and the United States have strengthened greatly over the past decade. The NAFTA process has been a central contributor to the improvement. The greater maturity of both nations in addressing sensitive bilateral issues and keeping individual problems from poisoning the overall relationship represents a historic breakthrough.

Indeed, the closer economic relations that have developed between the two countries were a critical ingredient in the U.S. government's decision to institute a massive financial aid package in the wake of the Mexican financial crisis. The United States had been helpful in the past, notably during Mexico's 1982 debt crisis. That assistance was much smaller ($1 billion), however, and more grudgingly offered than the $50 billion international support package the Clinton administration orchestrated in 1995. The rapid deployment of the funds, the quick adjustment of the Mexican economy, and early repayment of the U.S. loans clearly demonstrated the wisdom of that assistance for both nations.

One indicator of NAFTA's effects, aside from trade and investment statistics, is the opinion of business leaders themselves. This chapter will draw on the results of a survey conducted by the American Chamber of Commerce of Mexico (AmCham) in November 1996.[2] The survey questioned AmCham members about how NAFTA had affected their expectations of Mexico's growth prospects, trade flows, and investment strategies.

Of the 405 companies that returned the survey, nearly half (48.1 percent) were U.S.-owned businesses. Mexican firms represented 38.8 percent of the respondents, and firms headquartered in other countries constituted an eighth of the sample. Firms of all sizes—small, medium, large, and very large—were well represented in the sample. Large firms (those with gross sales of $8.1 to $40 million) made up 29.3 percent of the respondents. The remainder of the respondents were about equally divided between small and medium-size firms (companies with gross sales of up to $2 million for the former category and between $2.1 and $8 million for the latter), with each representing 22.5 percent of the sample, and very large firms (gross sales exceeding $40 million), making up 25.7 percent.[3] Companies with dollar income were overrepresented vis-à-vis their proportion of all

Mexican businesses, accounting for 56.2 percent of respondents. A little more than half of the responses (54 percent) came from manufacturing companies; service providers contributed 34.1 percent of the questionnaires returned; and the rest (11.9 percent) were provided by firms engaged in commerce.

To complement the survey results and enable a more in-depth understanding of NAFTA's impact, eleven interviews were conducted between December 1996 and January–February 1997 with the chief executive officers (CEOs) of companies in different key sectors: chemicals and petrochemicals, automobiles, tires, personal care products, computers, telecommunications and electronics, pharmaceuticals, consumer products, wood products, apparel, and banking. The CEOs head the leading firms in those sectors. Of the eleven CEOs interviewed, ten headed up major multinational firms; the eleventh owns and runs his firm. One of the multinational companies is European; the rest are headquartered in the United States. All of the firms have manufacturing facilities in Mexico.

Among the most important findings from the survey and interviews are these:

- Trade flows between Mexico and the United States have been growing rapidly since 1986, and Mexican exports to the United States stepped up a great deal beginning in 1994. Between 1994 and 1996 Mexico's trade with its NAFTA partners (the United States and Canada) rose 67 percent, while trade with non-NAFTA partners was up only 27 percent.
- Nearly every major manufacturing sector in Mexico increased exports at rates ranging from significant to spectacular between 1992 and 1996, the years during which NAFTA was negotiated and implemented. Mexico's agricultural exports have also grown rapidly in recent years. Manufacturing firms were more likely than companies in other sectors to have increased their exports. The larger the company, the more likely it was to report that its exports had risen because of NAFTA. About half the companies surveyed reported that their imports had risen as a result of NAFTA; very large firms were more likely than small firms to have increased imports.
- The average annual flow of direct foreign investment during the first three years of NAFTA (1994–1996) was $9.3 billion, more than double the average for the 1990–1993 period.[4] Since the implementation of NAFTA—which made it easier to invest in Mexico, according to the companies surveyed—foreign investment has shifted more heavily into the manufacturing sector. A majority reported that NAFTA had affected their own investment strategy,

with the very large companies more likely to have altered their investment strategies than the small firms.

- Fears of jobs fleeing to Mexico from the United States and Canada are unfounded. Rapid structural changes in Mexico have dampened employment growth in the formal sector of the economy. Employment levels in the industrial sector were only slightly higher in 1996 than in 1991.[5]
- The in-bond (maquiladora) industries have continued to grow very rapidly under NAFTA.
- Among all service industries in Mexico, the financial services firms have been most affected by NAFTA to date—favorably, from the perspective of users and of competition.
- According to the CEOs who were interviewed, NAFTA continued changes that had begun in their sectors when the economy was opened in the second half of the 1980s, except in the financial sector. In other words, the most wrenching adjustments took place before NAFTA was signed.
- The companies best able to take advantage of the opportunities offered by NAFTA are large firms and multinational companies.
- NAFTA has broadened the mix of products available in Mexico. Better service and higher quality are other outcomes of NAFTA and the economic opening.
- NAFTA has allowed companies to further rationalize production. Companies have also changed their sourcing and distribution strategies in response to NAFTA.
- NAFTA has not necessarily reduced firms' profit margins.
- Companies' banking relationships and financial strategies have not yet been affected by NAFTA, although NAFTA has in some cases opened up financing by suppliers.
- NAFTA has changed the way multinational firms perceive Mexico, which is now seen as a better place to do business.
- Almost all the companies surveyed expect that NAFTA will accelerate Mexico's overall economic growth rate. A smaller but still overwhelming majority expect the domestic market will grow more rapidly because of NAFTA.

TRADE FLOWS TO THE UNITED STATES

NAFTA did not create winners and losers in most manufacturing subsectors. It simply accelerated a process that began nine years before the treaty went into effect, a process initiated when Mexico's entry into the GATT opened a hitherto protected economy to competition from imports. Having faced the reality of world markets in the 1980s, most manufacturing companies were better prepared to take advantage of the opportunities NAFTA opened up than were firms in sectors that still enjoyed protection from foreign competition, thanks to legal exclusions enshrined in the constitution or in the direct foreign investment law.

Table 9.1, which details Mexico's trade with the United States over the seventeen-year period from 1980 to 1996, clearly shows that the highest growth of U.S.-Mexican trade dates from the opening of the Mexican economy in 1986. In eleven of the seventeen years, Mexico posted trade surpluses with the United States and did so continuously between 1982 and 1990; the surpluses were particularly large after the 1982 debt crisis and the 1994 peso crisis. Between 1991 and 1994, however, Mexico posted modest trade account deficits with the United States; the country's burgeoning trade deficits during the early 1990s were primarily with its non-NAFTA trading partners, notably Japan, South Korea, Taiwan, China, Germany, and Italy.

Mexico's exports to the United States grew more rapidly after NAFTA was implemented in 1994 than before, averaging just over 22 percent for 1994–1996, compared with an average annual growth rate of 13.1 percent over 1992 and 1993. Except in 1991, Mexico's exports to the United States

Table 9.1   Mexico's Merchandise Trade with the United States, 1980–1996
(millions of U.S. dollars unless otherwise indicated)

Year	Exports	Annual Percentage Change	Imports	Annual Percentage Change	Balance	Total Trade	Annual Percentage Change
1980	10,072	61.1	11,979	58.4	−1,907	22,051	59.6
1981	10,716	6.4	15,398	28.5	−4,682	26,114	18.4
1982	11,887	10.9	8,921	−42.1	2,926	20,808	−20.3
1983	13,034	9.7	4,958	−44.4	8,076	17,992	−13.5
1984	14,612	12.1	6,695	35.0	7,917	21,307	18.4
1985	15,029	2.9	11,132	66.3	3,897	26,161	22.8
1986	17,600	17.1	12,400	11.4	5,200	30,000	14.7
1987	20,270	15.2	14,569	17.5	5,701	34,839	16.1
1988	23,277	14.8	20,633	41.6	2,644	43,910	26.0
1989	27,186	16.8	24,969	21.0	2,217	52,155	18.8
1990	30,172	11.0	28,375	13.6	1,797	58,547	12.3
1991	31,194	3.4	33,276	17.3	−2,082	64,470	10.1
1992	35,200	12.8	40,600	22.0	−5,400	75,800	17.6
1993	39,930	13.4	41,636	2.6	−1,706	81,566	7.6
1994	49,492	24.0	50,843	22.1	−1,351	100,335	23.0
1995	61,706	24.7	46,312	−8.9	15,394	108,018	7.7
1996	72,962	18.2	56,763	22.6	16,199	129,725	20.1

Source: Annual Reports on U.S. Trade by Country, U.S. Department of Commerce, 1980–1996.

have grown at double-digit rates every year since 1986. Between 1986 and 1996 Mexico's exports to the United States jumped 315 percent, rising from $17.6 billion to $73.1 billion. Thus, while NAFTA apparently has accelerated the trend, it hardly started it.

Certain sectors did better than others from 1992 to 1995, according to data from both the United States and Mexico.[6] We use Mexican trade data to analyze sectoral performance, but either set of figures reveals the same trend: Both indicate that the manufacturing sector has done particularly well both as expectations grew during NAFTA negotiations and after NAFTA was implemented. Between 1992 and 1995 manufacturing as a whole accounted for almost all (93.6 percent) of Mexico's export growth. Within manufacturing, the metal products, machinery, and equipment sector accounted for 63.1 percent of Mexico's export growth over this three-year period. The automotive subsector led the way, alone accounting for 21.9 percent of total export growth during the period.

As noted earlier, almost every major manufacturing sector in Mexico grew at rates ranging from significant to spectacular between 1992 and 1995. Based on ten-month data, it appears that similar results were achieved in 1996. Growth rates ranged from a high of 175.5 percent for agricultural equipment (which started from a low base) to a low of 28.9 percent for petrochemicals.

Results from the AmCham survey affirm the aggregate trade statistics. Three-fifths of the 220 companies that answered AmCham's question about the impact of NAFTA on exports reported that their exports had indeed increased.[7] More than two-thirds (67.5 percent) of the 163 manufacturers who responded indicated that their exports had risen as a consequence of NAFTA.[8] U.S. and Mexican companies were more likely than other firms to have increased their exports: 64.8 percent of the 108 U.S. companies and 60.3 percent of the 73 Mexican firms that responded to the question reported that their exports had risen; roughly half (47.4 percent) of the 38 firms of other nationalities so reported. The most striking difference was by company size: More than three-quarters (76.1 percent) of the 67 very large firms that answered the question said their exports had increased since the implementation of NAFTA, compared with only 36 percent of the 25 small firms. Just over half (52.1 percent) of the 73 large firms that replied to the question indicated that their exports had increased. Of 47 medium-size firms, 59.6 percent reported higher exports. No firm indicated that exports had declined.

Reflecting the importance of imports in Mexico's production chains, a larger number of firms (253, or 62.5 percent of the sample) answered the question about how their imports have changed since the implementation of NAFTA. A little more than half (53.4 percent) of these indicated that their imports have risen since NAFTA took effect.[9] U.S. firms were more likely to have reported increased imports than either Mexican firms or those of other nationalities: 57.5 percent of U.S. companies (134) reported increases, compared with 48.2 percent of Mexican companies (81) and 48.7 percent of non-U.S. foreign firms (37). Size mattered: Over three-fifths (61.4 percent) of the 70 very large firms that responded to the question reported higher imports, compared with 48.6 percent of the 35 small companies. Of the companies that replied to the question, those with a dollar component in their revenue streams were less likely to have increased their imports since the inception of NAFTA: 48.4 percent of the 159 firms with some dollar revenue reported higher imports, compared with 60 percent of the 90 companies without dollar income.

DIRECT FOREIGN INVESTMENT AFTER NAFTA

Attractive as the potential of a domestic market of ninety million consumers may be, that potential remains to be realized. Until the decision to open the economy was taken in 1985, foreigners built plants in Mexico so that they could sell in Mexico. With the opening, foreigners put production capacity in Mexico to produce for other markets as well. The direct foreign investment (DFI) statistics speak for themselves: The more open the economy and the freer the trade, the more direct foreign investment flowed into Mexico (see Table 9.2). The first two-and-a-half years after NAFTA's implementation saw a dramatic increase in direct foreign investment. However, that DFI has not all come from NAFTA countries.

Historically, the bulk (about two-thirds) of direct foreign investment in Mexico has come from the United States. At the end of 1993 the United States accounted for almost 63 percent of authorized DFI in Mexico; Canada accounted for only 1.5 percent. Since NAFTA was implemented, these ratios have changed somewhat while total DFI has risen. The U.S. share of new DFI fell to 52.7 percent between 1994 and mid-1996, and that of Canada rose to 6.3 percent. Investments from other countries, notably Holland and India, have increased since NAFTA went into effect. During this two-and-a-half-year-period these two countries accounted for, respectively, 6.5 percent and 8.3 percent of new investments in Mexico, much more than in the past.[10] However, it would be premature to conclude that these countries' shares of DFI will continue at these levels. One major investment can represent a high percentage of DFI in a given year, but it does not necessarily represent a trend.

Because the Secretariat of Commerce and Industrial Development (Secofi) has changed the way it calculates foreign investment flows since 1994, it is difficult to compare the figures prior to and after that year. Under the old methodology Secofi reported DFI as it was approved rather than

Table 9.2   Accumulated Direct Foreign Investment in Mexican Firms, by Economic
Sector, 1984–1995 (millions of U.S. dollars)

Year	Total	Annual Flow	Sector				
			Manufacturing	Services	Commerce	Extractive	Agriculture
1984	12,899.9	1,429.9	10,213.3	1,406.9	1,015.9	258.0	5.8
1985	14,628.9	1,729.0	11,379.1	1,842.2	1,125.4	276.0	6.2
1986	17,053.1	2,424.2	13,298.0	2,165.3	1,276.6	306.8	6.4
1987	20,930.3	3,877.2	15,698.5	3,599.2	1,255.4	355.6	21.6
1988	24,087.4	3,157.1	16,718.5	5,476.6	1,502.2	380.5	9.6
1989	27,698.4	3,602.0	17,700.8	7,681.2	1,888.5	390.0	28.9
1990	31,411.8	3,722.4	18,893.8	9,884.2	2,059.8	484.0	90.0
1991	34,976.8	3,565.0	19,857.4	12,022.1	2,447.3	515.0	135.0
1992	40,681.9	5,705.1	21,420.1	15,305.2	3,258.7	523.6	174.3
1993	45,591.6	4,909.7	23,875.8	16,901.2	4,018.1	587.7	208.8
1994	52,499.7	6,908.1	28,264.6	18,379.1	5,032.2	606.5	217.3
1995	62,169.4	9,669.7	34,344.2	20,895.5	5,945.1	757.7	226.9

Source: Annual Reports of Foreign Investment in Mexico, Secretariat of Commerce and
Industrial Development (Secofi), 1987, 1991, and 1996.

when it was registered, but approved investments need not be made, and
firms have traditionally registered investments well after they have been
made. The change in methodology—to reporting DFI as it is registered—
can thus result in significant discrepancies between the approved and registered DFI numbers in any given year. In any event, assuming all approved
investment came into Mexico, DFI averaged $4.4 billion per year between
1984 and 1995. In the first thirty months after NAFTA implementation, DFI
from the United States alone was 58.8 percent higher, averaging $5.4 bil-
lion annually. The average annual level from all countries during the period
was $9.09 billion, more than twice the annual average between 1984 and
1995.[11]

The destination of direct foreign investment flows has also shifted
since NAFTA went into effect. In the 1970s and 1980s about two-thirds of
all direct foreign investment flows went to manufacturing. In the early
1990s, 63 percent of new foreign investments went into services and
commerce. However, in NAFTA's first thirty months, DFI has reverted to
manufacturing, which was the destination of most (57 percent) DFI.
Likewise, between 1994 and mid-1996, of the $12 billion in direct for-
eign investments U.S. firms brought into Mexico—52.7 percent of total
foreign investment during that period—51.2 percent went into the manufacturing sector, up from 35 percent from 1990 to 1993. Transportation
and communications has also received much more foreign investment in
recent years, a trend that promises to continue, given rapid advances in
technology.

Changes in Investment Strategies After NAFTA

The AmCham survey asked whether companies had changed their medium- and long-term investment strategies as a consequence of NAFTA. The answer was yes, according to 56 percent of the 350 companies that responded to the question. Companies replied affirmatively in about the same percentages, regardless of the currency in which their income stream was denominated. However, firm size and nationality did make a difference. About 7 out of 10 (69.8 percent) of the 86 companies classified as very large said their investment strategies had changed as a result of NAFTA, while only 46.4 percent of the 69 small companies reported a change. Non-U.S. foreign firms were much more likely than Mexican companies to have responded in the affirmative: Two-thirds of the 49 non-U.S. foreign companies answered yes, compared with 51.9 percent of the 129 Mexican companies.

Depending on whether one views the glass as half empty or half full, NAFTA's impact on attracting investment to North America (that is, in Mexico, the United States, and Canada) is either encouraging or disappointing. When firms were asked whether NAFTA had influenced them to shift investments from other parts of the world to North America, two-thirds of the 300 companies that responded answered no. Neither company size nor the currency mix in which income was denominated affected the answer. Foreign firms' decisions to shift investments from other parts of the world to North America were more likely to have been influenced by NAFTA: 36.8 percent of the 155 U.S. companies and 40 percent of the 45 non-U.S. foreign firms that responded said that NAFTA had influenced their decision to shift investment to North America, compared with 23.5 percent of the 98 Mexican companies that answered the question.

NAFTA has made it easier to invest in Mexico, according to 81.6 percent of the 359 firms that responded to the question. Foreign firms tended to perceive NAFTA's impact on ease of investing somewhat more positively than did Mexican firms: 86 percent of the 179 U.S. firms and 87.8 percent of the 49 other foreign firms replied in the affirmative, compared with 73.8 percent of the 130 Mexican companies that replied to the question.

The Nature of Investments in Mexico

The interviews also suggest that NAFTA encourages investment in Mexico, but these investments will not necessarily translate into significant new "greenfield" investments. The exception is in sectors such as wood products. Capital-intensive industries with obsolete plants face competition from imported goods produced with up-to-date technology. Firms must invest in plants that offer economies of scale and use new technology, said one CEO. But, added another, the investment is more expensive than in other countries "because of the Mexican risk" factor.

Another industry that "may see some manufacturers building plants in Mexico" is one in which barriers to open trade remain. Auto manufacturers, for instance, still must comply with local content requirements. If a tire company were to put a new plant in Mexico, one of the reasons would be to serve the OEM (original equipment manufacturer) market in Mexico:[12] Some of the OEMs still "will choose the tires they use based on the degree of local content," according to one CEO.

Many of the CEOs interviewed cited as an advantage of NAFTA the opportunities for rationalizing production. The "major restructuring of production" means that "incremental investments result in substantially more output," said the CEO of a consumer products manufacturer. The "working out of solutions within the North American region," as another put it, produces economies of scale that obviate the need to replicate production capacities within each of the NAFTA countries. "Where we need to upgrade significantly our equipment, it is more convenient to instead import production from the United States," said the CEO of the pharmaceutical firm.[13] However, the company is "bringing in more U.S. equipment because of the tariff advantage." The firm is also "investing more heavily in clinical trials in Mexico."

Although investments to upgrade manufacturing facilities are not as spectacular as the opening of a new plant, they are nonetheless significant. One CEO said that American pharmaceutical manufacturers in Mexico spent more (in dollars) to upgrade facilities in the crisis year of 1995 than in the boom year 1994. In 1996 investments were 42.9 percent higher than in 1995.

The apparel manufacturing industry is beginning to see the formation of strategic alliances, said the CEO interviewed. He reports investment in the sector from Europe and Asia; investment by Mexicans is insignificant, he says.

Another CEO, whose company inaugurated a manufacturing facility in Mexico in recent years, said, "We would have had a new plant there with or without NAFTA. However, that NAFTA was going to exist made us think about and design the new facility differently." The firm's leaders believe that NAFTA improves Mexico's growth prospects. The new plant was premised on the notion that domestic demand would grow more rapidly with NAFTA than without it.

CHANGES IN EMPLOYMENT AFTER NAFTA

One of the most contentious issues in the NAFTA negotiations concerned the fear that companies would flee to Mexico to take advantage of lower-cost labor there, and thus cause job losses in the United States. The Mexican data do not indicate that this is happening. Ironically, it appears that Mexico may have more to be worried about in terms of employment problems than either of its two NAFTA partners.

As the Mexican economy has become more open and competitive in recent years, job creation has become an increasingly complex problem. Pre- and post-NAFTA structural adjustments have contributed to stagnation in employment levels generally, and particularly in the manufacturing sector. Overall employment levels in Mexico fell sharply in the wake of the December 1994 devaluation of the peso. During the nine months after the peso crisis, the number of people employed in the formal economy fell by more than 850,000, or 7.4 percent.[14]

Nevertheless, the peso crisis was not the sole—or even the primary— source of Mexico's difficulties with job creation. The problem is a longer-standing one. In June 1991, 11.1 million people were permanently insured through the Social Security Institute. Despite the respectable performance of the economy over the following three years (GDP growth averaged 3.6 percent), only 11.3 million people were permanently insured by June 1994, an average annual increase of only 0.9 percent. By September 1996, the number of people covered had risen only marginally, to 11.4 million. With a workforce growing at more than 3 percent annually and open unemployment levels not changing significantly, the obvious implication is that most new employment has been in the informal sector.

A close look at the industrial sector in Mexico also shows disappointing results. Overall industrial employment grew at an average annual rate of 0.66 percent between 1991 and 1996. During that five-year period the large, mostly international companies and the in-bond industries have responded best to the opening of the economy. Most often such operations were those that either already focused on world markets or could shift production rapidly from domestic to international markets. Generally speaking, microenterprises (up to fifteen employees) and small enterprises (up to 100 employees) have suffered the greatest employment losses. Medium-size companies (up to 250 employees), whose losses were not as great, are rapidly recovering. Only large companies, as a group, have grown in terms of employment generation: The share of total industrial employment in large and medium-size firms rose from 65.3 percent in 1991 to 70.3 percent in 1996 (see Table 9.3).

THE IN-BOND (*MAQUILADORA*) INDUSTRIES

The maquiladora program begun in 1965, which permits temporary duty-free import of inputs for assembly and export, took advantage of low-cost Mexican labor and the fact that duties were paid only on the value added in

Table 9.3   Employment Levels in Mexico, by Industrial Sector, 1991, 1995, and
             1996

	Number of Employees			Net Jobs Created		
Sector	1991	1995	1996	1991–1995	1995–1996	1991–1996
Food	436,892	411,255	433,906	−25,637	22,651	−2,986
Beverages	140,853	139,651	143,138	−1,202	3,487	2,285
Tobacco	6,018	6,569	7,177	551	608	1,159
Textiles	176,102	133,221	155,445	−42,881	22,224	−20,657
Apparel	285,587	313,139	399,918	27,552	86,779	114,331
Shoes and leather	141,296	112,713	133,177	−28,583	20,464	−8,119
Wood products	53,131	49,198	55,286	−3,933	6,088	2,155
Furniture and accessories	83,880	64,201	74,568	−19,679	10,367	−9,312
Paper	71,057	61,983	67,319	−9,074	5,336	−3,738
Printing and publishing	121,358	111,349	117,956	−10,009	6,607	−3,402
Chemicals	237,029	199,074	207,742	−37,955	8,668	−29,287
Petrochemicals	9,647	5,866	6,916	−3,781	1,050	−2,731
Rubber and plastic	180,184	159,039	185,495	−21,145	26,456	5,311
Nonmetallic minerals	157,884	123,473	135,029	−34,411	11,556	−22,855
Basic metals	87,934	69,760	75,373	−18,174	5,613	−12,561
Metal products	366,700	262,222	304,698	−104,478	42,476	−62,002
Nonelectric machinery and equipment	92,987	74,529	84,884	−18,458	10,355	−8,103
Electrical machinery and apparatus	407,213	471,725	553,780	64,512	82,055	146,567
Transport equipment	219,744	204,052	222,776	−15,692	18,724	3,032
Other manufacturing	94,921	98,377	120,215	3,416	21,878	25,294
Total	3,370,417	3,066,356	3,479,798	−304,061	413,442	109,381

Source: January 1997 Economic Report (Mexico City: Grupo Financiero Bancomer,
1997), based on data from Secofi.

Mexico. The program has been a particular boost for the northern border
areas of the country. The cities of Tijuana, Mexicali, Ciudad Juarez,
Matamoros, Reynosa, Nogales, and Tecate house half the maquila plants
and generate about 60 percent of total employment. However, in spite of the
Mexican government's efforts to promote greater domestic integration in
the industries, local firms account for only about 2 percent of total inputs.
An equally minimal proportion—2 percent—of maquila products are sold
in Mexico. In-bond companies are far from wholly foreign-owned businesses. In 1994, 43 percent of the maquilas were owned by Mexican companies,
38 percent by U.S. companies, 14 percent by joint U.S.-Mexican operations, 2 percent by Japanese concerns, and 3 percent by others.

Since the late 1980s the in-bond industries have become one of the
most dynamic growth areas in the Mexican economy (see Table 9.4). Even
in the crisis year of 1995, the in-bond industry grew rapidly: Maquiladora
exports rose 18.4 percent, creating 80,000 net new jobs (see Table 9.5).

Table 9.4 Profile of the Mexican Maquiladora Industry, by Selected Indices, 1990–1996

| Year | Number of Firms | Total Employees (thousands) | Total Average Monthly Remunerations | | Average Hourly Wage for Laborers (U.S. dollars) | Value Added (millions of U.S. dollars) | Percent Growth of Maquila Exports | Maquila Share of Total Exports (percent) |
			Millions of 1994 Pesos[a]	Millions of Nominal Pesos[a]				
1990	1,920	446	217.4	432.6	0.88	3,635	18.4	34
1991	2,013	486	336.1	536.0	0.94	4,117	16.4	37
1992	2,129	511	533.7	681.0	1.03	4,805	16.7	40
1993	2,195	541	726.0	799.9	1.21	5,511	17.0	42
1994	2,064	600	961.3	961.3	1.23	5,839	20.2	43
1995	2,241	680	987.4	1,332.8	0.78	5,019	18.4	39
1996	2,520[b]	809[b]	1,077.3	1,964.0[c]	0.85[b]	6,300[c]	18.5[d]	38

Sources: Annual Reports on the Maquiladora Industry, National Institute of Statistics, Geography, and Information (INEGI) and Secretariat of Commerce and Industrial Development (Secofi), 1990–1996.

  a. Deflated by average annual consumer price index (CPI).
  b. October.
  c. Estimate.
  d. January–November.

Table 9.5 Sectoral Growth in Companies and Personnel in the Maquiladora Industry, October 1996

Sector	Number of Companies	Percent Growth from October 1995	Number of Employees	Percent Growth from October 1995
Food products	69	19.0	11,506	48.4
Clothing and textiles	632	30.6	146,484	46.6
Shoes and leather	58	7.4	7,816	3.0
Wood and metal furniture	314	13.8	43,976	18.3
Chemical products	105	1.9	14,874	13.0
Transport equipment	189	11.8	160,736	16.4
Nonelectric machinery and equipment	42	10.5	8,681	13.7
Electric machinery and equipment	127	4.1	76,683	12.3
Electronic materials and accessories	423	6.5	208,847	19.7
Games and sports equipment	46	7.0	12,958	−3.1
Other manufactured products	386	14.9	85,352	21.1
Total	2,520	15.4	809,434	21.2

Source: Monthly Report on Sectoral Development in the Maquiladora Industry, Secretariat of Commerce and Industrial Development (Secofi), February 1997.

Between the end of 1993 and November 1994, the number of people employed in the in-bond sector grew by a little more than 50 percent, from 541,000 to 811,000.

NAFTA's IMPLICATIONS FOR THE FINANCIAL SERVICES SECTOR

The manufacturing sector bore the brunt of the opening of the economy after 1990. The NAFTA negotiations spurred the pace of the opening of the nontradables sector and extended the opening to still protected sectors, such as banking.

The services sector that has felt the most impact from NAFTA, to date, is financial services. Ironically, because of the limitations on the operations of foreign financial institutions that existed until NAFTA, these institutions have been the least affected by the financial crisis in Mexico unleashed in December 1994. Foreign financial operations have suffered far fewer portfolio problems than their Mexican counterparts because their loan portfolios were much smaller and newer. Thus relieved of the need to worry about the quality of their loan portfolios, foreign financial institutions were able to focus almost exclusively on the profitable trading and capital markets business lines.

The crisis-driven modification of the laws governing foreign ownership of existing banks has allowed foreign banks to acquire ownership of several Mexican banks, as well as to set up their own operations. The share of total Mexican banking assets controlled by foreign financial institutions rose from 2 percent at the end of 1994 to 9.5 percent two years later. Third-country financial institutions have also reaped NAFTA rewards, because they can establish operations in Mexico through their affiliates incorporated in the United States and Canada.

The banking services sector of the economy, privatized only in 1991–1992, has been slower to adapt to international competition than the real sector of the economy. To help rectify this situation, NAFTA's financial services chapter was more generous to foreign investors than most observers had expected. In addition, under rules issued by the finance ministry (Secretaría de Hacienda y Crédito Público) in early 1995, foreign banks are permitted to acquire up to 100 percent ownership in existing banks—excluding only the three largest banks, Banamex, Bancomer, and Serfin—that hold less than 6 percent of the total capital of the banking system. Moreover, these rules allow foreigners to own up to 25 percent of the net capital for the banking system, as compared with the 11 percent that would have been allowed under NAFTA rules. Also, both Mexican and foreign individuals and companies, with approval from the Mexican finance ministry, may own up to 20 percent (instead of the 10 percent allowed under previous regulations) of a Mexican financial institution. The percentage of capital that foreigners, as a group, may acquire of majority–Mexican-owned banks, brokerage houses, and financial groups has been raised from 30 percent to 49 percent. Over the next several years, as heightened competition in the financial sector causes strong institutions to become more efficient and weaker ones to merge or disappear, Mexican businesses, investors, and consumers all will benefit.

THE AGRICULTURAL SECTOR AFTER NAFTA

In general, the agricultural sector in Mexico has been declining over the past several generations. It accounts for only about 5.3 percent of GDP, down from 11.6 percent in 1970 and 17.5 percent in 1940. Throughout much of the country subsistence farming dominates, with the notable exception of coffee-producing areas and certain northern parts of the country, where state-of-the-art technology has fostered success in exporting fresh fruits and vegetables to the United States.

As Table 9.2 shows, there has been comparatively little foreign investment in the Mexican agricultural sector over the years, mostly because of serious problems regarding land ownership and usage. Even so, agricultural trade, about 90 percent of which is with the United States and Canada, has grown rapidly in recent years. Mexico's most dynamic agricultural export products have been coffee, snack foods, fresh fruits and vegetables, tequila, beer, shrimp, and lumber.

Bulk agricultural products constitute Mexico's largest import categories, the most important of which are corn, soybeans, and cotton, as well as red meats, dairy products, and vegetable oils (excluding soybean oils). Because of the financial crisis in 1995, Mexico's agricultural imports from the United States were lower in that year than in 1992, but as the recovery began in 1996, agricultural imports swelled rapidly, rising by 53 percent over the previous year. Over the 1992–1996 period, excluding the economic crisis year 1995, Mexico's agricultural product trade deficit with the United States averaged $1.3 billion a year. This trend is expected to continue.

COMPANIES' STRATEGIES AFTER NAFTA

Consumers are one group that won big after NAFTA's implementation. The opening of the economy has given Mexican consumers access to a greater variety of better-quality, lower-priced products. Those products need not be imported: Mexican firms have risen to the occasion and improved the quality, variety, and pricing of domestically produced goods. This section examines how companies have met the challenge of international competition and how their actions have affected their margins.

Margins

Although the collapse of the peso in December 1994, less than a year after the implementation of the NAFTA treaty, cut short most consumers' ability to acquire imported products, the erosion of the peso's margin of underval- uation (in terms of purchasing-power parity) in 1996 kept pressure on domestic producers to limit price increases.[15] Margins contracted sharply in 1995.[16] Many of the CEOs who were interviewed reported that the margins of their firms had dropped when the Mexican government opened the econ- omy in the second half of the 1980s. There is no expectation that margins will recover to the levels that existed before the economic opening.

The reduction in tariffs brought about by NAFTA was a disaster for industry as a whole. The tire industry saw the low-end, price-sensitive seg- ment of the market (about 32 percent of the market) flooded by imports. Because of NAFTA "the industry must be more price sensitive," said one CEO. Because margins are higher in Mexico than in the United States, "when duties go to zero in 1998, it will hit margins."

Margins disappeared in the Mexican apparel industry, which was destroyed by the opening, according to the CEO who was interviewed. Most of the industry could not compete against products imported from countries with wage rates far lower than Mexico's. Those firms that sur- vived were the large producers "with strong ties to the stores," the CEO said.

The opening of the economy also transformed the electronics and information technology businesses. Margins fell, "a process accelerated by NAFTA," said one CEO. NAFTA's "small tariff benefits" had a favorable impact on margins, but those "were offset by the opening," according to another. Small competitors either found a niche in which they could com- pete or they closed down. Similarly, the opening brought world pricing to petrochemical products, hitting margins in that business.

Margins had been protected in the banking sector until NAFTA went into effect, but they fell—in some cases, to below precrisis levels—as new foreign competitors entered the banking sector in dollar lending, trading operations, and capital market transactions. The latter two activities are new with NAFTA, and all are aimed at a very narrow customer base.[17] The competition engendered by NAFTA for the business of a limited number of customers has "made it harder for us," said the banker interviewed.

He said also that those consequences of NAFTA forced them to think of "new products, new strategies," including diversification of trading and capital market products offered in the market. Mexican banks have signifi- cantly stepped up investment in their system capabilities and are strength- ening their organizational structures to compete, he continued. "When the economy recovers, we will go down market," taking the new products to more companies. Nonetheless, for competition to hit margins in a way that will benefit most companies in Mexico, foreign banks must establish local currency businesses, according to this CEO, and that will depend on the recovery of the economy. All of the CEOs interviewed agreed that most companies in Mexico will have to wait to benefit from NAFTA's opening of the financial sector.

Lower tariffs reduce costs, which, in turn, can feed through to prices either by causing price reductions or by limiting increases in prices. However, the CEO of the automotive manufacturing firm said that margins in his business are more sensitive to volume than to price changes. He sees NAFTA "as one more tool to implement our margin strategy." NAFTA's real importance for margins in the industry, in his view, derives from the opportunity it offers manufacturers to increase volume sales by rationalizing production.

Another CEO reported that margins in his firm, which manufactures a consumer product, depend more on transfer pricing policies than on trade agreements. The U.S. regulatory authorities' interest in transfer prices has affected margins, not NAFTA.

NAFTA has had a "negligible impact on margins" in the personal care products business, according to one CEO, although the reduction of tariffs produced "some improvement in margins." However, NAFTA has adversely affected the price of materials, especially raw materials. Under NAFTA, Mexican suppliers are trying to price their products at the world price, which means that firms must pay U.S.-equivalent prices for inputs although their products cost less in Mexico than in the United States. The impact on margins is bound to be direct and adverse.

Margins have improved for those firms in the pharmaceutical sector that have been able to take advantage of NAFTA's lower tariffs by switching to North American suppliers. The CEO interviewed felt that the "overall spirit of NAFTA" has contributed to relaxation of the price controls to which the industry is subject, a process that has improved margins.

The following sections describe some of the various strategies that companies have adopted in response to the attack on margins mounted by competition. NAFTA enhances some of them. Increasing productivity is one. Others involve cutting costs through changes in product mix, production rationalization, sourcing, and distribution.

Increased Productivity

In the tire industry the "low-end Mexican manufacturers started to get hit by competition in 1994. In 1995, the undervalued peso saved them," according to a tire company CEO, who believes the respite will not last much longer. So far, however, margin erosion has been minimal, thanks to productivity gains: "We've all hit home runs in terms of increases in productivity and efficiency," he stated. He credits better cooperation with the unions for much of the improvement in productivity, which has been accomplished with only "slight capital investment." In one of the few industries whose union contracts are still governed by the rigid *contrato ley*,[18] "NAFTA has awakened unions to the fact that jobs are in play," a realization that has led to better union-management relationships.

Measures to increase productivity were also necessary in the petrochemical sector. The CEO interviewed said his firm's efforts to make its Mexican operations competitive, which began in the aftermath of the 1982 crisis ("a wake-up call"), have allowed the firm to weather the fall in prices caused by the opening without hurting margins. However, that has not been the general experience in the sector, he said. The modification of processes and, above all, the change in attitudes under way for about fifteen years have enabled the company to compete in the world market.

Product Mix

As noted earlier, the opening of the Mexican economy and NAFTA have increased the range of products available to the consumer. The CEOs of major computer and electronics companies say that this opening has meant that more options exist in the market and that new products can be introduced into the Mexican market more quickly. Consumers have more options—ones that can save them money—in products ranging from dental drills to tires. In the case of dental drills, the wider variety of products means that dentists no longer have to buy the "Rolls-Royce" of drills to do their job. In the case of tires, the opening brought imports of nonmajor brands of tires aimed at the low-end, price-sensitive segment of the market.

The petrochemical sector saw "more product diversification" after the treaty, said the CEO of the company in that business. NAFTA "has opened our portfolio of products," according to the automotive company CEO. In fact, "more product was imported from the United States in 1995 than in any other period," an accomplishment made possible by the increase in exports and by NAFTA's relaxation of the sector's balance-of-payments requirements.

Personal care products that have been imported into Mexico have been principally premium goods. When the economic crisis struck, consumers switched to less-expensive products, thereby curtailing imports. Yet the CEO who was interviewed expects imports of premium products to pick up again as the economy and income levels recover.

Pharmaceuticals seem to be the exception to the general changes in product mix wrought by NAFTA. The CEO interviewed said that the market in that sector has followed its own dynamic. Although product mix in the pharmaceutical sector seems not to have been affected by the economic opening, NAFTA and the law on intellectual property rights enacted in the early 1990s have brought about significant changes in supply and production chains.[19]

The impact of the opening and of NAFTA have been equally dramatic, though perhaps less visible, for the production end of business. The flip side of the greater variety of products available in the Mexican market is less variety in manufactured products, according to the CEO of an information technology firm. In the wood products sector, products and production have had to become "more focused, more specialized," said one CEO. The CEO of an apparel manufacturer reported the same. In the automotive sector, NAFTA's easing of the balance-of-payments requirements applied to OEMs has permitted manufacturers to "better focus their production portfolio to meet the needs of the market," according to the CEO interviewed.

Rationalization of Production

Several of the CEOs interviewed cited the opportunities to rationalize production as an important benefit of NAFTA. With NAFTA, "economies of scale can be realized," said the CEO of a company that produces vehicles. The CEO of the petrochemical firm cited the rationalization of production undertaken by the automotive industry as a model for his own industry. The tire company CEO said his firm is "taking important first steps to rationalize production" of its plants in Central and South America—wherever the duty on tires is zero—as well as in the NAFTA countries. The CEO of an information technology company reported that his firm has been able to expand its manufacturing capacity because of NAFTA. The expanded capacity, part of the firm's strategy to rationalize production, has been used "to get economies of scale so that we can be competitive worldwide." The CEO of a company that manufactures consumer products said NAFTA had prompted a major restructuring of production in his company: "Scheduling can now be based on installed technology, not duties." The CEO of the firm that manufactures personal care products said there is no significant cost advantage in producing in either Mexico or the United States; his company has been sourcing some products from the United States, and he expects to see some consolidation of production going forward.[20] "As tariffs go to zero," he added, "NAFTA will become more important."

Sourcing

Judging by the interviews, NAFTA has had a much greater impact on how companies source than on exports. There has been a marked shift to sourcing within North America to reduce costs. The CEO of the pharmaceutical firm said, "Whenever possible, we are switching our sourcing to the United States." The reason is simple: The lower tariff on raw materials imported from NAFTA countries translates into higher margins. In the computer industry, raw materials and components are being sourced differently than in the past because of the "positive cost impact" offered by NAFTA's reduction of tariffs, according to one CEO. Servicing and parts availability reinforce the "bias towards buying locally."

The local supplier base also has improved as a result of the economic opening and NAFTA. The CEO of an automotive company praised "the speed at which Mexican suppliers are changing," citing improvements in quality, service, and cost competitiveness. Suppliers are "more professional, have more of a customer focus, and are willing to invest when they get long-term commitments" from the OEMs. The CEO of a consumer products firm said that before the opening his firm had to import inputs, if the firm's products were to meet international standards of quality. Thanks to the opening, his firm can now purchase locally produced inputs, because local suppliers can import the materials needed to produce the high-quality inputs required by the consumer products manufacturer.

Lower duties are only part of the savings. NAFTA has given companies "a bigger stick in dealing with local suppliers" who were protected before, according to one CEO. The availability of imports has allowed the manufacturer in the wood and paper products sector "to squeeze suppliers' margins more." Another CEO said, "We are obliged to be closer to our suppliers"; his company is "negotiating prices that are closer to world prices." The standard of world prices can cut both ways, however, as the manufacturer of personal care products found: That firm's domestic materials suppliers are attempting, with some success, to raise their prices to match world prices.

Long-term supply contracts are one tool for helping build a strong supplier base. CEOs in both the petrochemical and automotive industries commented on their firms' use of long-term supply contracts. The automotive manufacturer CEO offered this vignette: The trade association for auto parts suppliers strongly opposed the removal of restrictions on foreign participation in the sector in 1993, but that attitude had changed by 1996, after one of the OEMs had sourced more than $2 billion in Mexico over the next four years in parts for new exports.

Supplier development is not easy, according to the CEO of an electronics firm. Quality is the stumbling block. Nevertheless, companies work at supplier development because doing so is "a good corporate citizen issue," he said. His firm identifies potential suppliers, and government entities then work to develop them.

Distribution

The opening and NAFTA have improved not only the quality of the products available to Mexican consumers but also the service they receive. For example, a major electronics manufacturer has quadrupled the number of distributors of some product lines since 1991. At about the time NAFTA took effect, the firm opened an "integral service center," where all company products are serviced. The center is open around the clock. The number of technicians employed and the spare parts on hand have increased. Obviously, the turnaround for service has improved significantly.

Service, price, and flexibility have all been brought into play to reduce inventories in the petrochemical sector. Distribution systems have changed, redounding to the customers' benefit; in the petrochemical sector, for example, some U.S. distributors from Texas have begun distributing pesticides in northern Mexico. Because "dealers have more options, the tire industry has had to improve fill rates and inventory availability," according to another CEO.

Two CEOs said their firms have begun shipping directly from their Mexican manufacturing facilities to their customers in the United States. One is also shipping directly from its U.S. plants to Mexican customers. Direct shipment "shortens the cycle time to customers" and, for the manufacturer, means a "sharp reduction in expensive inventory requirements." In the personal care products sector, NAFTA has had only "limited impact" on the consolidation of distribution chains, however, because "trade concentration, a worldwide phenomenon, was already under way."

The crisis accelerated a profound change in the advertising industry. Advertisers must now think in terms of the "message," be it through promotions, sponsorships, or television and radio ads. Successful marketing is no longer just a matter of buying commercials, because of the growing sophistication of the consumer.

NAFTA has changed the distribution system in the apparel industry, too. Before NAFTA Mexican stores dictated what manufacturers produced: "It was a buyers' market totally," said the CEO interviewed. Because NAFTA opened up the possibility of exporting, "many manufacturers are beginning to leave existing distribution channels." Brand names are being manufactured in Mexico, and companies that own brand names sell to U.S. department stores. "Now, manufacturers and brand names are the distribution channels."

Conclusions

To the extent that a more rapidly growing economy benefits companies, NAFTA works, in the opinion of the companies surveyed by AmCham. Of the 365 firms that expressed an opinion about whether NAFTA will contribute to a higher growth rate for the Mexican economy, 92.6 percent answered yes. Four-fifths (80.2 percent) of respondents (358) believe that NAFTA will contribute to faster growth of the domestic market. U.S. and other foreign firms tended to be more optimistic about NAFTA's contribution to a more rapidly growing domestic market than were Mexican firms: 74.1 percent of the 131 Mexican firms that responded expected NAFTA to accelerate the growth rate of the domestic market, as compared with 83.1 percent of the 177 U.S. firms and 85.4 percent of the 48 firms of other nationalities that answered.

The companies that have done well in the more open economy share certain characteristics, as do those firms that have struggled to survive or failed. Although it is easier to be a winner in a dynamic sector, some firms in so-called losing sectors also have been able to do well. The survival process has made companies more competitive, lowered margins, prompted investment, improved quality, and reduced response time.

The interviews with CEOs indicate that those companies that have done well under free trade, regardless of the sector in which they fall,

- take advantage of the economies of scale offered by a larger market,
- rationalize production and sourcing,
- draw on international distribution chains,
- have access to capital or financing or both,
- have market power,
- use imported inputs, and
- have organizational structures that can adapt rapidly to change.

Multinational subsidiaries and very large Mexican firms, some of which are multinationals themselves, by definition possess the first five characteristics. Obviously, not all large firms have done well under NAFTA and not all small firms have suffered. However, the large companies and the subsidiaries of multinationals are most likely to have benefited from, or have been hurt the least by, the opening of Mexico's economy and NAFTA.

Being able to realize economies of scale in a country where production was previously limited to the domestic market requires investment. Investment means access to money, and in Mexico that has meant either owners with deep pockets or credit from banks. Without access to capital or bank financing since the financial crisis, most Mexican companies have been unable to invest to realize the economies of scale offered by NAFTA.

Those companies that have not prospered in a free-trade environment have often been handicapped by their size. However, "losers" from NAFTA share some traits that are independent of size. One is attitude.[21] Another related trait is inefficiency.[22]

Mexican-owned companies are almost always family-run businesses, even the largest firms traded on stock exchanges in Mexico and abroad. The transformation from a very closed economy to a very open one occurred in only half a decade. Unless owners have been able to adapt—and the challenge of changing a lifetime's way of doing business is formidable—their firms' products have not been able to compete effectively. Inefficiency can be tolerated in a closed economy, but it is not easily translated into profits in an open economy. The companies in Mexico that lost out with the opening of the economy often were those with inadequate systems that were run as a cash cow for the family and whose key staff positions were filled by people whose qualification was their surname.

The implications of NAFTA go beyond trade. Because NAFTA creates binding obligations on governments, it limits the discretion of bureaucrats. In Mexico that is an especially important step toward greater certainty, reduction of the cost of doing business, and fashioning of a less political business environment.

Easier to Operate?

The CEOs interviewed said that NAFTA has not eliminated the many *trámites* (bureaucratic hurdles) to investment and doing business about which businesspeople working in Mexico complain, but that it has had a salutary impact. Several cautioned that NAFTA must be seen as a part of an overall policy thrust designed to simplify the process of doing business, and thus improvements cannot be attributed simply to NAFTA. With that caveat, the producers of petrochemicals, electronics, telecommunications, computers, and tires all mentioned that moving merchandise across the border has become easier. Import-export procedures are better defined and customs clearance is smoother.

"Federal-level approvals for new investments and to open warehouses, and so on, have been cut out," said the CEO in the wood products sector, "but all the state and local requirements are still in place." The paperwork required to invest in the computer sector has "decreased greatly," according to one CEO.

The automotive and computer industries have benefited from the gradual elimination of the performance requirements the Mexican government had imposed on their industries. In the electronics industry, NAFTA has accelerated the move toward uniform regulations concerning, for example, product safety standards set by Underwriters Laboratories and followed by the NAFTA partners.

Several CEOs highlighted a change in the governmental-business relationship, which is partly attributable to NAFTA. One CEO, head of a consumer products company, cited "a very different attitude on the part of the government" that "is filtering down, but it takes time." According to the CEO of a pharmaceutical firm, the "whole system has become more flexible; there are fewer requirements." The CEO of the petrochemical manufacturer said communication with governmental authorities has improved.

Trade Disputes

By and large, the companies in the AmCham survey do not perceive that NAFTA has helped resolve trade disputes. Of the two-fifths of the sample that responded to the question "If your firm has had a commercial dispute, has NAFTA helped you to resolve it?" 78.9 percent answered that NAFTA had not helped resolve the dispute. Foreign firms were more likely than Mexican firms to report that NAFTA had helped in resolving commercial disputes: 27.1 percent of the seventy U.S. companies and 27.3 percent of the twenty-two other foreign firms answered yes, as compared with 9.8 percent of the fifty-one Mexican companies that responded to the question. Large firms were most likely to answer yes: 27.1 percent of the forty-eight large firms answered affirmatively, almost double the percentage of medium-size and very large firms that responded to the question (respectively, 15.4 percent of twenty-six businesses and 14.3 percent of thirty-five firms). Small firms were also more likely to have found NAFTA useful: 23.1 percent of the twenty-six companies answered affirmatively. The number of respondents in each category is small, however, which means that the relationship between firm size and the utility of NAFTA's dispute resolution mechanisms can be considered only a working hypothesis.

The one CEO of the eleven interviewed that reported any need to use NAFTA's dispute resolution mechanism said that the Mexican government had discouraged the sector from bringing dumping charges against foreign competitors. NAFTA has also diminished the power of Mexican monopolies and oligopolies. The CEO interviewees agreed that the exposure of key sectors of the economy (such as finance) to competition will ultimately benefit Mexican consumers and companies, yet they all stressed that the opening up of those sectors will not occur in the near future.

Focus

NAFTA has changed the way firms look at Mexico. "NAFTA has reduced uncertainty," said one CEO, "and that is comforting to our shareholders and management." The CEO of a consumer products manufacturing firm said NAFTA "has introduced a positive bias in favor of North America."

Echoing that sentiment, another CEO commented that, because of NAFTA, "we see North America as one market and are working out solutions within the region." According to the CEO of another manufacturing company, "With NAFTA, Mexico began to figure in our plans. The plant in Mexico is no longer the last plant fixed."

The move toward rationalization of production reflects the redefinition of the market that NAFTA has brought about. NAFTA and the opening of the Mexican economy in general have also changed the level of consumer awareness. As one CEO summarized, "Consumers demand more quality, more service, and expect to have more to choose from."

The regulatory authorities are taking advantage of the presence of foreign bank branches to inform oversight procedures, according to the banker who was interviewed. The Comisión Nacional Bancaria y de Valores (National Banking and Securities Commission) is "very interested in seeing how we use technology," accounting standards, and compliance and review procedures.

Finally, NAFTA has highlighted the underlying structural obstacles to competitiveness that some sectors face. A good example is the wood products sector, a "losing" sector in an open economy. The land tenure system in Mexico has made the country "fiber deficient." When the economy was closed, companies could import pulp, process it in plants too small to achieve economies of scale with outdated technology, and yet make a profit. When the barriers to imports came down, manufacturers in Mexico were at a decided disadvantage. They had to compete against producers whose nonimported raw materials were processed in large, up-to-date facilities. The Mexican manufacturers who can invest in new plants can now achieve economies of scale in production by using export markets, but they still have the competitive disadvantage of manufacturing in a fiber-deficient market. Until there is greater certainty about the land tenure system, few dare to invest in forests, an investment with a thirty-year time frame. Without those investments, Mexico cannot be self-sufficient in fibers, and manufacturers will be unnecessarily handicapped.

NOTES

1. All dollar amounts are U.S. dollars.

2. AmCham-Mexico is the largest U.S. Chamber of Commerce outside of the United States; some three-fifths of its 2,700 members are non-U.S. companies. It represents 85 percent of U.S. direct foreign investment (DFI) in Mexico. AmCham-Mexico is supported entirely by sales of publications and services, in addition to members' dues. It does not receive financial support from any government.

3. The Secretariat of Commerce and Industrial Development (Secofi) classifies companies by size: Companies with 16 to 100 employees are considered small;

those employing 101 to 250 people are classified as medium-size; and large firms are those employing more than 250 people. Companies considered medium-size according to the AmCham survey criterion would most likely be classified as large firms under the Secofi criterion.

4. Figures are from Secofi.

5. The industrial sector encompasses manufacturing, mining, electricity, gas and water, and construction.

6. Substantial discrepancies exist between Mexican and U.S. trade data. The two governments recently established a task force to try to reconcile the differences. Figures in this section are authors' calculations, using data from Bank of Mexico, Mexico City.

7. The increases ranged from 1 percent to 1,000 percent. The median increase was 50 percent. Firms classified as small reported a median increase of 25 percent; all other firms reported a median increase of 50 percent. U.S. firms reported a median increase of 60 percent, compared with a 40 percent median increase for Mexican companies.

8. Not surprisingly, manufacturers represented a higher proportion of exporting companies than of the overall sample: 74.1 percent of the companies responding to the question about exports were manufacturers, although they constituted only 54.1 percent of the firms responding to the survey.

9. The minimum increase reported was 2 percent; the maximum was 600 percent. The median increase was 30 percent. Small firms reported a median increase in imports of 55 percent. The median increase reported by other firms was 20 percent (medium-size companies) and 30 percent (large and very large companies). Foreign firms reported a higher median increase (40 percent for U.S. firms and 45 percent for others) than Mexican companies (20 percent).

10. Figures are from Secofi.

11. Ibid.

12. There would be a cost savings from displacing old plant capacity in the United States with a new plant in Mexico.

13. For other of its products, the company brings in raw materials from the United States, produces the pharmaceutical in Mexico, and then exports it to Europe, Asia, and Latin America.

14. Instituto Nacional de Estadística, Geografía e Informática (INEGI).

15. In 1995 the peso's average margin of undervaluation in purchasing-power parity terms was about 20 percent. By the end of 1996 that margin of undervaluation had dropped to around 4 percent.

16. According to AmCham surveys conducted between 1994 and 1995, the average margin of manufacturing firms in November 1994 was 7.3 percent; the median was 8 percent. In mid-1995, the average margin had dropped to 4.3 percent, and the median to 3.1 percent. American Chamber of Commerce, *Planeación de negocios: Análisis del mercado Mexicano '96* (Business planning: Analysis of the Mexican marketplace '96) (Mexico City: American Chamber of Commerce, A.C., October 1995), p. III-19.

17. The CEO of the foreign bank branch estimated the customer base at about 100 names drawn from the government, Mexican banks, and multinational and very large Mexican corporations. Only a few government entities, banks, and multinationals fall within that premier group. The banks, for example, are divided into three tiers, and "almost nobody is banking the third-tier" banks, according to the banker who was interviewed. Which multinationals fall within the select few depends on the size of their Mexican operations, so the Mexican subsidiary of a very large

multinational firm might find itself in the same situation vis-à-vis its bank as a medium-size Mexican-owned company.

18. A *contrato ley* is an industry-wide contract that must be explicitly approved by the government.

19. Changes in supply and production chains are derived from comparative costs (NAFTA) and protection versus patent infringement (intellectual property rights).

20. The term *sourcing* means "purchasing inputs."

21. When talking about his firm's thirteen-year campaign to raise productivity, the CEO of the petrochemicals firm said that changing attitudes had been the most difficult part of the task.

22. The degree of penetration of information technology is an indicator of the efficiency with which a firm is managed. It also can serve as an indicator of access to capital and financing. According to the CEO interviewed from the information technology sector, the coefficient in Mexico is 0.55 percent compared with 2.2 percent in the United States and about 2 percent in Canada.

10

Educating and Training the Mexican Labor Force for a Global Economy

Javier A. Elguea and Pilar Marmolejo

The world has suddenly changed before our eyes. The Soviet Union has disintegrated, allowing the rise of various emerging, democratic economies, and the Cold War and the bipolar world order are no more. As we approach the turn of the century, for the first time in history there is a consensus that market economies are the best path to prosperity and peace.

Another cause of the powerful changes taking place in the world is the technological innovation of recent decades and its powerful influence on productivity gains, robotics, and artificial intelligence. The amalgamation of computer science with the new telecommunications technologies has evolved into information networks, such as the Internet, which have transformed the workplace for practically all of the companies in the industrialized countries, as well as for many others elsewhere.

As a result of this dramatic transformation, parts of the world are now reinventing their economies. Large and powerful regions are reorganizing their productive systems and developing their human resources for the next century. The industrialized countries discovered some time ago that an ever-increasing proportion of their populations is employed in jobs that require intellectual potential, not manual labor. This trend has accelerated since the late 1980s, during which time the development of information technology has created more "smart jobs" than ever before.

The transformation of the labor markets is not, as often claimed, a simple exodus of manual labor from the First to the Third World, nor is it the result of differences in wage levels in industrialized and developing countries. The reasons for the transformation are far more profound and have greater long-term consequences for the labor markets of all countries. In the industrial age, strategic resources were essentially raw materials such as grains, steel, and oil, products that came directly from the soil and subsoil. In the new world order, the strategic resources are ideas and information. In these new economies, which are information intensive rather than labor intensive, the critical mass is deposited in a specialized and highly educated labor force with crucial skills and the capability to manage complex information. Indeed, the defining feature of the new labor force in the twenty-first century will be the ability to solve problems using information.

This transformation of the labor force is already apparent in the developed countries, as prospective studies by the U.S. Department of Labor confirm. Jobs now abound in, among other fields, systems analysis, computer science and applications, information systems, computer programming, medical technology, management analysis, and legal services. At the same time, there is a downward trend in the number of jobs for assemblers, machine and equipment operators, domestic help, and manufacturing workers in general.[1] The better-paid positions are those that require more education, and jobs calling for less education and skill receive the lowest wages.

UNDERDEVELOPMENT AND EDUCATION

Developing countries believing that the profound change in the international economy is the result of manufacturing jobs moving to countries with lower labor costs—such as their own—can find only passing comfort. The phenomenon is both temporary and limited—the harsh reality is that, in absolute terms, these jobs are disappearing in the underdeveloped countries and are being replaced by new jobs usually associated with more productive technologies. Clearly, the prospect of a multipolar world divided into economic blocs forces emerging economies to make a drastic choice: Either they become integrated into the international economy as mature, active members or they must become resigned to occupying only residual niches of prosperity in the foreseeable future.

Those developing countries that wish to bring the living standards of the developed world to their own populations—and Mexico is among them—have no choice but to educate their workers to compete in these new labor markets. Only by bringing about a fundamental change in the type of work, and by educating workers for these new jobs, will it be possible to bolster productivity per worker in Mexico. In other words, in Mexico as in the rest of the world the reorganization of labor will have to be accompanied by the reorganization of education.

EDUCATION AND GLOBALIZATION

With the end of the bipolar international order, the world has been reorganized into trading blocs that compete for global markets. Three blocs now contend for world leadership in the next century: Europe, Japan and Southeast Asia, and North America. Each of these blocs is working to develop competitive industries in the 1990s to ensure their inhabitants the highest living standards in the twenty-first century.

In most cases the development of education and research systems has preceded the takeoff of these countries' industries and economies; in others, investment in education has been a strategic element of economic growth policy. In all cases investments in education and training have placed these countries and regions in a privileged and highly competitive position in the world. Some data illustrate the point.

The European Bloc

The bloc that is most advanced in terms of political integration and economic unity is undoubtedly Europe. With 337 million inhabitants, Europe has the largest number of highly educated people. Even the countries of eastern Europe, although they may have failed in their economic policies, have among the best basic educational systems worldwide.

Countries in this bloc are in the vanguard of research, innovation, and educational development, particularly in Germany and France, where technical schools turn out the most productive industrial workers in the world, and more recently in the United Kingdom, where the curricular and administrative reform of education has already produced signs of recovery in academic performance indicators. The integration funds, which the European Union will soon implement to integrate its members' policies on education and training, will be a major step toward the adoption of uniform standards throughout the continent. Clearly, in a relatively short time the European bloc will be capable of taking on any challenge from any bloc in any field; it will also pose new and complex challenges that will make the international economic environment even more competitive and difficult.

The Southeast Asian Bloc

The Southeast Asian bloc, which until recently had thrived because of its privileged access to North American and European markets, has grown enough to substitute much of the demand from these external markets with internal demand. Japan, for example, has become both a major market for goods produced in other Southeast Asian countries and an exporter of capital in the region, thus beginning a trend toward integration and tremendous economic strength.

The ideals of work and education, nurtured over hundreds of years by Confucianism, are held in almost cultlike status by the populations of Southeast Asia. In the Asian educational system learning is a group activity, and institutional evaluations emphasize that all members of the group must strive to achieve high standards in verbal and numerical skills, in addition to acquiring practical knowledge. Learning in the schools is systematically reinforced at home through the well-known system of *juku,* in which the role of parents and employers is equally as important as that of teachers.

Competition is a fundamental element of the education and training systems of Asia. The best students compete intensely for access to the best schools, whereas schools and companies engage in fierce competition for access to financial and human resources. The result is an educational system with a clear sense of purpose, one in which companies are allowed to influence academic contents and standards, thus ensuring that they will be able to draw on a highly skilled and productive labor force.

Education is an investment in human capital, and no other nation is investing as much in the future as Japan, which has earmarked more investment per person to education and research and development than any other country in the world. As a result, Japan's high school graduates consistently obtain the best scores in international standardized evaluations. Some researchers maintain that because of the length and intensity of the school year in Japan, a fourteen-year-old Japanese student has received as much education as an eighteen-year-old American or European student.[2] In standardized intelligence tests, the average Japanese student obtains a score of 117, whereas his European or American counterpart scores 100, on average. Approximately 800,000 Japanese are dedicated full time to research and development, more than the total for France, Germany, and the United Kingdom combined.

The North American Bloc

The heavily populated North American region boasts the largest, richest market in the world, large-scale economies, and the leading edge in scientific and technological research in several strategic areas of production: high technology, biogenetic research, aeronautics, and telecommunications.

It has often been said that the educational system of the United States is the least advanced in the developed world, although the evidence does not appear to bear out that assertion. The United States has invested heavily in education in recent years; for example, in 1989 more than $350 billion went to improve public and private education in a system that served forty-five million elementary and secondary schools and almost thirteen million university students.[3] In comparative terms, the United States earmarks a higher percentage—6.8 percent—of its gross national product to education than either Germany or France. In addition, its universities and research centers have long been the best and most productive in the world. U.S. universities, which attract the best professors and students, hold the record for active Nobel prize winners.

A commonly leveled criticism of the U.S. educational system is that it lacks specialized technical schools, such as those in Germany and France, that can quickly educate highly productive technical personnel. Such criticisms fail to consider the fundamental role of education and training centers for workers in private enterprises, however. In the United States there are no large or medium-size firms that have not developed their own educational systems. These training centers actively and efficiently foster the transfer of knowledge and refinement of skills according to specific, production-related objectives. These in-house educational systems have absolute freedom in curriculum design and great flexibility, enabling them to adjust quickly to technological and organizational changes that affect their labor forces. No assessment of the U.S. educational system can be complete without taking into account the impact of these numerous training centers on the working population and on the competitiveness of the United States.

EDUCATION AND TRAINING IN MEXICO

Compared with the attainments of the educational systems of the developed world that Mexico aspires to join, the gains of the Mexican educational system seem meager, but the demands on that system have been pressing indeed: The Mexican population is still very young—people between two and twenty-nine years of age accounted for 63 percent of the total population in 1990, far above the average (47 percent) for the member countries of the Organization for Economic Cooperation and Development (OECD). In 1994 approximately 29 percent of the country's population was in school (25.8 million students out of a total population of 89.6 million); if the four million other people who receive educational services in nonacademic settings (in on-the-job training, for example) are included, students make up 33 percent of the population. The growth in the student population has been greatest for preschool, secondary *(bachillerato),* undergraduate *(licenciatura),* and graduate-level education.

Nationwide demand for education, as measured by the percentage of people between the ages of four and twenty-four years who are in school, has been just over 60 percent since 1980. Table 10.1 compares the educational levels attained by the Mexican population (ages fifteen years and older) in 1970 and 1990; the decline in the percentage of those with no education—from 31.6 in 1970 to 13.4 in 1990—clearly demonstrates that the educational system is successfully reaching more people. The increase in

Table 10.1   Distribution of the Population Fifteen Years and Older, by Level of
Education, 1970 and 1990

Level of Education	1970 Population	Percent	1990 Population	Percent
No education	8,199,383	31.6	6,667,481	13.4
Incomplete primary	10,080,693	38.9	11,289,043	22.8
Completed primary	4,358,971	16.8	9,553,163	19.3
Postprimary education	3,290,396	12.7	21,087,094	42.5
Not specified	9,115	0.0	1,014,095	2.0
Total	25,938,558	100.0	49,610,876	100.0

Source: "Perfil Socio-demográfico," *XI Censo General de Población y Vivienda, México:*
1990 (Mexico City: Instituto Nacional de Estadística, Geografía e Informática, 1996).

the number of people receiving postprimary education is particularly
impressive: from 12.7 percent of the population in 1970 to 42.5 percent in
1990. Undoubtedly, the quantitative increase in the supply of education is
what has enabled Mexico to win its decades-long battle against illiteracy;
the country's literacy rate now stands at 88.6 percent.[4]

Average schooling for those fifteen years old and over rose from 5.8
years in 1984 to 7 years in 1995. The upward trend is encouraging,
although Mexico's trading partners and competitors register figures considerably higher: 12.3 years for the United States and 12.1 years for Canada.

Nonetheless, these modest yet important gains in education have
enabled Mexico to claim fifty-third place in the United Nations
Development Programme's human development index.[5] Above it are the
Southeast Asian "tigers," several countries of the former Soviet Union, and
all of the developed countries. Below it are countries in Latin America,
Africa, and part of the Middle East.

EDUCATION FOR WORK: SECONDARY AND HIGHER EDUCATION

Upper secondary education, which comprises the *bachillerato* degree and
its equivalents, has the greatest potential impact on training of the productive workforce, because it is the last stage of formal schooling prior to entry
in the job market. Both the public and private sectors finance upper secondary education; 80 percent of those who receive upper secondary education go to public schools, with the remainder attending private schools.
This educational level, which takes approximately three years to complete,
can take three forms: (1) *the bachillerato,* or general preparatory studies,
whose function is to contribute to the general education of those preparing
to continue their studies; (2) vocational education, which contributes to the
training of specialized technical personnel for the job market; or (3) the

bachillerato tecnológico bivalente, a two-track program offering students both technical training and the background necessary for higher education. Higher education can be pursued after the *bachillerato* in universities, technological institutes, or in teacher-training schools.

A total of 748 higher education institutions in Mexico grant the *licenciatura* degree (the equivalent of a B.A. or B.S. degree). Again, one must distinguish between private and public investment in education. It is important to point out that by the 1960s higher education was provided almost entirely by public institutions. After that, public universities suffered a blow to their academic standards because of increasing politicization, and private universities, which offered better standards, proliferated. Nowadays, private universities account for about 21 percent of enrollment, with the two largest of these schools enrolling just over 41,000 students. The growing role of the private sector in education is reflected also in technology and teacher training: More than one-fourth of all students enrolled in these programs attend private institutions.

As for public institutions, one must distinguish among federal, state, and autonomously funded schools. Federal authority extends over a large part of technological education and upper secondary institutions; state authorities play a greater role in basic education, and some teacher-training schools come under state auspices. Universities, however, are autonomous.

Private sector investment in training—that is, in nonacademic forms of education—has increased in recent years. Such investments now account for 64.7 percent of the total investment in education for work (see Table 10.2).

Table 10.2   Education in Technical and Vocational Training Programs, by Source of Funding, 1992 (percent)

Field of Education	Federal	State	Autonomous	Private Sector
Training	25.6	9.7	—	64.7
Professional	52.9	7.6	8.8	31.2
Technical	32.4	23.5	21.5	22.6

Source: Organization for Economic Cooperation and Development, *Sistema Nacional de Educación Tecnológica (México), 1992* (Paris, 1997), p. 171.

Private Sector Investments in Science and Technology

Notwithstanding the growing public and private investment in secondary and higher education, curricular content still fails to adequately address the changing needs of the productive system. If the social function of education is to prepare students to face life, then training for the workplace should be a fundamental goal. Lamentably, however, the education students receive at secondary and higher schools prepares them for jobs that businesses no longer need. Because the course of industry development and policies concerning technology adoption determine not only the special needs of a country for scientific and technological knowledge but also the nature of available jobs, it is important that education be influenced by the dynamics of the productive system.

Those dynamics have changed since the mid-1980s, when Mexico mounted an effort to reorganize and transform the business sector to make it more competitive, vigorous, and productive. The decisive step toward this goal was taken with the opening of the economy in 1985; deregulation followed in 1989. In this context a new interrelationship sprung up between technologies and businesses, centered upon the transfer of technology. This development implied new demands for the higher education and research systems and a general restructuring of Mexico's science and technology policy.

The response to these new demands so far has been insufficient to meet current challenges. The resources allocated to scientific and technological research in both infrastructure and human resources, measured as a proportion of gross domestic product (GDP), are meager compared with the allocations of other countries, especially the industrialized ones. The Mexican scientific and technological community is small, and data from the early 1990s show that the number of students interested in pursuing a scientific career had decreased: In 1991, 56,625 students were enrolled in this area; by 1993, that figure had fallen to 33,440.[6]

In 1985 a survey of twenty-five businesses in Monterrey revealed that 70 percent of the large businesses and 39 percent of the medium-size businesses were interested in their technological development; by 1988 these figures had increased to 89 percent and 81 percent, respectively. The survey also showed that the businesses that funded their own research and development did so with less than 1 percent of their sales revenues.[7]

Yet despite the increasing amounts that Mexican businesses have been investing in science and technology, their contributions lagged far behind those made by the business sectors in the member countries of the OECD in 1991 (see Table 10.3). Expenditures for science and technology are distributed fairly evenly between the state and the private sector in all of the industrialized countries except Japan, where contributions from the private sector predominate. In the poorest OECD countries this spending is concentrated in the public sector, as it is in Mexico, where the private sector accounted for only 22 percent of such investment. In absolute numbers, Mexico's expenditures for research and development amounted to 0.8 percent of U.S. expenditures and to 1.99 percent of Japan's.

Table 10.3   Selected Indicators of Investment in Science and Technology (S&T) by
OECD Member Countries, 1991

OECD Member	Expenditures for S&T (percentage of GDP)	Expenditures for S&T (millions of dollars)	Source of Financing (percent)[a]		S&T Personnel per Thousand People
			Industry	Government	
Sweden	2.90	4,179.8	59.2	37.6	12.0
Japan	2.87	67,349.0	77.4	16.8	14.1
Switzerland	2.86	3,827.8	24.5	22.6	14.2
United States	2.75	154,348.0	50.7	46.8	12.2
Finland	2.02	1,617.2	56.3	40.9	11.6
Norway	1.84	1,314.5	44.5	49.5	9.5
European Union	1.69	106,393.3	48.1	43.0	10.5
Austria	1.51	2,043.2	50.3	46.5	6.7
Canada	1.50	7,782.8	41.3	44.0	8.2
Australia	1.34	3,670.7	40.3	54.9	8.0
Iceland	1.01	45.5	24.0	65.5	8.5
Turkey	0.47	884.2	27.6	71.3	0.8
Mexico	0.36	1,345.2	22.0	78.0	0.9

Source: OECD, 1994 data, as cited in Pablo Mulás del Pozo, *Aspectos Tecnológicos de la Modernización Industrial de México* (Mexico City: Academia de la Investigación Científica en México, 1995), p. 218.
   a. Contributions from external sources are not reported here.

Links Between the Private Sector and Academia

In the early 1980s, before Mexico opened its economy, research in applied basic sciences and in engineering was carried out in public sector institutions for the most part. In academia, such research was concentrated mainly in public schools of higher education. In both instances that research was performed with little direction from industry, either public or private. The first ties between academia and private industry were established to train personnel who could later dedicate themselves to industrial scientific and technological research. By the late 1980s institutions of higher education had gone one step further by exploring the possibility of establishing ties with the private sector for research.

As a result of these attempts to link university research and the private sector, the first agreements were adopted for cooperation between private businesses and public and private universities. Examples include the work carried out between Industrias Resistol S.A. (IRSA) and the Universidad Nacional Autónoma de México, the Universidad Autónoma Metropolitana, and the Universidad de Guadalajara in 1988; the IRSA-Universidad agreement ran for five years at a cost of $1 million to IRSA.[8]

Based on the IRSA-Universidad experience, an agreement was entered into by RAYCHEM and the Universidad Autónoma Metropolitana, which included the possibility of seeking funding from foreign businesses for graduate-level programs, the training of graduate-level students, and the production of international publications.[9] In 1990 the Universidad Autónoma Metropolitana entered into an agreement with CONDUMEX and the same year negotiated another agreement with the Mexican Petroleum Institute.

PUBLIC SECTOR EXPENDITURES FOR EDUCATION

Spending on education constitutes an investment in human capital whose social and private yields are equal to or greater than other investment opportunities. Spending on education has a multiplier effect in developing countries: It increases productivity, improves income distribution and employment, promotes social mobility, and accelerates the pace of economic growth. Also important are the indirect, nonmonetary effects of investment in education: Reduced poverty, improved health conditions, diminished crime rates, and technological innovations are among them.

Public and private spending for education increased significantly from the late 1980s to the mid-1990s, rising from 141 billion pesos in 1988 to 292 billion pesos in 1994 (see Table 10.4). This growth in resources devoted to education accounts for the increase in coverage and the improvement in other educational indicators during the 1988–1994 period.

Table 10.4   Public and Private Expenditures for Education, by Total and as a Percentage of GDP

	Total Expenditures for Education (millions of pesos at 1980 prices)	Public Sector Expenditures (percent of total)		Private Sector Expenditures (percent of total)	Total Expenditures (percentage of GDP)
Year		Federal	State and Municipal		
1988	141,410	80.3	10.8	8.9	3.6
1989	165,467	77.0	14.6	8.4	3.9
1990	197,389	75.1	16.8	8.1	4.3
1991	220,050	79.4	15.4	5.2	4.7
1992	249,517	80.1	13.5	6.4	5.2
1993	282,963	84.8	11.9	5.8	5.9
1994	292,106	83.6	11.0	5.4	6.2

Source: Secretariat of Public Education (SEP), based on data from the Secretariat of the Treasury and Public Credit, and OECD, *Exámenes de las Políticas Nacionales de Educación—México: Educación Superior* (Paris, 1997), p. 49.

DEVELOPMENT OF HUMAN RESOURCES IN THE PRODUCTIVE SECTOR

Although the technical or professional training of its employees is not one of the express purposes of the productive sector, such training is a prerequisite for its ability to function. In an ever more competitive environment, training is essential for enhancing quality, flexibility, productivity, and mobility. When training in the educational system is deficient or nonexistent, private businesses themselves become the training institutions.

In 1994, when the North American Free Trade Agreement entered into force, Mexico's public and private sectors began to adapt to a model of development based on productivity, quality, and competitiveness. Job training initiatives, which some businesses had already undertaken, soon became part of that effort, but much remains to be accomplished in this area: Of the thirty-three million people who make up the economically active population in Mexico, only about 62 percent have at least six years of formal schooling, and, despite private sector efforts, the number of those who receive training for the job or on the job remains small.

In Mexico there is a clear distinction between training for the job and training on the job. Job training, which may be formal or nonformal, is administered by the secretariat for public education. On-the-job training is provided by businesses, through the National System for Education and Training, which is under the secretariat for labor; the objective of on-the-job training is to teach workers the skills they need to fill available positions. Private sector involvement in these training programs is intensive: Businesses serve 51.63 percent of the students, contribute 74.18 percent of the teachers, and account for 82.27 percent of the schools and training centers.

According to the Mexican Association of Labor Relations Executives (AMERI), of the 157 businesses surveyed throughout Mexico in 1995, 73 percent carried out training assessments; the average time spent in training was 106 hours (about thirteen working days); and the average investment per person trained was 605 pesos. The percentage of the total payroll earmarked for training was 3.53 percent;[10] another AMERI report put that figure at 3 percent in 1997.[11] A 1994 study on small and medium-size industries, however, reported that even though most businesspeople stated that education and training of personnel could give them an edge over their competitors, their investment in training was scant (see Table 10.5).[12] Nevertheless, an exception to this perverse rule may be found in the investment in training made by the maquiladora industries. The maquiladoras are now of great importance to the Mexican economy, both in the generation of employment and in attracting foreign currency.

A survey of fifty-five businesses in Matamoros with ties to manufac-

Table 10.5   Percentage of Sales Devoted to Education and Training by the Business
Sector, by Personnel Category, 1993

Percentage of Sales	Management, Administrative, and Support Staff	Technical and Engineering	Workers
None	14.2	20.0	28.6
Less than 0.25	34.2	31.4	40.0
0.25–0.50	22.9	14.3	11.4
0.51–1.00	17.1	22.9	5.7
More than 1.00	11.4	11.4	8.5

Source: Creación de Capacidades Tecnológicas Internas en Pequeñas y Medianas Empresas (Mexico City: Consejo Consultivo de Ciencias de la Presidencia de la República, 1994).

turers on both sides of the border revealed dissatisfaction with workers' capabilities—respondents said they needed more employees who had graduated from basic programs of study. The study emphasized that 87 percent of the businesses need educational and training programs to increase their competitiveness. Ninety-five percent of the businesspeople in the survey stated that they would participate in training programs.[13] All of the surveyed firms agreed that they already spend a considerable part of their budget, 1 percent on average, on training and retraining programs; these programs focus on total quality, ISO 9000,[14] world-class manufacturing, implementation, computer systems applied to manufacturing processes, statistical control of processes, quality control, and textile manufacturing systems.

As for the manufacturing industry, two-thirds of the manufacturing establishments included in a study of technical personnel reported that they carried out formal training activities. Other private sector businesses are also active in the administration of training: They account for 41.4 percent of all training; other important sources of training are centers operated by sectorial groupings (22.8 percent), public training centers (12.5 percent), and independent instructors (12.2 percent). Technological institutions of higher education play a very modest role, accounting for only 5.6 percent of training.[15]

In 1993 about half of the establishments in the manufacturing industry said they would increase their training activities in coming years. The other half offered a variety of reasons for not offering training, among which were that they did not see any value added in such training (44.6 percent), they did not see the need for continuing education (14.3 percent), or they were skeptical about the abilities of the trainers (8 percent); only 8.6 percent of the firms cited cost as their main objection.[16]

In 1994 a study was released that detailed the number of workers who had participated in training programs from 1980 to 1994.[17] Training increased over the period for workers in all sectors, but the expansion in absolute numbers was especially marked in processing, commerce, and services (see Table 10.6). The communications and transportation sector also showed substantial gains in training, which is linked to the process of privatization and modernization of Mexican telecommunications that began in 1990 with the sale of Teléfonos de México.

Table 10.6   Number of Workers Enrolled in Training Courses, by Sector, 1980, 1985, 1990, and 1994

Sector	1980	1985	1990	1994
Agriculture	1,225	1,916	5,055	9,912
Commerce	50,895	79,304	104,299	168,382
Communications and transportation	735	11,831	47,918	50,985
Construction	11,822	15,274	22,262	37,384
Electricity	24	229	106,698	59,898
Extractive activities	5,003	13,187	11,080	26,795
Processing	151,528	293,349	531,808	947,381
Services	140,209	61,095	100,507	206,493
Total	361,441	771,067	929,627	1,507,229

Source: Creación de Capacidades Tecnológicas Internas en Pequeñas y Medianas Empresas (Mexico City: Consejo Consultivo de Ciencias de la Presidencia de la República, 1994).

TELÉFONOS DE MÉXICO: AN INSTRUCTIVE SUCCESS STORY

The case of Teléfonos de México merits special attention, for it illustrates the benefits of investment in human capital. During the past several years the telecommunications sector, through Teléfonos de México, has experienced the most profound and accelerated technological transformation in its history. Thanks to the unprecedented investment of more than $10 billion, the obsolete analog infrastructure was replaced by a state-of-the-art digital infrastructure that enables the now-private company to compete with the infrastructure of any phone company in the industrialized world.

Since its privatization in 1990, Teléfonos de México has focused on the development of instruments to help the company change. In 1991, for example, it announced the creation of the Technological Institute of Teléfonos de México (Inttelmex), which was charged with transforming the company's human resources by giving them the skills and knowledge they needed to manage the new technologies, offer better service to customers, and improve their productivity.

The following data demonstrate the magnitude of the company's investment in human capital: In a five-year period Inttelmex gave 59,193 courses, with 513,978 participants. In other words, each of the almost 50,000 employees of Teléfonos de México took ten courses from 1991 to 1996, or two courses per year, with the training per worker averaging fourteen days a year. Consequently, the company can now boast a highly trained workforce with high standards of productivity.

The number of employees per 1,000 telephone lines is one of the international standards for gauging the productivity of telecommunications companies. Teléfonos de México employed 9.6 employees per 1,000 lines in 1990 and 5.7 employees per 1,000 lines in 1996, which indicates that workers were 40 percent more productive in 1996 than in 1990. This gain in productivity took place without resorting to massive layoffs. The annual growth in lines of 12 percent during these years was completely absorbed by the same personnel, now better trained and motivated.

CONCLUSIONS AND RECOMMENDATIONS

Globalization and changes in the international economic order posit a central role for education of the workforces of businesses and countries. The heightened role of education in modem societies necessitates a series of changes in social organization. For example, the rapidity of technological changes requires that a permanent system for retraining be in place at all levels of the economy. Countries that are unable to reorganize their educational structures to perform this function will find themselves at a decided disadvantage.

This reorganization of education calls for a planned, concerted effort on the part of governments and regulatory bodies in education, business, schools, technological institutes, and universities. In Mexico, as in the rest of the world, the public and the private sectors must both work toward the reorganization of education, and the costs and responsibilities should be distributed between them.

To date, the public sector has invested heavily in education and training, yet much of that investment has been squandered on administrative structures and bureaucratic excess and a lot of the rest has been misused, given that curriculum contents and teacher training are out of step with the requirements of the new labor markets. It is essential that the public sector gear its efforts toward the qualitative reform of the education system, principally in terms of content and preparation of teachers. The public sector should, more than anything else, guarantee the quality of basic education— that is, ensure proficiency in verbal, mathematical, and computer languages—which is a prerequisite for any form of secondary or higher education.

The private sector should step up its investment in human capital to the levels spent by firms in the developed world, because these are the firms against which Mexican businesses must compete. The aim of education and training investments should be to help workers acquire relevant skills and knowledge and to increase employee productivity. In this context, the private sector should reflect on successes in the manufacturing and maquiladora sectors and in telecommunications, where investments in training have proven highly profitable. Finally, the need for adequate transfer of technology, and in some cases for research and development, should bring businesses to the doorsteps of universities and technological institutes, where they might motivate and influence the content of curricula and research programs.

Someone once said that the human species, since its origins, has been caught up in a race between education and evolutionary catastrophe. This observation is more significant now than ever before: Competition among commercial blocs will generate enormous wealth during the next century, but the risk is great that, without the necessary education, the enormity of poverty will be exacerbated for the other two-thirds of the world's population.

NOTES

1. C. Burger, "Knowledge and Productivity," *Newsweek,* June 1993.
2. Paul Kennedy, *Preparing for the Twenty-First Century* (New York: Random House, 1993).
3. All dollar amounts are U.S. dollars.
4. United Nations Development Programme, *Human Development Report* (Madrid: UNDP, 1994).
5. United Nations Development Programme, *Human Development Report* (Madrid: UNDP, 1995).
6. *Indicators of Scientific and Technological Activities* (Mexico City: Consejo Nacional de Ciencia y Tecnología [Conacyt], 1995), p. 58.
7. Pablo Mulás del Pozo, *Aspectos Tecnológicos de la Modernización Industrial de México* (Mexico City: Academia de la Investigación Científica en México, 1995).
8. Ibid.
9. Ibid.
10. Asociación Mexicana de Ejecutivos en Relaciones Industriales (AMERI), *Anuario Benchmark 1995: Las Mejores Prácticas de Recursos Humanos en México* (Mexico City: AMERI, 1995), p. 23.
11. Asociación Mexicana de Ejecutivos en Relaciones Industriales, *Anuario Benchmark 1997: Las Mejores Prácticas de Recursos Humanos en México* (Mexico City: AMERI, 1998), p. 29.
12. J. L. Solleiro, *Creación de Capacidades Tecnológicas Internas en*

Pequeñas y Medianas Empresas (Mexico City: Consejo Consultivo de Ciencias de la Presidencia de la República, 1994).

13. University of Texas, *Industrial Training Needs in Brownsville/Matamoros* (Austin: University of Texas, July 1994).

14. ISO 9000 is a set of guidelines developed by the Geneva-based International Organization of Standards for Quality Management. The goal of ISO 9000 is to ensure quality control at all steps in the production process.

15. Pablo Mulás, *Aspectos Tecnológicos de la Modernización Industrial de México*, pp. 81–112.

16. Ibid.

17. Instituto Nacional de Estadística, Geografía e Informática, *Encuestas Nacionales de Capacitación, 1995* (Mexico City: INEGI, 1996).

11

Strategies of Mexican Firms Toward Global Markets: Theory and Representative Cases

Arturo Fernández Pérez and Ramiro Tovar Landa

Producers and governments in every country often complain that business is not conducted on a "level playing field." Adjustments therefore have to be made, they say, to moderate or eliminate competitive inequities. Their argument is specious, however, because international trade arises out of the differences among countries in physical resources, human capital, and even consumer tastes—countries specialize in the production of those goods and services that they can provide more efficiently than other countries. International trade exists precisely because the playing field is not level.

THEORETICAL OVERVIEW OF FIRMS' STRATEGIES

As competition from imported goods becomes more vigorous, domestic companies' share of the market declines, their profit margins shrink, and the pressure on them to cut costs for production and marketing mounts. In response to this new market environment, firms change strategies to reallocate resources and to expand into foreign markets.

For example, after Mexico opened its economy through the General Agreement on Tariffs and Trade and signed on to the North American Free Trade Agreement, trade flows increased. Consequently, multinational firms began to expand their operations into Mexico, and Mexican firms were obliged to give serious attention to the development of an international business strategy.

Foreign expansion into domestic markets is accomplished in mainly three ways: (1) firms export their goods directly to the target market; (2) their local affiliates import their goods; and (3) they sell goods produced by their affiliates in domestic markets. To hurdle import barriers, reduce transport costs, and satisfy market-specific demands, the new expanding firms therefore seek to establish foreign production operations or to implement cooperation agreements with firms in the target markets.

Regionalization by free trade areas and customs unions are only transition steps toward firm and trade globalization, however. The normal progression starts from an environment in which only the national firms of low-income countries serve foreign markets, and they do so only by exporting; when firms from higher-income countries enter the picture, competition among national and multinational firms leads to a mixed equilibrium and a substantial trade volume. As countries converge relative to incomes and capital endowments, multinational companies eventually begin to displace trade in goods with trade in services such as banking, telecommunications, and information.[1]

In recent years Mexican firms have adopted a mix of strategies to redimension their activities not only in the domestic market but also in foreign markets; their goal is to exploit their relative advantages and to use several forms of capital more efficiently. The strategies they have employed range from capital diversion, specialization, and diversification to direct foreign investment and international cooperation agreements.

Access to Foreign Capital Markets

To realize the benefits of international capital flows, Mexico, like other countries, has reformed its laws and regulations to attract foreign investments. As economies develop, so too do the ways in which firms are financed. In the usual course of financial development, at the outset firms make their own capital investments and then move to bank-intermediated financing of debt. In the absence of barriers to international capital flows, equity markets eventually emerge, first at the domestic level and later at the global level.

Stepping up firms' activities in the stock market and opening the domestic stock market to foreign investors help create liquidity and improve information. Having access to a country's domestic stock market induces participation by foreign investors who otherwise would not trade, and the heightened trading on both sides following cross-listing reduces spreads and increases information and liquidity in both markets. Liquid equity markets make investment less risky through diversification as well as more attractive, because they allow savers to acquire assets and sell them, if need be, without sustaining substantial financial penalties. With transaction costs low, ownership of capital can be transferred efficiently, which has implications for the array of investments undertaken; and with risks diversified, traders in internationally integrated stock markets can invest in risky projects that promise higher returns. The combined result is better capital allocation and increased savings and investments.

In highly integrated and liquid markets, firms must produce information about their operations, plans, and finances, which enables investors to closely monitor their performance. That information serves firms as well as investors: It helps firms allocate their resources better, and it abets the alignment of the interests of owners and managers. The firms' financial structure and debt-equity ratio also change in the move to integrated, liquid markets: As the stock market develops, firms not only issue new equity but also increase their debt, because greater market participation improves monitoring and corporate control, thus making creditors more willing to lend. As markets continue to develop and grow, firms tend to substitute equity for debt.

Foreign investors, recognizing the need for international diversification, and firms that seek to broaden their shareholder base and raise capital then undertake equity diversification by means of (a) direct equity operations by foreign investors in domestic stock markets; (b) investments in country funds; (c) issue of rights on equity, held by depository institutions (American and global depository receipts); and (d) foreign equity offerings by domestic firms in international stock markets. Firms from emerging markets figure prominently in the stocks issued through depository schemes: In the United States in 1994, 73 percent of all new depository receipts were for non-U.S. firms in emerging markets.

Empirical evidence suggests that dual listing in a domestic market and in a foreign market boosts firms' value by providing more liquidity, enlarging the shareholder base, and imposing stricter disclosure requirements, all of which increase shareholder wealth. When firms in emerging markets like Mexico's raise new equity capital in a public offering, their initial returns are quite high, whereas their perceived riskiness is lower after they are listed on a major international stock market. The implications for the domestic market are important as well: When the stakes are high—that is, when firms can do business in foreign markets—intermarket competition mounts, which lowers local transaction costs. Because deregulation and the removal of barriers to capital flows allow the transition from segmented capital markets to globally integrated capital markets, the market portfolio of developing countries will tend to move beyond the domestic market to comprise individual stocks. Firms that have delayed their integration into global capital markets have experienced large and probably unexpected changes in their market valuation.

The greater liquidity arising from foreign investments in the domestic capital market is key to the participation of medium-size firms. Between 1993 and 1996 more than forty Mexican firms of various sizes and activities issued initial public offerings totaling more than $1.6 billion, or about 0.5 percent of Mexico's average annual gross domestic product (GDP) for that period.[2] Among emerging markets, however, at the end of 1996 Mexico ranked only sixteenth relative to listed stocks and thirteenth relative to the ratio of stock market value to GDP,[3] because overregulation and adverse macroeconomic events slowed the process of capital market integration and made it costly.

DIVERSIFICATION AND SPECIALIZATION

Firms operating in a closed economy have only a limited market for their goods; hence, to increase their profits, those firms must expand their product line—in other words, they seek to diversify their operations. In an open economy with extensive markets, however, firms can realize economies of scale by expanding their production of a particular good, or specializing. Also in an open economy, competition from imported goods may force firms in relatively inefficient lines of business to reallocate their resources to areas in which they are more efficient than their foreign competitors. Thus, in this new market environment inefficient businesses either close down or capital is diverted from inefficient operations and redirected to those whose efficiency can meet international trade benchmarks.

Firms that diversify are less vulnerable to import competition than those that do not diversify. Even if profit margins were no higher than they were before diversification, at least some of the diversified firm's product line would survive competition from lower-cost imports. Another advantage to diversification is that the experience gained with the firm's base product is portable: The marginal cost for the new business is lower than it would have been had such market experience not already been acquired.

The benefits of diversification accrue not only from the adoption of new business lines but also from the expansion of operations into foreign markets. Engineering and construction activities provide one example. Because construction tends to be a cyclical activity in most countries, contracting firms might well increase their profits by operating in several markets whose construction business cycles do not run concurrently; moreover, the experience gained from overseas construction jobs enables firms to more accurately estimate their costs and submit bids that stand a chance of being accepted—inexperienced firms must build large margins into their bids to cover cost uncertainties.

FOREIGN INVESTMENT

Because transportation costs, tariffs, and other barriers to trade often prevent firms from achieving full economies of scale in only one location, firms may seek to serve most of their national markets by investing in plants inside the target markets. The decision facing a multinational firm is whether to enter a new market via direct investment or by contracting with a local firm and investing later. Ventures with a local agent allow the multinational firm to avoid costly mistakes by finding out whether the market is large enough to support direct investment, although the agent can extract information rents from the multinational firm because it is better informed about market characteristics. Direct investment is the desirable mode of entry when the market is relatively large and the variability in profits is not. Such foreign direct investments also offer a way to avoid problems with property rights concerning the use of intangible assets such as know-how and market reputation, as well as the rents captured from them. Moreover, firm-specific, intangible assets—human resources, brand reputation, or other forms of capital—can give local firms cost advantages over foreign producers. Generally speaking, multinational firms tend to have a high ratio of intangible assets to total market value.

Transportation costs within an expansive target market affect firms' foreign investment strategy as well: Because the cost of transporting low-value items throughout the market is likely to be high relative to the cost of production, firms may choose to operate several geographically dispersed plants. If, however, firms can make a good profit on the sale of high-value items even after paying transportation costs (that is, if the cost of transportation is low relative to the cost of production), they will probably produce from a central location. The decision to invest in multinational or multiplant production weighs the added fixed costs of multiple plants against the transport savings from exporting at the plant level. The larger the potential market to be served, the more likely it is that firms will choose the high fixed costs of multiplant operations.

The establishment of production branches in the target market is an attractive option when goods are expensive to produce and service and the monitoring cost of distribution partnerships are costly and uncertain (that is, when the potential behavior of the partner in business is not in the multinational firm's best interests). Yet, when a potential foreign distribution partner's costs are lower than those of the expanding firm, or when information about the market is not readily available, a cooperation agreement or contract will be the dominant strategy.

Foreign direct investment is desirable, then, in at least three situations: (1) when transport costs are high; (2) when domestic firms have a high level of intangible assets; or (3) when institutional barriers to foreign direct investment are absent or negligible.

Foreign Investment by Acquisitions or Mergers

A merger in the legal sense assembles two or more firms under the same legal structure. An entirely new business entity may be created, or one company may simply absorb the other. In the first case, the shares of the merging firms are exchanged for those of the new entity; in the second case, all assets transfer to the absorbing firm, which makes payments to the shareholders of the absorbed firm.

Acquisition and merger usually lead to significant changes in the composition of the managerial staff and to consolidation or reorganization of the incoming firm's market strategy. Because acquisition or merger of firms combines existing assets, profitability may be achieved faster thereby than by building assets through a relatively long and uncertain investment process. The two major incentives for acquiring or merging firms are (1) to realize pecuniary and real economies—that is, savings from increased specialization, better economies of scale, and, in the case of mergers of firms making noncompeting products, new economies of scope gained by using related production processes and distribution channels; and (2) to extend the market, in cases in which firms sell the same product but in separate geographic markets.

STRATEGIC ALLIANCES

Another way to enter foreign markets is to contract with foreign firms, which allows the local firm to exploit any superior information the potential partner may possess about the characteristics of the market. The decision to contract hinges on whether the benefits of efficient market entry outweigh the potential costs of reciprocal nonexcludability, asymmetric information, moral hazard, adverse selection, and incomplete contracting.

A firm that wants to sell its product in a new market faces uncertainty about the foreign market environment. To enter that market the firm might invest in its own sales facilities, including production facilities, which entail sunk costs that make the investment relatively irreversible. Alternatively, the firm might implement a cooperation agreement with a foreign firm to gain ready access to information about the new market, if both parties believe they can profit from the arrangement. Investment in irreversible set-up operations and a low contract-termination cost make the firm a more attractive potential cooperation partner.

Of course, that foreign firm knows that its contracting partner may eventually use the market information it gains to extract rents from it, and it also knows that if it reveals demand to be high, the other firm may decide to produce directly. The multinational firm could then avoid sharing rents with a partner by making direct investments in, for example, wholesaling and servicing subsidiaries.

A special case is joint ventures between firms that are owned by two or more independent companies but managed collectively. This form of coordinated entrepreneurship occurs among firms on the periphery of their business, which find it difficult and expensive to be up-to-date about the environment surrounding their product areas and regions. Joint ventures make it possible to spread risks and share resources, and thereby to achieve goals that would be too costly to pursue alone, given the high levels of investment, technology, or market knowledge necessary for coping with uncertainties.

In a joint venture, information is generated for, about, and among partner firms. Feedback manifests itself in changes not only in physical capital (plants and capacity) but also in intangible assets (technology, marketing, and networks, for example). That evolution eventually leads either to convergence of partner firms' competitive capabilities or to cooperative specialization, arrived at by mutual recognition of the firms' different but complementary capabilities.

SOME REPRESENTATIVE CASES

Whether a particular firm chooses to become multinational or make foreign investments is determined by the new market structure and the industry's own characteristics. The major fast-growing firms in emerging economies may be relatively behind in research and development, but they do possess intangible assets such as location and superior knowledge of the domestic market.

The following cases illustrate different strategies for different markets. Domestic firms with high-technology requirements or superior domestic market knowledge (or both) tend to favor strategic alliances with foreign partners when such foreign firms have large setup costs relative to the host market size and the agency costs involved are relatively low (Alfa, Grupo Modelo, Cifra). In industries in which the scale economies are large, transportation costs are high, and the potential foreign partner can become a local competitor, the preferred strategy is to make a foreign direct investment in the target market (Cemex and Femsa); if the evolution of the market is not taken into account, however, that strategy may turn out to be deficient and very costly (Vitro).

Alfa

Alfa is one of Mexico's largest corporations in terms of revenues, assets, and diversification. Since the early 1990s Alfa has renovated 60 percent of its fixed assets to match international standards for competitiveness. Alfa has become the lowest-cost steel producer in North America and is involved in the production of various high-growth chemical products, such as purified terephthalic acid (PTA) and dimethyl terephthalate (DMT), both of which are in strong demand worldwide as primary materials for synthetic fibers and packing materials used by the soft drink industry and others related to nylon, polyester, Lycra, expandable plastics, and urethanes.

Alfa is currently Mexico's largest exporter of manufactured goods, with products delivered to more than fifty countries. Exports account for 38 percent of the company's total sales, or $1.1 billion. Two of its subsidiaries—Alpek, one of the largest private petrochemical plants in Latin America, and Hylsamex, its steel products division—make up 81 percent of Alfa's total revenues and 88 percent of its consolidated exports.

A key part of Alfa's business strategy is forging strategic alliances with international partners to gain access to advanced technology and foreign markets. At present, Alfa has established strategic alliances with seventeen different firms worldwide, such as Amoco, DuPont, and BASF. Also taking advantage of the new opportunities presented by deregulation policies in Mexico, Alfa has entered into a joint venture with CSW International to build a 120-megawatt, gas-fired cogeneration electricity plant to supply energy to petrochemical complexes in northern Mexico. Through another joint venture, this one with AT&T and a Mexican financial group, Bancomer, an Alfa subsidiary provides telecommunications services as a long-distance carrier. Other joint ventures are listed in Table 11.1.

Table 11.1   Alfa's Strategic Foreign Alliances in Various Sectors

Sector	Product or Service	Strategic Alliances
Steel	Flat and nonflat steel, rebar, wire, pipe, galvanized sheet metal, insulated metal panels	Kawasaki Heavy Industries (Japan), Kvaerner Davy (United States), MAN GHH (Germany)
Petrochemicals and synthetic fibers	DMT and PTA (raw materials for polyester), nylon and Lycra, polypropylene resins, and specialty chemicals	Amoco (United States), DuPont (United States), BASF (Germany), Montell (United States)
Refrigerated food	Processed meats, dairy products	Oscar Mayer (United States), Tyson Foods (United States), Sodima (France)
Miscellaneous	Aluminum engine heads, mattresses, carpets, rugs, retail home construction, and repair of related materials	Ford (United States), Shaw Industries (United States)
Telecommunications	Long-distance carrier	AT&T (United States)

Source: Alfa Annual Report, 1996.

Cemex

The cement industry is a classic example of a field in which global competition takes place among multinational firms with multiplant operations, because transportation costs are high relative to production costs. When transportation costs—including tariffs and the danger of countervailing duties—are significant, the firm's least-cost strategy is to establish multiple plants over a geographic expanse, with each serving the customers nearest its location. Cement plants also have substantial sunk costs and scale economies, but because the unit transport cost rises along with output when more distant markets are served, a firm will minimize costs by locating a plant in each regional market; in general, the higher the transportation costs, the larger the number of regional plants.

Multinational firms can compete in a foreign market either through exporting or through domestic production by subsidiaries. In the case of cement, profits decline if penetration of the market is accomplished by exporting, given high transportation costs and the potential entry of new firms in the market. The most likely ways that the cement industry will defend and expand its market share, therefore, are through acquisition of domestic firms or investment in new plants.

With over forty-seven million metric tons of production capacity, Cemex is the largest cement firm in the Americas and the fourth largest worldwide. Cemex has more than half of its assets in operations in twenty-two countries outside Mexico, with extensive distribution centers and maritime terminals in the Dominican Republic, Mexico, Panama, Spain, the United States, and Venezuela. In 1992 Cemex acquired the two biggest cement plants in Spain,[4] followed in early 1994 by the acquisition of the largest cement producer in Venezuela.[5] In recent years Cemex has bought assets in the Dominican Republic, Panama, the Philippines, and the United States.

Cemex operations in Spain are a strategic response to acquisitions of domestic plants in that country by other leading multinational firms in the cement industry, such as Holderbank, all of which aim to penetrate the European Union market. The desire to compete globally led Cemex to acquire holdings in Venezuela and Panama as well. Holderbank is active in Venezuela, and the location of both countries is well suited for export-oriented production aimed at the Caribbean and Central and South American market (and to a lesser extent the U.S. market). In the same drive to consolidate in Latin America, Cemex acquired the second and third largest cement producers in Colombia in 1996.[6]

In 1995 Cemex traded internationally more than eight million metric tons of cement and clinker; exports accounted for approximately 55 percent of its sales. However, exports to the United States are constrained by a 62 percent punitive tariff from an antidumping resolution against cement imports from Mexico, a tariff that was upheld by a NAFTA dispute-resolution panel in 1996. Nevertheless, Cemex has consolidated its position in the U.S. southern market by acquiring assets in a firm with operations in Texas, Arizona, California, and Florida,[7] and it recently acquired a cement plant in Texas with a production capacity of 1.1 million tons per year.

Empresas La Moderna

Empresas La Moderna, which belongs to the conglomerate Pulsar International, has operations in three divisions. Two are oriented mainly toward the domestic market, where the company is a leading producer: In cigarette production Empresas La Moderna has a 53 percent market share, and in packaging, a 49 percent market share. In the third field, vegetable seeds, which is aimed at the international market, the company is a world-wide leader with a 22 percent market share. Empresas La Moderna has been traded on the New York Stock Exchange since 1994; as a result of its globalization, it has been able to diversify its revenue sources, of which around 45 percent are in hard currencies, derived mostly from its agribusiness operations.

The firm's main global operations are in agrobiotechnology. La Moderna's experience in growing and processing tobacco—the company is vertically integrated in this field—made it aware of the demand for high-end agricultural technology. Consequently, the firm entered into joint ventures with leading U.S. and other international biotechnology and genetic engineering firms to investigate propagation and development of seeds and vegetables. Empresas La Moderna, through acquisitions or mergers with foreign firms, has agrobiotechnology operations in fresh produce marketing, seeds, and research and development (R&D) in genetic engineering.

The worldwide seed market is divided into agronomic seed (grains, animal feed, and oil products) and vegetable seed, with margins varying substantially among the seed varieties. The operating margins for agronomic seeds are approximately 6 percent to 7 percent, whereas for vegetable seeds they run from 12 percent to 22 percent. The firm's strategy has been to pick niche markets for its fresh products.

La Moderna bought Asgrow Seeds in 1994 and later sold part of that acquisition to Monsanto (a U.S. corporation), coupled with a nonexclusive technology transfer agreement regarding vegetable and fruit seed production. Other vegetable seed divisions of La Moderna were consolidated in its subsidiary, Seminis,[8] which has captured around 22 percent of the global market for vegetable seeds, making it one of the top five seed firms worldwide. This subsidiary spends about 11 percent of sales on R&D annually, in line with the top competitors in the industry. Seminis has research stations in thirteen countries in the Americas, Europe, the Middle East, and Asia, with sales in more than 100 countries (95 percent of which are in North America and Europe) and production facilities in more than twenty-five.

Grupo Modelo

The beer industry is characterized not only by relatively significant transportation costs but also by brand loyalty and extensive networks of distribution. Very few of the world's major brewing companies have become multinational firms; instead, they reach foreign markets through their exports. Brand name recognition and its protection seem to outweigh the benefits of licensing or establishment of multiplant operations in foreign countries.

Modelo, which is ranked tenth in worldwide beer production, has a 55 percent domestic market share and accounts for 71 percent of Mexico's exported volume of beer. Among the 450 brands of imported beer sold in the United States—the world's largest beer importer—Modelo has been second only to Heineken since 1986. Modelo distributes in Canada as well as in the United States; it also has distribution subsidiaries in Brussels and Spain and exports directly to Asia, Oceania, the Caribbean, and Central and South America.

The joint venture undertaken in mid-1993 by Grupo Modelo and Anheuser-Busch (A-B),[9] the biggest brewer in the world, is a prime example of the benefits to be realized from two countries' gaining access to distribution networks in each other's domestic markets. Through an exclusive distribution agreement between the two companies, which anticipated intense global competition among brand names from the United States and Europe, Anheuser-Busch gained access to the Mexican market and Modelo procured the instrument to increase its leadership among imported beers in the U.S. market. A-B has reached a 30.3 percent market share among imported beers in Mexico through a Modelo subsidiary, and Modelo has consolidated its leadership in the U.S. import market, increasing volume sales by 8 percent in 1993 and 13 percent in 1994.

Vitro S.A.

Glass manufacturing is characterized by scale economies but also by significant sunk and transportation costs and vertical integration. Consequently, in the globalization process the trend is to operate multiple, geographically diverse plants.

Vitro ranks as one of the largest glass container manufacturers in the world, producing also flat glass, windshields, glassware, and household and commercial appliances; the glass container sales account for around 60 percent of total revenues. Vitro's corporate division encompasses more than seventy companies in North, Central, and South America (most of which are in the food and beverage industry and in the construction and automotive sector); it operates manufacturing plants in six of those countries, and it exports to more than sixty countries worldwide. Forty percent of its assets are located outside Mexico—these foreign operations accounted for 66 percent of Vitro's total sales in 1995. In the same year exports constituted 35 percent of total sales from Mexican operations.

Since the mid-1960s this firm has been engaged in many international joint ventures. In 1965 in alliance with Pilkington PLC, a British glassmaker, Vitro established Comegua, with glass container production facilities in Guatemala and Costa Rica. In 1996 Vitro acquired a 51 percent stake in Vitemeco, a Colombian automotive and architectural glass processor. Vitro also has associations with Monsanto Corporation for the production of windshield film and with PQ Corporation for work with silicates and other chemicals. Recently, in 1995, Vitro acquired Vidrio Lux S.R.L., a leading Bolivian producer of glass containers for the soft drink and beer industries, and it has minority participation in the leading glass container production company in Peru and in a Brazilian firm dealing in glass oven products.

An important step in the firm's globalization was the acquisition of Anchor Glass Container Corporation in the United States, which was the third-ranked producer of glass containers worldwide. In September 1996, Anchor filed for protection under Chapter 11 of the U.S. bankruptcy code; Vitro sold Anchor in February 1997 and used the proceeds to repay creditors.

Plastic containers offer many of the advantages traditionally unique to glass—impermeability, transparency, and heat resistance, for example—as well as others, such as nonbreakability and lower shipping costs. Vitro has therefore begun diversifying into the plastics sector. In 1994 Vitro and Pechiney International, a European group, entered into a strategic alliance to supply the beverage-container market in Mexico and Central America. Other diverse interests include manufacture of household appliances in alliance with Whirlpool Corporation; gas stove components in alliance with Delta Sourdillon, a leading French manufacturer; and glassware through a joint venture with Libbey Inc., whereby Libbey became a 49 percent equity holder in Vitrocrisa, the largest manufacturer of glass tableware in Mexico.

Femsa

Fomento Económico Mexicano S.A. de C.V. (Femsa) is the largest beverage producer in Latin America. This firm produces packing materials, as well as beverages, and owns an extensive chain of convenience stores. The main operations of the firm comprise an own-brand brewery and a bottling company for the Coca-Cola Company.

In 1993 Coca-Cola acquired a 30 percent stake in its subsidiary, which produces, advertises, and distributes Coca-Cola soft drinks in the Mexico City area and southeast Mexico. Femsa, appointed the anchor bottler for Coca-Cola in Latin America, is now one of the largest Coca-Cola franchise holders in the world. In 1994 it acquired a 51 percent stake in Argentina's franchise bottler in Buenos Aires, and it currently has a 55 percent share of the market in that region. It extended its reach in 1996 by the franchise acquisition of the territory adjoining Buenos Aires.

Femsa has the largest range of beer brands in Mexico, with an estimated 46 percent share of the domestic market. Exports to Latin America and Europe constitute 38 percent of Femsa's total exports, but the United States is the major export target. In 1994 Femsa's beer-producing subsidiary formed a strategic alliance with the Canadian brewery John Labatt Ltd., with the objective of consolidating its participation in Canadian and U.S. markets. Under this agreement Labatt acquired 22 percent of Femsa, with the option to acquire an additional 8 percent during the next four years, an arrangement similar to the one between Modelo and Anheuser-Busch.

More recently (in mid-1995), Femsa and the U.S.-based Amoco Oil Company entered into a joint venture to offer retail and automotive service at gas stations in Mexico. Amoco currently owns about 2,800 convenience stores at service stations in the United States; Femsa, through its parent company Oxxo, operates approximately 700 small convenience stores in Mexico.

Cifra

Cifra is the biggest chain retail discount store and restaurant operator in Mexico. Since 1991 Cifra has been party to a joint venture agreement with Wal-Mart, the largest U.S. retailer, which until then had no foreign operations. Wal-Mart now runs 314 stores outside the United States and has become the world's largest retailer.

The joint venture currently operates 145 units, including eighteen supercenters and twenty-eight wholesale clubs, whose sales total approximately $2 billion. Cifra, which operates 228 stores outside the joint venture, in 1996 posted an excellent performance compared with other retail discount stores, despite the widespread economic crisis in 1995. Although retail sales fell 28 percent in 1995 and another 23.5 percent in 1996, Cifra still reported a net income of $257 million on total sales of approximately $2.9 billion. In mid-1997 Wal-Mart acquired a majority stake in Cifra for $1.2 billion, its first direct foreign investment operation; the joint venture units were merged with Cifra, with purchasing and distribution consolidated.

CONCLUSIONS

Globalization increases the flow of capital and technology to developing economies, thus generating higher growth rates than would be possible in a less-integrated economy. All four of the factors associated with globalization—international trade, foreign direct investment, international interfirm agreements, and integrated capital markets—are present in the Mexican case. Macroeconomic stability, the first requisite for a sound business environment that allows long-term participation in the global market, also appears to be in the offing for Mexico: The economy has been opened wide to competition through trade liberalization and deregulation, which have promoted efficiency gains in domestic businesses.

The response of Mexican firms to this new environment has important implications for domestic industrial and trade policy. Before economic reforms, Mexico's industrial and trade policy was aimed at supporting certain sectors, often to the detriment of other sectors, because the resources that were transferred to the target sectors—skilled labor and capital, for example—were in finite supply. Now that the economy has been opened, any such transfer of resources would have to take into account the effect on dividend payments across countries, and no government can obtain the information necessary for weighing the marginal gains to targeted sectors against the resources' opportunity costs.

In short, any policy that involves the transfer of resources is inferior to the firms' own strategies. Like firms in any open economy, successful firms in Mexico have heeded market incentives and seized market opportunities; the very diversity of their responses to globalization undermines and severely diminishes the operational value of direct policy interventions. The global marketplace itself will determine which firms succeed or fail.

NOTES

1. James R. Markusen and Anthony Verables, "Multinational Firms and the New Trade Theory," working paper 5036, National Bureau of Economic Research, Cambridge, Mass., 1995.

2. Authors' calculations. All dollar amounts are U.S. dollars.

3. Mexico listed 200 firms; Chile ranked twelfth with 251, and Brazil seventh with 544. Mexico's percentage of stock market value to GDP was 34.8 percent (Chile ranked third with 135.5 percent, and Brazil twelfth with 35.1 percent). *Bolsa Mexicana de Valores* (Mexican stock exchange).

4. Compañía Valenciana de Cementos Portland S.A. and La Auxiliar de la Construcción S.A., consolidated since September 1993 as Grupo Valenciana.

5. In September 1995 Cemex had control of Corporación Venezolana de Cementos S.A.C.A., with 59.5 percent of voting shares.

6. Cementos Diamante and Cementos Samper.

7. Cemex acquired assets from Lafarge, which was renamed Sunbelt Asphalt and Materials, Inc.

8. Seminis arose from the merger of Asgrow, Petoseed Company, and Royal Sluis B.V.

9. A-B acquired 17.7 percent of Modelo, with an option to acquire up to 35.12 percent until the end of 1997, plus a fixed annual dividend equivalent to 6.3 percent over the price shares participation.

PART THREE

Conclusion

12

Prospects for Mexico's Private Sector: Toward the Twenty-First Century

Riordan Roett

Mexico's private sector has modernized rapidly and under highly inauspicious circumstances, both domestic and international. The opening of the economy in the 1980s followed a dramatic collapse of the old economic model. North American regional integration offered new opportunities but raised important questions about the competitiveness of the Mexican private sector. Political uncertainty became a component of national life in recent years, with opposition parties claiming a more significant role in national life.

As we approach the twenty-first century, several tasks remain to be done to make the private sector regionally and globally competitive. These are daunting but not impossible to accomplish. Ironically, those challenges are largely ones that the private sector itself cannot control. Although its participation in the process is vital, the business community in Mexico must rely, first, on a modernizing state to play a more constructive role in introducing and consolidating a set of much-needed microlevel reforms. These will provide the enduring twenty-first-century structure required for a deepening of the market-driven economic model now in place. That is the first task to be realized.

The second task is to recognize that the Mexican private sector's continued modernization will be impacted by the twin trends of globalization and regionalization. The future of the North American Free Trade Agreement (NAFTA) and of the Free Trade Area of the Americas (FTAA) needs to be considered in devising an appropriate strategy for the private sector in the next century.

And, finally, whatever strategy is identified as appropriate by the business community should take into account the momentum of political liberalization now under way in Mexico. Although it is not clear what the twenty-first century holds for Mexico in political-institutional terms, it is clear that the old order is receding, the elements of a new system are emerging, and the Mexican private sector will be both an actor in and an object of those systemic changes.

THE MEXICAN STATE AND THE PRIVATE SECTOR

Until very recently, state-directed economic development was predominant in Mexico. Linked in an unusual symbiotic relationship, the private sector and the government, dominated by the Institutional Revolutionary Party (PRI), arrived midcentury at an understanding regarding their respective roles in society. Protection, favoritism, cronyism, and obedience were the hallmarks of the relationship. Although not officially part of the ruling establishment, an effective private sector became a sine qua non for the success of the Mexican state. The model succeeded for decades. By the 1960s, however, it was clear that change was in the air. The state had become sclerotic. The factionalism and cronyism within the private sector and between its leaders and the party-state were egregious. The instability and incompetence that characterized the administrations of Luis Echeverría Alvarez (1970–1976) and José López Portillo (1976–1982) resulted in the collapse of the Mexican state in the early 1980s. Banking on the country's dramatic increase in oil revenues and borrowing heavily from abroad, the government ignored a burgeoning current-account deficit, an overvalued peso, and a large fiscal deficit. Those factors resulted in the onset of the debt crisis in 1982, which was only symptomatic of a deeper malaise in Mexico.

After a brief moment of self-denial, the government of Miguel de la Madrid Hurtado (1982–1988) undertook the heroic task of modernizing the state and liberating the private sector. Those efforts continued under the regime of Carlos Salinas de Gortari (1988–1994) and are still under way in the *sexenio* of Ernesto Zedillo Ponce de León (1994–2000). The first half of the De la Madrid administration was dominated by a recession, debt restructuring, the 1985 Mexico City earthquake, and low oil prices. Reform began in earnest in 1986–1987 and accelerated sharply during Salinas's term of office. What now needs to be done is to continue the process of modernization as Mexico moves into the next century.

There is no magic to the list of reforms that need to be implemented. But these are political initiatives of the state authorities, initiatives that will affect key actors, many of whom are reluctant to change or who fear change itself. Labor is perhaps the best example. To successfully compete in the twenty-first century, the Mexican state will need to address the structural distortions and rigidities in the labor market that now prevent growth from producing higher levels of employment. As a recent study indicates, "These distortions include high labor taxes, restraints on firms seeking to adjust their labor forces, and excessive government involvement in setting wages. The result is segmentation of the labor market, which greatly reduces the flexibility required to adapt the productive structure to the dictates of the increasingly competitive global economy."[1] What is needed are initiatives that, for example, give employers greater flexibility in terms of employment contracts and downsizing, reduce mandated payroll taxes, reform the severance payment system, reduce or eliminate the government's role in wage determination, and decentralize the collective bargaining process. All of these will help attenuate the segmentation of labor markets and should result in a sharp increase in employment.

Another critical cluster of policy changes that the state must oversee and implement is in the development of efficient capital markets for the twenty-first century. Financial intermediation margins are too high in Mexico, as they are in almost all of the countries in the hemisphere. Bond and equity markets are shallow, illiquid, and highly concentrated. Microenterprises and small businesses have poor access to credit, and rural and housing financial markets are often isolated, inefficient, and limited. In the short run, improvements must be made in the regulation and supervision of banks and other financial institutions, and the government needs to give priority to increasing competition in the banking sector, developing efficient bond and equity markets, and integrating segmented sectoral finance.[2]

The Mexican state is faced with the daunting task, too, of improving the existing legal and regulatory frameworks. For sustained growth and competition in Mexico, it is imperative that greater protection be given to property rights, to the enforcement of contracts, and to the establishment of credible and stable regulatory frameworks. Competition laws must be well designed and properly enforced to foster efficient markets. Investment, innovation, and economic transactions will be slight if the individuals and businesses that save, innovate, and transact are not reasonably certain that they will be able to reap the results of their efforts. Good land titling and registry are basic for the operation of land, housing, and credit markets. The inadequate protection of property rights, together with cumbersome legal and regulatory procedures, has contributed to the widespread informality that still characterizes "doing business" in Mexico.

Crucial to the future competitiveness of the private sector is the promotion of quality investment in human capital. It is generally agreed that one of the most important determinants of a country's long-term growth and robust competitiveness is the education of its people. And it is the caliber of basic education that Mexico needs to stress. The current catalog of problems is daunting: low levels of academic achievement, too few years spent in schooling because of high rates of grade repetition, and the lack of access by the poor to quality education, which results in unequal educational opportunities across social classes. Teacher quality must be upgraded. Time in school needs to be extended, and public expenditures for education need to be reallocated. Mexico's private sector can play a role in education at the plant and shop level. But it can play only the role of lobbyist with the state, which will remain the principal allocator of resources for promoting human capital for the foreseeable future. That lobbying mission, however, is as important as any of the other reforms that will be needed by the private sector for its expanding role in the twenty-first century.

And, finally, it is critical that the Mexican state move to establish credible and efficient government practices. That, combined with the rule of law, will go a long way toward providing an appropriate framework for the private sector, for foreign investors, and for the challenges of competition in the twenty-first century. Some of the principal issues to be confronted are the poor quality of bureaucratic structures, unreliable judiciaries, and high levels of corruption, crime, and violence. The accountability and transparency of the Mexican government are key to the continuing success of the market-oriented economic model now in place.

THE CHALLENGES OF GLOBALIZATION AND REGIONALIZATION

The Mexican private sector is confronted in the twenty-first century with the two challenges of competing in a global marketplace and preserving the advantages of the North American market. These two challenges are not incompatible, but success in meeting both of them requires that the state reforms discussed above move forward. And the private sector needs to think through and reconcile the often competing demands of the globalized economy and the rapidly changing, somewhat volatile regional North American market.

Mexico has replaced Japan as the second most important trading partner of the United States (Japan moved to third place, with Canada retaining its lead role). The trade—and investment—relationship between Mexico and its northern neighbors will undoubtedly deepen and broaden in the twenty-first century. With the failure of the Clinton administration to gain fast-track negotiating authority from the U.S. Congress in late 1997, the future of regional trade arrangements is in question. It is not clear that the vision of an FTAA by 2005 is feasible. The inability of the U.S. administration to win approval for fast-track authority means that the original goal of extending NAFTA throughout the hemisphere is on hold. For the Mexican private sector, this is both an opportunity and a risk. The opportunity is clear. The North American market proved to be a significant lifeline for Mexico after the peso devaluation crisis of late 1994. And that market should continue to offer extensive opportunities for Mexican exports in the next century, given the vitality and projected growth rates in the United States in particular but also in Canada.

But is it in the interests of the Mexican private sector to ignore trade and investment developments elsewhere in the region and globally? Obviously not. The success of Mexico's bilateral trade agreement with Chile is a prime example of pragmatic policy with regard to hemispheric trade. The bilateral link with Chile has resulted in a number of new business opportunities for the Mexican private sector. In the absence of a free trade arrangement between the United States and Chile, firms in Mexico and Canada are dramatically increasing their trade. As recently reported, "There has . . . been a boom in the number of U.S. companies shipping products from plants in Canada or Mexico to Chile."[3] This trend will continue so long as there is no comprehensive trade agreement for the Americas. The twin advantages for the Mexican private sector in regional terms, then, are that it can consolidate its strong position in the North American market and pursue targets of opportunity regionally, following the Mexican government's adept strategy of seeking bilateral trade ties in the Americas.

The issue of globalization is critical for the Mexican private sector in the twenty-first century. In addition to the state-led reforms already discussed, which provide the basis for any globally competitive strategy that Mexico will follow, the private sector needs continued access to capital and technology. These will determine the pace and the degree to which that country can be a world player in the twenty-first century. Credit or capital will be available as long as creditors believe the reform process is moving forward. Technology will follow investment, mergers and acquisitions, joint ventures, and more sophisticated production methods. These will be drawn to Mexico if the government attends to needed reforms and if Mexico is seen as an appropriate production platform for exporting to other countries in the hemisphere with which Mexico has free trade agreements.

The Mexican private sector is in a competitive position regarding regional trade. It benefits strongly from the multilateral links within North America, and it is in a position, absent a broader FTAA, to pragmatically select its trading partners in the hemisphere. That, in turn, will make the Mexican economy more attractive to foreign investors. Investors will seek strategic alliances with partners in the private sector, leading to an expansion of the capital and technology available for the deepening of industry and services in the twenty-first century.

POLITICAL LIBERALIZATION

Current efforts to open the political system, to make it more competitive and more transparent, constitute the third movement that will deeply affect the Mexican private sector in the next century. A key juncture will be the presidential election of 2000 to choose a successor to Ernesto Zedillo. More generally, the broader political process, if increasingly democratic, will involve government in new ways in the management of the economy. That involvement will obviously impact on doing business.

One trend that will accelerate, if the Mexican Congress gains greater voice in the broad lines of economic policymaking, is decentralization. Although still a highly centralized state, Mexico may well move toward greater decentralization in the twenty-first century, as is slowly happening elsewhere in the Americas. It is generally agreed that decentralization needs to be speeded up in the delivery of public services, in particular. Local governments in the future can be expected to respond more efficiently to the demand for services, to be more adaptable to changing local circumstances, and to be more accountable to the local population. Decentralization should improve the quality of local institutions and processes that are associated with effective local governance, including curbs on corruption.

To the degree that the Mexican Congress, which is regionally and locally oriented, expands its mandate, the pressure to decentralize, to increase revenue sharing, and to move services and institutions out of Mexico City will grow. The private sector will need to factor into its strategic planning the increased political role of local and state institutions that have been weak and dependent on the central government throughout the twentieth century. State governments and legislatures, town councils, and the federal Congress may well begin to play a broader role in policymaking in the twenty-first century. These will be developments that the private sector must take into consideration. Until now, the business community dealt either with a highly centralized, secretive state (before De la Madrid) or (since that *sexenio*) with a more transparent but still centralized state bureaucracy. The private sector cannot ignore the implications of decentralization and local sources of power in the twenty-first century.

At the national level, the pace and quality of political reform will be linked directly to perceptions of political risk by actual and potential investors. The efforts to deepen the legitimacy of the Congress and local offices, the expansion of the role of opposition political parties in decision-making, and the acceptance by the dominant Institutional Revolutionary Party in overseeing and participating in this political change will be essential to the future and continued success of the private sector.

For decades the PRI was Mexico's only serious political force, and its candidates routinely won not only the presidency but virtually all other political posts as well. Only in the past decade has the decision been taken at the center of the political system to gradually open space for rival parties. In recent years, the opposition has won six state governorships, and in July 1997 it won the first direct election for the government of Mexico City and gained a majority of the seats in the lower house of the national legislature. The current volatility in the Mexican political system causes some concern.[4] Investors abhor the possibility of political instability. The risk-return factor drives markets today, and Mexico needs to be sure that the investor community is comfortable with political risk levels. The uncertainty about the future of Mexican politics is good for political scientists and journalists and other pundits; it is possibly less so for a skittish investor community with a wide variety of opportunities for direct and portfolio investment.

The transition from this century to the next in political terms will impinge on the private sector. If that transition is open and relatively stable—even if it means a change of parties in control of the executive in 2000—the private sector should benefit from continued investment flows. Should the transition be sidelined or marked by uncertainty and violence, the private sector will suffer the consequences. Politics and business are inseparable in today's global economy.

CONCLUSIONS

None of these challenges are impossible to achieve nor need they take place simultaneously. Sequencing of reform is crucial in any society, and particularly so in Mexico. The reform of the state is probably the first priority. In turn, a new role for the Mexican state will involve needed political reform and transparency. The private sector's strategies for the twenty-first century, whether global or regional, will follow from the success or failure of the first two processes. The achievements to date cannot be overlooked and should not be denigrated, but in an increasingly competitive global economy all developing countries compete with other developing countries. Mexico must continue to move forward to compete effectively. Mexico already has a strong advantage in its central role in North America, yet that role will grow and deepen only if the twenty-first-century reforms that I have discussed are taken seriously and the decision of the country's policymakers to pursue them is genuine. The opportunities for the next century for the Mexican private sector are open-ended. The lessons learned in the past decade by the private sector will not be forgotten. Now is the time to provide the support and the institutional infrastructure to enable the private sector to move to the next plateau of economic success.

NOTES

1. Shahid Javed Burki and Guillermo E. Perry, *The Long March: A Reform Agenda for Latin America and the Caribbean in the Next Decade* (Washington, D.C.: World Bank, 1997), p. 8.

2. Ibid.

3. Anthony Faiola, "Chile Takes Its Trade Elsewhere," *Washington Post,* December 25, 1997, p. A29.

4. Sam Dillon ("'Dinosaur' Stirs Mexico's Old Guard," *Washington Post,* February 27, 1998, p. A6) discusses the possible reaction of the more traditional wing of the government party to the advances made by the political opposition in recent years. Should that wing prevail, the level of political uncertainty in Mexico would increase sharply.

Bibliography

Acosta Córdova, Carlos, and Fernando Ortega Pizarro. "Prioridad de los banqueros, cuatro años después de la reprivatización: Obtener utilidades." *Proceso,* 23 May 1994, 35.

Alba, Carlos. "El empresariado mexicano ante el tratado de libre comercio con norteamérica." Working paper, Centro de Estudios Internacionales, El Colegio de México, Mexico City, August 1993.

Allen, Michael, Craig Torres, and Dianne Solis. "Populist Backlash: Mexican Leftists Gain Wide Support, Posing Threat to Ruling Party." *Wall Street Journal,* 27 June 1997, A1.

Alós, María Luisa. "Disgusta a la IP perfil de consejo." *Reforma,* 11 May 1995, 15A.

Alós, María Luisa, and Osiel Cruz. "Apoyan calzado y textil." *Reforma,* 10 April 1995, 15A.

Althaus, Dudley. "Mexican Middle Class in Crisis: Desperate Citizens Form Group to Halt Economic Downslide." *Houston Chronicle,* 26 February 1995, 18A.

Alvarez, Carmen. "Molesta a empresarios negociación financiera." *El Norte,* 8 October 1992.

American Chamber of Commerce. *Planeación de negocios: Análisis del mercado Mexicano '96* (Business planning: Analysis of the Mexican marketplace '96). Mexico City: American Chamber of Commerce, A.C., October 1995.

"Apoyaremos a quien asegure continuidad: CCE." *Excélsior,* 27 September 1993, 28.

Asian Development Bank. *Managing Financial Sector Distress and Industrial Adjustment: Lessons for Developing Countries.* Manila, Philippines: Asian Development Bank, 1992.

Asociación Mexicana de Ejecutivos en Relaciones Industriales. *Anuario Benchmark 1995: Las Mejores Prácticas de Recursos Humanos en México.* Mexico City: Asociación Mexicana de Ejecutivos en Relaciones Industriales, 1995.

———. *Anuario Benchmark 1997: Las Mejores Prácticas de Recursos Humanos en México.* Mexico City: Asociación Mexicana de Ejecutivos en Relaciones Industriales, 1998.

Aspe, Pedro. *El camino mexicano de la transformación económica.* Mexico City: Fondo de Cultura Económica, 1993.

Aspen, Chris. "The Auction's Over: What Lies Ahead for Mexico's Newly Private Banks." *Business Mexico,* August 1992, 44.

Banamex. "Deuda privada en el exterior." *Examen de la Situación Económica de México* 72, no. 844 (1996): 97–101.

Banco de México. *Informe Anual: 1994,* April 1995.

Banco de México. *Informe Anual: 1996,* April 1997.

Banco de México and Secretaría de Hacienda y Crédito Público. *Boletín de Prensa,* 30 July 1997.

Bancomer. *Reporte Económico,* Mexico City, July 1996.

Bancomext compilation. "Lecciones recientes sobre el desarrollo de la economía mexicana y retos para el futuro." In *México: Transición económica y comercio exterior,* 89–97. Mexico City: Bancomext, 1997.

Bartley, Robert. "Mexico's Money Theorists Need a Tip from Hong Kong." *Wall Street Journal,* 20 December 1996, A17.

Becerril, Isabel, and Leticia Rodríguez. "Política industrial promotora de la inversión, exigen empresarios: Necesario un diseño que rebase la frontera sexenal." *El Financiero,* 6 December 1994, 31.

———. "Urge resolver discrepancias entre macro y microeconomía." *El Financiero,* 6 December 1994.

Brailovsky, Vladimir. "Las implicaciones macroeconómicas de pagar: Las respuestas de política económica ante la 'crisis' de la deuda en México, 1982–1988." In *La economía mexicana: Un enfoque analítico,* edited by Gonzalo Castañeda Ramos, 275–331. Mexico City: Limusa-Noriega Editores, 1994.

Bruno, Michael. "Opening Up: Liberalization with Stabilization." In *The Open Economy: Tools for Policymakers in Developing Countries,* edited by Rudiger Dornbusch and F. Leslie C. H. Helmers, 223–248. New York: Oxford University Press, 1988.

Burger, C. "Knowledge and Productivity." *Newsweek,* June 1993.

Burki, Shahid Javed, and Guillermo E. Perry. *The Long March: A Reform Agenda for Latin America and the Caribbean in the Next Decade.* Washington, D.C.: World Bank, 1997.

"Business Leaders Renew Criticism of Zedillo Administration's Economic Policy and Urge Government to Increase Public Spending." *SourceMex,* 3 April 1996.

Calva, José Luis. "Régimen Cambiario." *El Universal,* 11 July 1997, 11.

Calvo, Guillermo, and Enrique Mendoza. "Petty Crime and Cruel Punishment: Lessons from the Mexican Debacle." *American Economic Review* 86 (1996): 170–175.

Calvo, Guillermo A., Leonardo Leiderman, and Carmen M. Reinhart. "Inflows of Capital to Developing Countries in the 1990s." International Monetary Fund, Washington, D.C., 1996. Photocopy.

Cárdenas, Enrique. *La política económica de México, 1950–1994.* Mexico City: El Colegio de México–Fondo de Cultura Económica, 1996.

Castañares Priego, Jorge. "Desventajas ante el TLC." *El Nacional,* 23 September 1992, 24.

Castañeda Ramos, Gonzalo. "La empresa mexicana y su gobierno corporativo: Antecedentes y desafíos para el siglo XXI." Department of Economics, Universidad de las Américas, Puebla, Mexico, 1997. Photocopy.

Clavijo, Fernando, and José I. Casar, eds. *La industria mexicana en el mercado mundial.* 2 vols. Mexico City: Fondo de Cultura Económica, 1994.

Comisión Nacional Bancaria y de Valores. *Capital, provisiones y utilidades de la banca desde su privatización a la fecha.* Mexico City: Dirección General de Vigilancia y Análisis, Comisión Nacional Bancaria y de Valores, 1998.

— — —. *La crisis bancaria en México: Evolución reciente y medidas instrumentadas hasta el primer semestre de 1997.* Mexico City: Comisión Nacional Bancaria y de Valores, 1997.

— — —. *La crisis bancaria en México: Orígenes, consecuencias y medidas instrumentadas para superarla.* Mexico City: Comisión Nacional Bancaria y de Valores, 1996.

Conger, Lucy. "Tilting at Neoliberalism," *Institutional Investor,* May 1997, 103.

Congressional Budget Office. *The Changing Business of Banking: A Study of Failed Banks from 1987 to 1992.* Washington, D.C.: Congressional Budget Office, 1994.

Contreras Salcedo, Jaime. "El industrial mexicano no va a entregar su mercado a cambio de nada." *El Financiero,* 7 February 1992.

Córdoba, José. "México." In *The Political Economy of Policy Reform,* edited by John Williamson, 232–284. Washington, D.C.: Institute for International Economics, 1994.

De Juan, Aristóbulo. "A Sum Up, or False Friends in Banking Reform." Paper prepared for the annual meeting of the European Bank for Reconstruction and Development, London, April 1995.

De la Cuadra, Sergio, and Salvador Valdés. "Myths and Facts About Financial Liberalization in Chile: 1974–1983." In *If Texas Were Chile: A Primer on Banking Reform* (A Sequoia Seminar), edited by Philip L. Brock. San Francisco: Institute for Contemporary Studies, 1992.

Del Castillo, Gustavo. "Private Sector Trade Advisory Groups in North America: A Comparative Perspective." In *The Politics of Free Trade in North America,* edited by Gustavo del Castillo and Gustavo Vega Cánovas. Ottawa: Center for Trade Policy and Law, Carleton University, 1995.

Del Castillo, Gustavo, and Gustavo Vega Cánovas. *The Politics of Free Trade in North America.* Ottawa: Center for Trade Policy and Law, Carleton University, 1995.

De Remes, Alain. "Debe el estado permitir la competencia financiera." *Excélsior,* 3 July 1993, 1.

Diamond, Douglas W. "Financial Intermediation and Delegated Monitoring." *Review of Economic Studies* 198 (1984): 393–414.

Diamond, Douglas, and Philip Dybvig. "Bank Runs, Deposit Insurance, and Liquidity." *Journal of Political Economy* 91, no. 31 (1983): 401–419.

Díaz de León, Alejandro, and Moisés Schwartz. "Crisis Management and Institutional Change Aimed at the Prevention of Future Crisis." In *The Banking and Financial Structure in the NAFTA Countries and Chile,* edited by George M. von Furstenberg, 184–198. Boston: Kluwer, 1997.

Dillon, Sam. "'Dinosaur' Stirs Mexico's Old Guard." *Washington Post,* 27 February 1998, A6.

Dornbusch, Rudiger, and Alejandro Werner. "Mexico: Stabilization, Reform, and No Growth." *Brookings Papers on Economic Activity* 1 (1994): 253–317.

Edith Rudiño, Lourdes. "Fuera del esquema de UDI 95% de los miembros de El Barzón." *El Financiero,* 5 April 1995, 8.

— — —. "Legítimas las demandas de El Barzón contra la banca." *El Financiero,* 27 April 1995, 9.

Edwards, Sebastian. "Exchange-Rate Policy in Mexico: Options and Recommendations." University of California at Los Angeles, 1997. Photocopy.

— — —. "Exchange Rates and Capital Flows in Emerging Latin American Markets." Paper presented at the Dallas Federal Reserve Symposium, Dallas, 14 September 1995.

Fadl, Sergio. "El papel del Banco Nacional de Comercio Exterior como factor de apoyo del sector exportador." In *México: Transición económica y comercio exterior*, 42–43. Mexico City: Bancomext, 1997.

Faiola, Anthony. "Chile Takes Its Trade Elsewhere." *Washington Post*, 25 December 1997, A29.

Feldstein, Martin. "Overview." Paper presented at the symposium "Financial Stability in a Global Economy," Federal Reserve of Kansas City, Jackson Hole, Wyo., 28 August 1997.

Flores, Armando. "Desconfían empresarios de la política industrial." *El Economista*, 8 May 1995, 1.

Flores, G., et al. "Macroplan de rescate financiero para empresas medianas y pequeñas." *El Financiero*, 19 March 1995.

Flores, Mauricio. "Reformarán leyes de intermediarios." *Reforma*, 18 January 1995.

Folkerts-Landau, David, Ito Takatoshi, and Marcel Cassard. *International Capital Markets: Developments, Prospects, and Policy Issues*. Washington, D.C.: International Monetary Fund, 1995.

Frías Santillán, Amalia. "La desinformación aumenta la vulnerabilidad de México: ANIT." *Uno Más Uno*, 28 July 1992.

Galbis, Vicente. "Financial Sector Liberalization Under Oligopolistic Conditions and a Bank Holding Structure." *Savings and Development* 2 (1986): 117–140.

Gallardo, Juan. "La Coordinadora de Organizaciones Empresariales de Comercio Exterior (COECE)." In *Hacia un Tratado de Libre Comercio en América del Norte*. Mexico City: Miguel Angel Porrúa, 1991.

Gallegos, Elena, and Emilio Lomas. "Se simplificará la ley para crear empresas, anuncia Herminio Blanco." *La Jornada*, 10 May 1995, 43.

García, José de Jesús. "Se modifica la relación entre bancos y el gobierno federal." *Excélsior*, 8 October 1993, 1.

Gavito, Javier, Aarón Silva, and Guillermo Zamarripa. "Mexico's Banking Crisis: Origins, Consequences, and Countermeasures." In *Regulation and Supervision of Financial Institutions in the NAFTA Countries and Beyond*, edited by George M. von Furstenberg, 228–245. Boston: Kluwer, 1997.

Gavito, Javier, and Ignacio Trigueros. "Los efectos del TLC sobre las entidades financieras." In *Lo negociado del TLC*, edited by Georgina Kessel, 223. Mexico City: Instituto Tecnológico Autónomo de México and McGraw Hill, 1994.

Gil Díaz, Francisco, and Agustín Carstens. "Some Hypotheses Related to the Mexican 1994–1995 Crisis." Working paper 9601, Bank of Mexico, Mexico City, 1996.

Gómez U., Alonso. "La política económica de México, respuesta a la altura del cambio mundial: Canacintra." *Excélsior*, 8 February 1992.

González Gómez, Mauricio. "Memoranda on the Recent Performance of the Mexican Economy." Paper prepared for the Group of Associated Economists, 22 July 1997.

Greenspan, Alan. "Globalization of Finance." Paper presented at the Fifteenth Annual Monetary Conference, Cato Institute, Washington, D.C., 14 October 1997.

Güémez, Guillermo. "Mexico's Business Associations and the Free Trade Agreement." *Comercio Internacional Banamex*, October 1991, 64.

Gutiérrez, Vicente. "Cuesta el dinero en México trece veces más que en Estados Unidos." *Excélsior*, 3 May 1993, 1.

Hale, David. "Comments." In *Private Capital Flows to Emerging Markets After the Mexican Crisis*, 142–146. Washington, D.C.: Institute for International Economics, 1996.

———. "Will Mexico Follow the Monetary Path of Chile or Argentina?" Chicago: Kemper Financial Services, 1995.

Herrera, Victor, and John Chambers. *Bank System Report*. New York: Standard & Poor's, 1996.

Indicators of Scientific and Technological Activities. Mexico City: Consejo Nacional de Ciencia y Tecnología, 1995.

Izquierdo, Rafael. *Política hacendaria del desarrollo estabilizador*. Mexico City: El Colegio de México–Fondo de Cultura Económica, 1995.

J. P. Morgan. "The Mexican Peso Will Continue to Surprise," *Market Brief*. 16 May 1997.

J. P. Morgan. *Special Report*, New York, June 1996.

Katz, Isaac. "Efecto regional de la apertura comercial." In *México: Transición económica y comercio exterior*, 341–343. Mexico City: Bancomext, 1997.

Kennedy, Paul. *Preparing for the Twenty-First Century*. New York: Random House, 1993.

Kravis, Marie Josée. *Lessons of the Mexican Peso Crisis: Report of an Independent Task Force*. New York: Council on Foreign Relations, 1996.

Krueger, Anne O. "The Political Economy of the Rent-Seeking Society." *American Economic Review* 64 (1974): 291–303.

Krugman, Paul. "Dutch Tupis and Emerging Markets." *Foreign Affairs* 74, no. 4 (July–August 1995): 28–44.

———. *Pop Internationalism*. Cambridge: MIT Press, 1996.

La industria mexicana en el mercado mundial: Elementos para una política industrial, edited by Fernando Clavijo and José I. Casar. Mexico City: Fondo de Cultura Económica, 1994.

Luna, Matilde. "Las asociaciones empresariales mexicanas y la apertura externa." Working paper, Universidad Nacional Autónoma de México, Mexico City, August 1992.

———. "Los retos de la globalización: La reforma microeconómica." In *Los empresarios ante la globalización*, edited by Ricardo Tirado, 211–217. Mexico City: Universidad Nacional Autónoma de México and Instituto de Investigaciones Sociales, 1994.

Luna, Matilde, and Ricardo Tirado. *El Consejo Coordinador Empresarial: Una radiografía*. Mexico City: Facultad de Ciencias Políticas y Sociales and Instituto de Investigaciones Sociales, Universidad Nacional Autónoma de México, 1992.

Lustig, Nora. *Mexico: The Remaking of an Economy*. Washington, D.C.: Brookings Institution, 1992.

Markusen, James R., and Anthony Verables. "Multinational Firms and the New Trade Theory." Working paper 5036, National Bureau of Economic Research, Cambridge, Mass., 1995.

Maxfield, Sylvia. *Governing Capital: International Finance and Mexican Politics*. Ithaca, N.Y.: Cornell University Press, 1990.

Medina-Mora, Eduardo. "Managing Market Expectations in Latin America: Lessons from Mexico's 1994 Crisis." Paper presented at the Forbes Magazine and Council of the Americas Conference on the Latin American Market, New York, 7–9 November 1996.

Mena, Yadira. "Modifica estrategia: Apoyará Bancomext 10 ramas productivas." *Reforma*, 31 March 1995, 22A.

Mercado, Luis E. "Política industrial." *El Economista*, 30 March 1995, 11.

Mishkin, Frederich. "Asymmetric Information and Financial Crisis: A Developing Country Perspective." Federal Reserve Bank of New York, March 1996.

Mulás del Pozo, Pablo. *Aspectos tecnológicos de la modernización industrial de*

México. Mexico City: Academia de la Investigación Científica en México, 1995.

Musalem, Alberto, Dimitri Vittas, and Asli Demirguc-Kunt. "North American Free Trade Agreement: Issues on Trade in Financial Services for Mexico." PRE working paper 1153, World Bank, Financial Sector Development, Washington, D.C., July 1993.

Olivas, Mireya. "Herminio Blanco Mendoza: La clave es la competitividad." *El Economista,* 11 May 1995, 33.

Organization for Economic Cooperation and Development. *Economic Surveys: Mexico 1995.* Paris: Organization for Economic Cooperation and Development, 1995.

Ortiz, Guillermo. *La reforma financiera y la desincorporación bancaria.* Mexico City: Fondo de Cultura Económica, 1994.

Pastor, Manuel, and Carol Wise. "The Political Economy of North American Trade: The Origins and Sustainability of Mexico's Free Trade Policy." *International Organization* 48 (summer 1994): 459–489.

Pérez U., Matilde. "Entregará El Barzón 400 mil escritos de consignación de pagos." *La Jornada,* 24 April 1995, 13.

"Protegen demasiado al sistema bancario." *El Norte,* 13 May 1992.

Przeworski, Adam. *Democracy and the Market: Political and Economic Reforms in Eastern Europe and Latin America.* New York: Cambridge University Press, 1991.

Puga, Cristina. "Business Elites and Political Change in Mexico." Paper presented at the American Sociological Association Congress, Miami Beach, Fla., 13 August 1993.

———. "Las organizaciones empresariales en la negociación del TLC." In *Los empresarios ante la globalización,* edited by Ricardo Tirado. Mexico City: Universidad Nacional Autónoma de México and Instituto de Investigaciones Sociales, 1994.

———. "Medianos y pequeños empresarios: La difícil modernización." *El Cotidiano* 50 (September–October 1992).

Quintero, Silvia, and Erick Luna. "El impacto de la apertura comercial en la función importaciones: México." Undergraduate thesis (tesis de licenciatura), Universidad de las Américas–Cholula, Puebla, Mexico, 1997.

Ramírez de la O, Rogelio. "The Budget for 1997: Uncertain Cost of Rescuing the Banking System." Ecanal Special Report 1, February 1997.

———. "A Mexican Vision of North American Economic Integration." In *Continental Accord: North American Economic Integration,* edited by Steven Globerman, 23–24. Vancouver: Fraser Institute, 1991.

Rangel, Enrique. "Middle-Class Militancy." *Dallas Morning News,* 16 December 1996.

Reynolds, Alan. "Another Dornbusch Disaster?" Hudson Institute, Indianapolis, Ind., 1996. Photocopy.

Rodríguez López, Leticia. "Ignora el gobierno las demandas de la IP para reactivar la economía." *El Financiero,* 27 May 1995, 6.

Ros, Jaime. "La Enfermedad Mexicana." *Nexos,* July 1997, 57–61.

Rubio, Luis. "El sector privado en el pasado y futuro de México." In *Industria y trabajo en México,* edited by James Wilkie and Jesús Reyes Heroles G., 243–262. Mexico City: Universidad Autónoma Metropolitana, 1990.

———. "¿Existe un modelo económico alternativo?" *El Norte,* 1 May 1997.

Rubio, Luis, and Alain de Remes. *¿Cómo va a afectar a México el Tratado de Libre Comercio?* Mexico City: Fondo de Cultura Económica, 1992.

Sachs, Jeffrey, and Andrés Velasco. "Lessons from Mexico." Working paper, New York University, 1995.

Salgado, Alicia. "Acelerado proceso de fusiones y alianzas bancarias, en puerta." *El Financiero,* 10 April 1995, 4.

Salinas-León, Roberto. "Don't Cry for Mexico's Current Account Deficit." *Wall Street Journal,* 21 February 1992, A13.

———. "From Stability to Stagflation: Lessons from the Mexican Fiasco." In *Money and Markets in the Americas,* edited by James A. Dorn and Roberto Salinas-León, 115–126. Vancouver: Fraser Institute, 1996.

———. "Exchange Rate Mercantilism." *Barrons,* July 1997.

———. "Mexican Money Post-Mancera." *International Economy,* November–December 1997, 38–41.

———. "Peso Stability Is Now Ortiz's New Job." *Wall Street Journal,* 19 December 1997, A13.

Secretaría de Hacienda y Crédito Público. *Criterios generales de política económica.* Mexico City: Secretaría de Hacienda y Crédito Público, 1997.

Solís, Leopoldo. *Economic Policy Reform in Mexico.* New York: Pergamon Press, 1981.

Solleiro, J. L. *Creación de Capacidades Tecnológicas Internas en Pequeñas y Medianas Empresas.* Mexico City: Consejo Consultivo de Ciencias de la Presidencia de la República, 1994.

Story, Dale. "Trade Politics in the Third World: A Case Study of the Mexican GATT Decision." *International Organization* 36 (autumn 1982): 767–794.

Summers, Lawrence. "Summers on Mexico: Ten Lessons to Learn." *The Economist,* 23 December 1995 to 5 January 1996, 46–48.

Sundarajan, V., and Tomás J. T. Baliño. "Issues in Recent Banking Crises." In *Banking Crises: Cases and Issues,* edited by V. Sundarajan and Tomás J. T. Baliño, 1–57. Washington, D.C.: International Monetary Fund, 1991.

"Survey: Banking in Emerging Markets." *The Economist,* 12 April 1997, 34.

Tomlin, Brian W. "The Stages of Prenegotiation: The Decision to Negotiate North American Free Trade." *International Journal* 44, no. 2 (spring 1989): 254–279.

Torres, Craig. "In Mexico, Banks Face Pressure to Unite." *Wall Street Journal,* 5 October 1993, C22.

United Nations Development Programme. *Human Development Report.* Madrid: United Nations Development Programme, various years.

University of Texas. *Industrial Training Needs in Brownsville/Matamoros.* Austin: University of Texas, July 1994.

"Urge nueva política industrial." *La Jornada,* 19 September 1993, 35.

Vargas Saldívar, Norma. "Recomienda la cúpula empresarial hacer más eficiente la sustitución de importaciones." *El Financiero,* 15 May 1995, 27.

Vázquez Tercero, Héctor. "El CCE y sus propuestas de política económica." *El Financiero,* Comercio Exterior section, 22 May 1995.

Vega Cánovas, Gustavo. "La promoción de las exportaciones, el TLCAN y el futuro del libre comercio en América del Norte." In *México: Transición económica y comercio exterior,* 368–369. Mexico City: Bancomext, 1997.

Vidal, Francisco Javier. "Lo que el tiempo se llevó: La industria paraestatal." In *La restructuración industrial en México, cinco aspectos fundamentales,* edited by Josefina Morales, 118–119. Mexico City: Instituto de Investigaciones Económicas, Universidad Nacional Autónoma de México, 1992.

Villarreal, René. *El desequilibrio externo en la industrialización de México (1929–1975): Un enfoque estructuralista.* Mexico City: Fondo de Cultura Económica, 1976.

Wheat, Andrew. "The Mexican Debtors' Revolt." *Multinational Monitor* 17 (June 1996).

Williams, Heather. "Planting Trouble: The Barzón Debtors' Movement in Mexico." Current Issue Brief Series 6. Center for U.S.-Mexican Studies, University of California, San Diego, 1996.

"Zedillo's Mexico." *Institutional Investor,* March 1997, 13.

Zúñiga, J. Antonio, and Salvador Guerrero Chiprés. "La venta de los bancos, para reducir la deuda interna: Hacienda." *La Jornada,* 26 May 1990, 15.

About the Contributors

Enrique Cárdenas Sánchez is rector of the Universidad de las Américas (UDLA) in Puebla, Mexico, where he is also a member of the economics faculty.

Javier A. Elguea is president of the Technological Institute of Teléfonos de México (Inttelmex).

Everardo Elizondo Almaguer, who was chief economist of Grupo Financiero Bancomer, S.A., when he wrote his chapter, was recently appointed deputy governor of the Banco de México, the Mexican central bank.

Arturo Fernández Pérez is rector of the Instituto Tecnológico Autónomo de México (ITAM) and a member of the university's economics faculty.

Javier Gavito Mohar is vice chairman of financial analysis and development at the National Banking and Securities Commission in Mexico City. Until 1994, he was Antonio Carrillo Flores Professor of Finance at the Instituto Tecnológico Autónomo de México (ITAM).

Jonathan Heath is founder and president of Jonathan Heath and Associates, an independent consulting firm located in Mexico City that provides analysis on the political and economic environment in Mexico.

Kristin Johnson Ceva is a Ph.D. candidate in political science at Stanford University and a visiting scholar at the Pacific Council on International Policy, working to complete her doctoral dissertation on economic liberalization and business-government relations in Mexico.

Pilar Marmolejo is a human resources analyst at the Technological Institute of Teléfonos de México (Inttelmex).

Deborah L. Riner is chief economist at the American Chamber of Commerce in Mexico City.

Riordan Roett is Sarita and Don Johnston Professor of Political

239

Science and director of the Latin American Studies Program at the Paul H. Nitze School of Advanced International Studies (SAIS), Johns Hopkins University. He is also founding director of the SAIS Program on U.S.-Mexico Relations and the Center of Brazilian Studies.

Roberto Salinas León is an economic analyst and director of economic strategy at Televisión Azteca in Mexico City. He is the former executive director of the Center for Research on Free Enterprise (CISLE).

Aarón Silva Nava is director of accounting projects at the National Banking and Securities Commission in Mexico City. He also served as deputy director of financial planning at the Ministry of Finance in Mexico, and has taught specialized courses in public finance and financial planning at the Instituto Nacional de Administración Pública (INAP) and the Centro de Estudios Monetarios Latinoamericanos (CEMLA).

Clint E. Smith is senior research scholar at the Institute for International Studies at Stanford University. He is a consultant on international and public policy to leading U.S. foundations, and is author of a forthcoming volume on United States–Mexico relations through the 1990s.

John V. Sweeney is managing director at Vector Casa de Bolsa, a financial services firm in Mexico City. From 1984 to 1997, he served as the U.S. Treasury's Representative in Mexico and helped negotiate the 1988 debt restructuring, NAFTA, and the 1995 emergency financing facility.

Ramiro Tovar Landa is a member of the economics faculty of the Instituto Tecnológico Autónomo de México (ITAM).

Raymundo Winkler is director of the Center for Economic Studies of the Private Sector (CEESP) in Mexico City.

Guillermo Zamarripa Escamilla is general director for development and economic research at the National Banking and Securities Commission in Mexico City. He is adjunct professor at the Instituto Tecnológico Autónomo de México (ITAM) and conducts research in the areas of finance and economics.

Index

About the Book

Mexico's private sector continues to confront challenges imposed not only by reforms in the country's economic and political systems but also by demands of the international economic community for transparent and fair business dealings. In this book, scholars and business leaders examine the responses to these challenges, weighing the goals of economic reform against its results, assessing the effect of economic modernization on sectors of the Mexican economy, and evaluating the political, economic, and social prospects for further reforms.

Riordan Roett is Sarita and Don Johnston Professor of Political Science and director of the Latin American Studies Program at the Paul H. Nitze School of Advanced International Studies (SAIS), Johns Hopkins University. He is also founding director of the SAIS Program on U.S.-Mexican Relations and the Center of Brazilian Studies. He is author of numerous books and articles on Latin America and recently edited *The Challenge of Institutional Reform in Mexico* and *The Mexican Peso Crisis: International Perspectives.*